Ia 39
30

AN ENGLISHMAN IN PARIS.

AN ENGLISHMAN IN PARIS.

1250 copies First Edition, June 1892.
1000 ,, Second Edition, July 1892.

AN ENGLISHMAN IN PARIS

(NOTES AND RECOLLECTIONS)

IN TWO VOLUMES

VOL. I.

REIGN OF LOUIS-PHILIPPE

SECOND EDITION REVISED

LONDON: CHAPMAN & HALL, LD.
1892

CONTENTS.

CHAPTER I.

PAGE

The Quartier-Latin in the late thirties—The difference between then and now—A caricature on the walls of Paris—I am anxious to be introduced to the quarter whence it emanated—I am taken to "La Childebert," and make the acquaintance of the original of the caricature—The story of Bouginier and his nose—Dantan as a caricaturist—He abandons that branch of art after he has made Madame Malibran burst into tears at the sight of her statuette—How Bouginier came to be immortalized on the façade of the Passage du Caire—One of the first co-operative societies in France—An artists' hive—The origin of "La Childebert"—Its tenants in my time—The proprietress—Madame Chanfort, the providence of poor painters—Her portraits sold after her death—High jinks at "La Childebert"—The Childebertians and their peacefully inclined neighbours—Gratuitous baths and compulsory douches at "La Childebert"—The proprietress is called upon to repair the roof—The Childebertians bivouac on the Place St. Germain-des Prés—They start a "Society for the Conversion of the Mahometans"—The public subscribe liberally—What becomes of the subscriptions?—My visits to "La Childebert" breed a taste for the other amusements of the Quartier-Latin—Bobino and its entertainments—The audience—The manager—His stereotyped speech—The reply in chorus—Woe to the bourgeois intruder—Stovepipe hats a rarity in the Quartier-Latin—The dress of the collegians—Their mode of living—Suppers when money was flush, rolls and milk when it was not—A fortune-teller in the Rue de Tournon—Her prediction as to the future of Joséphine de Beauharnais—The allowance to students in those days—The Odéon deserted—Students' habits—The Chaumière—Rural excursions—Père Bonvin's 1

CHAPTER II.

My introduction to the celebrities of the day—The Café de Paris—The old Prince Demidoff—The old man's mania—His sons—The furniture and attendance at the Café de Paris—Its high prices—A mot of Alfred de Musset—The cuisine—A rebuke of the proprietor to Balzac—A version by one of his predecessors of the cause of Vatel's suicide—Some of the *habitués*—Their intercourse with the attendants—Their courteous behaviour towards one another—Le veau à la casserole—What Alfred de Musset, Balzac, and Alexandre Dumas thought of it—A silhouette of Alfred de Musset—His brother Paul on his election as a member of the Académie—A silhouette of Balzac, between sunset and sunrise—A curious action against the publishers of an almanack—A full-length portrait of Balzac—His pecuniary embarrassments—His visions of wealth and speculations—His constant neglect of his duties as a National Guard—His troubles in consequence thereof—L'Hôtel des Haricots—Some of his fellow-prisoners—Adam, the composer of "Le Postillon de Lonjumeau"—Eugène Sue; his portrait His dandyism—The origin of the Paris Jockey Club—Eugène Sue becomes a member—The success of "Les Mystères de Paris"—The origin of "Le Juif-Errant"—Sue makes himself objectionable to the members of the Jockey Club—His name struck off the list—His decline and disappearance 34

CHAPTER III.

Alexandre Dumas père—Why he made himself particularly agreeable to Englishmen—His way of silencing people—The pursuit he loved best next to literature—He has the privilege of going down to the kitchens of the Café de Paris—No one questions his literary genius, some question his culinary capacities—Dr. Véron and his cordon-bleu—Dr. Véron's reasons for dining out instead of at home—Dr. Véron's friend, the philanthropist, who does not go to the theatre because he objects to be hurried with his emotions—Dr. Véron, instigated by his cook, accuses Dumas of having collaborateurs in preparing his dishes as he was known to have collaborateurs in his literary work—Dumas' wrath—He invites us to a dinner which shall be wholly cooked by

CONTENTS.

him in the presence of a delegate to be chosen by the guests—The lot falls upon me—Dr. Véron and Sophie make the *amende honorable*—A dinner-party at Véron's—A curious lawsuit in connection with Weber's "Freyschutz"—Nestor Roqueplan, who became the successor of the defendant in the case, suggests a way out of it—Léon Pillet virtually adopts it and wins the day—A similar plan adopted years before by a fireman on duty at the opéra, on being tried by court-martial for having fallen asleep during the performance of "Guido et Génevra"—Firemen not bad judges of plays and operas—They were often consulted both by Meyerbeer and Dumas—Dumas at work—How he idled his time away—Dumas causes the traffic receipts of the Chemin de Fer de l'Ouest to swell during his three years' residence at Saint-Germain—M. de Montalivet advises Louis-Philippe to invite Dumas to Versailles, to see what his presence will do for the royal city—Louis-Philippe does not act upon the advice—The relations between Dumas and the d'Orléans family—After the Revolution of '48, Dumas becomes a candidate for parliament—The story of his canvass and his address to the electors at Joigny—Dumas' utter indifference to money matters—He casts his burdens upon others—Dumas and his creditors—Writs and distraints—How they are dealt with—Dumas' indiscriminate generosity—A dozen houses full of new furniture in half as many years—Dumas' frugality at table—Literary remuneration—Dumas and his son—"Leave me a hundred francs" 62

CHAPTER IV.

Dr. Louis Véron—The real man as distinguished from that of his own "Memoirs"—He takes the management of the Paris Opéra—How it was governed before his advent—Meyerbeer's "Robert le Diable" *underlined*—Meyerbeer and his doubts upon the merits of his work—Meyerbeer's generosity—Meyerbeer and the beggars of the Rue Le Peletier—Dr. Véron, the inventor of the modern newspaper puff—Some specimens of advertisements in their infancy—Dr. Véron takes a leaf from the book of Molière—Dr. Véron's love of money—His superstitions—His objections to travelling in railways—He quotes the Queen of England as an example—When Queen Victoria overcomes her objection, Véron holds out—"Queen Victoria has got a successor: the Véron dynasty begins and ends with me"—Thirteen at table—I make the acquaintance of Taglioni—The woman and the ballerina—Her adventure at Perth—An improvised performance of "Nathalie, la Laitière Suisse"—Another adventure in Russia—A modern Claude Du-Val—My last meeting with Taglioni—A dinner-party at De Morny's—A comedy scene between husband and wife—Flotow, the composer of "Martha"—His family—His father's objection to the composer's profession—The latter's interview with M. de Saint-Georges, the author of the libretto of Balfe's "Bohemian Girl"—M. de Saint-Georges prevails upon the father to let his son study in Paris for five years, and to provide for him during that time—The supplies are stopped on the last day of the fifth year—Flotow, at the advice of M. de Saint-Georges, stays on and lives by giving piano-lessons—His earthly possessions at his first success—"Rob Roy" at the Hôtel Castellane—Lord Granville's opinion of the music—The Hôtel Castellane and some Paris salons during Louis-Philippe's reign—The Princesse de Lieven's, M. Thiers', etc.—What Madame de Girardin's was like—Victor Hugo's—Perpetual adoration; very artistic, but nothing to eat or to drink—The salon of the ambassador of the Two Sicilies—Lord and Lady Granville at the English Embassy—The salon of Count Apponyi—A story connected with it—Furniture and entertainments—Cakes, ices, and tea; no champagne as during the Second Empire—The Hôtel Castellane and its amateur theatricals—Rival companies—No under-studies—Lord Brougham at the Hôtel Castellane—His bad French and his would-be Don Juanism—A French rendering of Shakespeare's "There is but one step between the sublime and the ridiculous," as applied to Lord Brougham—He nearly accepts a part in a farce where his bad French is likely to produce a comic effect—His successor as a murderer of the language—M. de Saint-Georges—Like Molière, he reads his plays to his housekeeper—When the latter is not satisfied, the dinner is spoilt, however great the success of the play in public estimation—Great men and their housekeepers—Turner, Jean Jacques Rousseau, Eugène Delacroix 90

CHAPTER V.

The Boulevards in the forties—The Chinese Baths—A favourite tobacconist of Alfred de Musset—The price of cigars—The diligence still the usual mode of travelling—Provincials in Paris—Parliamentary see-saw between M. Thiers and M. Guizot—Amenities of editors—An advocate of universal suffrage—Distribution of gratuitous sausages to the working man on the king's birthday—The rendezvous of actors in search of an engagement—Frédérick Lemaître on the eve of appearing in a new part—The Legitimists begin to leave their seclusion and to mingle with the bourgeoisie—Alexandre Dumas and Scribe—The latter's fertility as a playwright—The National Guards go shooting, in uniform and in companies, on the Plaine Saint-Denis—Vidocq's private inquiry office in the Rue Vivienne—No river-side resorts—The plaster elephant on the Place de la Bastille—The sentimental romances of Loïsa Puget—The songs of the working classes—Cheap bread and wine—How they enjoyed themselves on Sundays and holidays—Théophile Gautier's pony-carriage—The hatred of the bourgeoisie—Nestor Roqueplan's expression of it—Gavarni's—M. Thiers' sister keeps a restaurant at the corner of the Rue Drouot—When he is in power, the members of the Opposition go and dine there, and publish facetious accounts of the entertainment—All appearances to the contrary, people like Guizot better than Thiers—But few entries for the race for wealth in those days—The Rothschilds still live in the Rue Lafitte—Favourite lounges—The Boulevards, the Rue Le Peletier, and the Passage de l'Opéra—The Opéra—The Rue Le Peletier and its attractions—The Restaurant of Paolo Broggi—The Estaminet du Divan—Literary waiters and Boniface—Major Fraser—The mystery surrounding his origin—Another mysterious personage—The Passage de l'Opéra is invaded by the stockjobbers, and loses its prestige as a promenade—Bernard Latte's, the publisher of Donizetti's operas, becomes deserted—Tortoni's—Louis-Blanc—His scruples as an editor—A few words about duelling—Two tragic meetings—Lola Montès—Her adventurous career—A celebrated trial—My first meeting with Gustave Flaubert, the author of "Madame Bovary" and "Salambô"—Emile de Girardin—His opinion of duelling—My decision with regard to it—The

CONTENTS.

original of "La Dame aux Camélias"—Her parentage—Alexandre Dumas gives the diagnosis of her character in connection with his son's play—L'Homme au Caméllia—M. Lautour-Mézerai, the inventor of children's periodical literature in France—Auguste Lireux—He takes the management of the Odéon—Balzac again—His schemes, his greed—Lireux more fortunate with other authors—Anglophobia on the French stage—Gallophobia on the English stage .. 124

CHAPTER VI.

Rachel and some of her fellow-actors—Rachel's true character—Her greediness and spitefulness—Her vanity and her wit—Her powers of fascination—The cost of being fascinated by her—Her manner of levying toll—Some of her victims, Comte Duchâtel and Dr. Véron—The story of her guitar—A little transaction between her and M. Fould—Her supposed charity and generosity—Ten tickets for a charity concert—How she made them into twenty—How she could have made them into a hundred—Baron Taylor puzzled—Her manner of giving presents—Beauvallet's precaution with regard to one of her gifts—Alexandre Dumas the younger, wiser or perhaps not so wise in his generation—Rachel as a raconteuse—The story of her *début* at the Gymnase—What Rachel would have been as an actor instead of an actress—Her comic genius—Rachel's mother—What became of Rachel's money—Mama Félix as a pawnbroker—Rachel's trinkets—Two curious bracelets—Her first appearance before Nicholas I.—A dramatic recital in the open air—Rachel's opinion of the handsomest man in Europe—Rachel and Samson—Her obligations to him—How she repays them—How she goes to Berryer to be coached in the fable of "The Two Pigeons"—An anecdote of Berryer—Rachel's fear of a "warm reception" on the first night of "Adrienne Lecouvreur"—How she averts the danger—Samson as a man and as an actor—Petticoat-revolts at the Comédie-Française—Samson and Régnier as buffers—Their different ways of pouring oil upon the troubled waters—Mdlle. Sylvanie Plessy—A parallel between her and Sarah Bernhardt—Samson and Régnier's pride in their profession—The different character of that pride—"Apollo with a bad tailor, and who dresses without a looking-glass"—Samson gives a lesson in declamation to a procureur-impérial—The secret of Régnier's greatness as an actor—A lesson at the Conservatoire—Régnier on "make-up"—Régnier's opinion of genius on the stage—A mot of Augustine Brohan—Giovanni, the wigmaker of the Comédie-Française—His pride in his profession—M. Ancessy, the musical director, and his three wigs 183

CHAPTER VII.

Two composers, Auber and Félicien David—Auber, the legend of his youthful appearance—How it arose—His daily rides, his love of women's society—His mot on Mozart's "Don Juan"—The only drawback to Auber's enjoyment of women's society—His reluctance to take his hat off—How he managed to keep it on most of the time—His opinion upon Meyerbeer's and Halévy's genius—His opinion upon Gérard de Nerval, who hanged himself with his hat on—His love of solitude—His fondness of Paris—His grievance against his mother for not having given him birth there—He refuses to leave Paris at the commencement of the siege—His small appetite—He proposes to write a new opera when the Prussians are gone—Auber suffers no privations, but has difficulty in finding fodder for his horse—The Parisians claim it for food—Another legend about Auber's independence of sleep—How and where he generally slept—Why Auber snored in Véron's company, and why he did not in that of other people—His capacity for work—Auber a brilliant talker—Auber's gratitude to the artists who interpreted his work, but different from Meyerbeer's—The reason why, according to Auber—Jealousy or humility—Auber and the younger Coquelin—"The verdict on all things in this world may be summed up in the one phrase, 'It's an injustice'"—Félicien David—The man—The beginnings of his career—His terrible poverty—He joins the Saint-Simoniens, and goes with some of them to the East—Their reception at Constantinople—M. Scribe and the libretto of "L'Africaine"—David in Egypt at the court of Mehemet-Ali—David's description of him—Mehemet's way of testing the educational progress of his sons—Woe to the fat kine—Mehemet-Ali suggests a new mode of teaching music to the inmates of the harem—Félicien David's further wanderings in Egypt—Their effect upon his musical genius—His return to France—He tells the story of the first performance of "Le Désert"—An ambulant box-office—His success—Fame, but no money—He sells the score of "Le Désert"—He loses his savings—"La Perle du Brésil" and the Coup-d'Etat—"No luck"—Napoleon III. remains his debtor for eleven years—A mot of Auber, and one of Alexandre Dumas père—The story of "Aïda"—Why Félicien David did not compose the music—The real author of the libretto 217

CHAPTER VIII.

Three painters, and a school for pifferari—Gabriel Decamps, Eugène Delacroix, and Horace Vernet—The prices of pictures in the forties—Delacroix' find no purchasers at all—Decamps' drawings fetch a thousand francs each—Decamps not a happy man—The cause of his unhappiness—The man and the painter—He finds no pleasure in being popular—Eugène Delacroix—His contempt for the bourgeoisie—A parallel between Delacroix and Shakespeare—Was Delacroix tall or short?—His love of flowers—His delicate health—His personal appearance—His indifference to the love-passion—George Sand and Delacroix—A miscarried love-scene—Delacroix' housekeeper, Jenny Leguillou—Delacroix does not want to pose as a model for one of George Sand's heroes—Delacroix as a writer—His approval of Carlyle's dictum, "Show me how a man sings," etc.—His humour tempered by his reverence—His failure as a caricaturist—His practical jokes on would-be art-critics—Delacroix at home—His dress while at work—Horace Vernet's, Paul Delaroche's, Ingrès'—Early at work—He does not waste time over lunch—How he spent his evenings—His dislike of being reproduced in marble or on canvas after his death—Horace Vernet—The contrast between the two men and the two artists—Vernet's appearance—His own account of how he became a painter—Moral and mental resemblance to Alexandre Dumas père—His political opinions—Vernet and Nicholas I.—A bold answer—His opinion on the mental state of the Romanoffs—The comic side of

Vernet's character—He thinks himself a Vauban—His interviews with M. Thiers—His admiration of everything military—His worship of Alfred de Vigny—His ineffectual attempts to paint a scene in connection with the storming of Constantine—Laurent-Jan proposes to write an epic on it—He gives a synopsis of the cantos—Laurent-Jan lives "on the fat of the land" for six months—A son of Napoleon's companion in exile, General Bertrand—The chaplain of "la Belle-Poule"—The first French priest who wore the English dress—Horace Vernet and the veterans of "la grande armée"—His studio during their occupancy of it as models—His budget—His hatred of pifferari—A professor—The Quartier-Latin revisited 234

CHAPTER IX.

Louis-Philippe and his family—An unpublished theatrical skit on his mania for shaking hands with every one—His art of governing, according to the same skit—Louis-Philippe not the ardent admirer of the bourgeoisie he professed to be—The Faubourg Saint-Germain deserts the Tuileries—The English in too great a majority—Lord ——'s opinion of the dinners at the Tuileries—The attitude of the bourgeoisie towards Louis-Philippe, according to the King himself—Louis-Philippe's wit—His final words on the death of Talleyrand—His love of money—He could be generous at times—A story of the Palais-Royal—Louis-Philippe and the Marseillaise—Two curious stories connected with the Marseillaise—Who was the composer of it?—Louis-Philippe's opinion of the throne, the crown, and the sceptre of France as additions to one's comfort—His children, and especially his sons, take things more easily—Even the Bonapartists admired some of the latter—A mot of an Imperialist—How the boys were brought up—Their nocturnal rambles later on—The King himself does not seem to mind those escapades, but is frightened at M. Guizot hearing of them—Louis-Philippe did not understand Guizot—The recollection of his former misery frequently haunts the King—He worries Queen Victoria with his fear of becoming poor—Louis-Philippe an excellent husband and father—He wants to write the libretto of an opera on an English subject—His religion—The court receptions ridiculous—Even the proletariat sneer at them—The *entrée* of the Duchesse d'Orléans into Paris—The scene in the Tuileries gardens—A mot of Princesse Clémentine on her father's too paternal solicitude—A practical joke of the Prince de Joinville—His caricatures and drawings—The children inherited their talent for drawing and modelling from their mother—The Duc de Nemours as a miniature and water-colour painter—Suspected of being a Legitimist—All Louis-Philippe's children great patrons of art—How the bourgeoisie looked upon their intercourse with artists—The Duc de Nemours' marvellous memory—The studio of Eugène Lami—His neighbours, Paul Delaroche and Honoré de Balzac—The Duc de Nemours' bravery called in question—The Duc d'Aumale's exploits in Algeria considered mere skirmishes—A curious story of spiritism—The Duc d'Aumale a greater favourite with the world than any of the other sons of Louis-Philippe — His wit — The Duc d'Orléans also a great favourite—His visits to Decamps' studio—An indifferent classical scholar—A curious kind of black-mail—His indifference to money—There is no money in a Republic—His death—A witty reply to the Legitimists 264

CHAPTER X.

The Revolution of '48—The beginning of it—The National Guards in all their glory—The Café Grégoire on the Place du Caire—The price of a good breakfast in '48—The palmy days of the Cuisine Bourgeoise—The excitement on the Boulevards on Sunday, February 20th, '48—The theatres—A ball at Poirson's, the erstwhile director of the Gymnase—A lull in the storm—Tuesday, February 22nd—Another visit to the Café Grégoire—On my way thither—The Comédie-Française closes its doors—What it means, according to my old tutor—We are waited upon by a sergeant and corporal—We are no longer "messieurs," but "citoyens"—An eye to the main chance—The patriots do a bit of business in tricolour cockades—The company marches away—Casualties—"Le patriotisme" means the difference between the louis d'or and the écu of three francs— The company bivouacs on the Boulevard Saint-Martin—A tyrant's victim "*malgre lui* —Wednesday, February 23rd—The Café Grégoire once more—The National Guards *en negligé*—A novel mode of settling accounts—The National Guards fortify the inner man—A bivouac on the Boulevard du Temple—A camp scene from an opera—I leave—My companion's account —The National Guards protect the regulars—The author of these notes goes to the theatre—The Gymnase and the Variétés on the eve of the Revolution—Bouffé and Déjazet —Thursday, February 24th, '48—The Boulevards at 9.30 a.m. —No milk—The Revolutionaries do without it—The Place du Carrousel—The sovereign people fire from the roofs on the troops—The troops do not dislodge them—The King reviews the troops—The apparent inactivity of Louis-Philippe's sons—A theory about the difference in bloodshed —One of the three ugliest men in France comes to see the King—Seditious cries—The King abdicates—Chaos—The sacking of the Tuileries—Receptions and feasting in the Galerie de Diane—" Du café pour nous, des cigarettes pour les dames "—The dresses of the princesses—The bourgeois feast the gamins who guard the barricades—The Republic proclaimed—The riff-raff insist upon illuminations—An actor promoted to the Governorship of the Hôtel de Ville— Some members of the " provisional Government " at work —Méry on Lamartine—Why the latter proclaimed the Republic 298

AN ENGLISHMAN IN PARIS.

CHAPTER I.

The Quartier-Latin in the late thirties—The difference between then and now—A caricature on the walls of Paris—I am anxious to be introduced to the quarter whence it emanated—I am taken to "La Childebert," and make the acquaintance of the original of the caricature—The story of Bouginier and his nose—Dantan as a caricaturist—He abandons that branch of art after he has made Madame Malibran burst into tears at the sight of her statuette—How Bouginier came to be immortalized on the façade of the Passage du Caire—One of the first co-operative societies in France—An artists' hive—The origin of "La Childebert"—Its tenants in my time—The proprietress—Madame Chanfort, the providence of poor painters—Her portraits sold after her death—High jinks at "La Childebert"—The Childebertians and their peacefully inclined neighbours—Gratuitous baths and compulsory douches at "La Childebert"—The proprietress is called upon to repair the roof—The Childebertians bivouac on the Place St. Germain-des-Prés—They start a "Society for the Conversion of the Mahometans"—The public subscribe liberally—What becomes of the subscriptions?—My visits to "La Childebert" breed a taste for the other amusements of the Quartier-Latin—Bobino and its entertainments—The audience—The manager—His stereotyped speech—The reply in chorus—Woe to the bourgeois-intruder—Stove-pipe hats a rarity in the Quartier-Latin—The dress of the collegians—Their mode of living—Suppers when money was flush, rolls and milk when it was not—A fortune-teller in the Rue de Tournon—Her prediction as to the future of Joséphine de Beauharnais—The allowance to students in those days—The Odéon deserted—Students' habits—The Chaumière—Rural excursions—Père Bonvin's.

LONG before Baron Haussmann began his architectural transformation, many parts of Paris had undergone changes, perceptible only to those who had been brought up among the inhabitants, though distinct from them in nationality, education, habits, and tastes. Paris became to a certain extent, and not altogether voluntarily, cosmopolitan before the palatial mansions, the broad avenues, the handsome public squares which subsequently excited the admiration of the civilized world had been dreamt of, and while its outer aspect was as yet scarcely modified. This was mainly due to the establishment of railways, which caused in the end large influxes of foreigners and provincials, who as it were drove the real Parisian from his haunts. Those visitors rarely penetrated in large numbers to the very heart of the Quartier-Latin. When they crossed the bridges that span the Seine, it was to see the Sorbonne, the Panthéon, the Observatory, the Odéon, and the Luxembourg; they rarely stayed after nightfall. The Prado, the Theatre Bobino, the students' taverns, escaped their observation when there was really something to see; and now, when the Closerie des Lilas has become the Bal Bullier, when the small theatre has been demolished, and when the taverns are in no way distinguished from other Parisian taverns—when, in short, commonplace pervades the whole—people flock thither very often. But during the whole of the forties, and even later, the *rive gauche*, with its Quartier-Latin and adjacent Faubourg St. Germain, were almost entirely sacred from the desecrating stare of the deliberate sightseer; and, consequently, the former especially, preserved its individuality, not only materially, but mentally and morally—immorally would perhaps have been the word that would have risen to the lips of the observer who lacked the time and inclination to study the life led there deeper than it appeared merely on the surface. For though there was a good deal of roystering and practical joking, and short-lasted *liaison*, there was little of deliberate vice, of strategic libertinism—if I may be allowed to coin the expression. True, every Jack had his Jill, but, as a rule, it was Jill who had set the ball rolling.

The Quartier-Latin not only sheltered sucking lawyers and doctors, budding professors and savans and literateurs, but artists whose names have since then become world-renowned. It was with some of these that I was most thrown in contact in that quarter, partly from inclination, because from my earliest youth I have been fonder of pictures than of books, partly because at that time I had already seen so many authors of fame, most of whom were the intimate acquaintances of a connection of mine, that I cared little to seek the society of those who had not arrived at that stage. I was very young, and, though not devoid of faith in possibilities, too mentally indolent when judgment in that respect involved the sitting down to manuscripts. It was so much easier and charming to be able to discover a budding genius by a mere glance at a good sketch, even when the latter was drawn on charcoal on a not particularly clean "whitewashed" wall.

I was scarcely more than a stripling when one morning such a sketch appeared on the walls of Paris, and considerably mystified, while it at the same time amused, the inhabitants of the capital. It was not the work of what we in England would call a "seascape and mackerel artist," for no such individual stood by to ask toll of the admirers; it was not an advertisement, for in those days that mode of mural publicity was scarcely born, let alone in its infancy, in Paris. What, then, was this colossal, monumental nose, the like of which I have only seen on the faces of four human beings, one of whom was Hyacinth, the famous actor of the Palais-Royal, the other three being M. d'Argout, the Governor of the Bank of France; M. de Jussieu, the Director of the Jardin des Plantes; and Lasailly, Balzac's secretary? What was this colossal nose, with a ridiculously small head and body attached to it? The nasal organ was certainly phenomenal, even allowing for the permissible exaggeration of the caricaturist, but it could surely not be the only title of its owner to this sudden leap into fame? Was it a performing nose, or one endowed with extraordinary powers of smell? I puzzled over the question for several days, until one morning I happened to run against my old tutor, looking at the picture and laughing till the tears ran down his wrinkled cheeks. It was a positive pleasure to see him. "C'est bien lui, c'est bien lui," he exclaimed; "c'est absolument son portrait craché!" "Do you know the original?" I asked. "Mais, sans doute, je le connais, c'est un ami de mon fils, du reste, tout le monde connait Bouginier." "But I do not know him," I protested, feeling very much ashamed of my ignorance. "Ah, you! that's quite a different thing; you do not live in the Quartier-Latin, but everybody there knows him." From that moment I knew no rest until I had made the acquaintance of Bouginier, which was not very difficult; and through him I became a frequent visitor to "La Childebert," which deserves a detailed description, because, though it was a familiar haunt to many Parisians of my time with a taste for Bohemian society, I doubt whether many Englishmen, save (the late) Mr. Blanchard Jerrold and one of the Mayhews, ever set foot there, and even they could not have seen it in its prime.

But before I deal with "La Childebert," I must say a few words about Bouginier, who, contrary to my expectations, owed his fame solely to his *proboscis*. He utterly disappeared from the artistic horizon in a few years, but his features still live in the memory of those who knew him through a statuette in *terra cotta* modelled by Dantan the younger. During the reign of Louis-Philippe, Dantan took to that branch of art as a relaxation from his more serious work; he finally abandoned it after he had made Madame Malibran burst into tears, instead of making her laugh, as he intended, at her own caricature. Those curious in such matters may see Bouginier's presentment in a medallion on the frontispiece of the Passage du Caire, amidst the Egyptian divinities and sphinxes. As a matter of course, the spectator asks himself why this modern countenance should find itself in such incongruous company, and he comes almost naturally to the conclusion that Bouginier was the owner, or perhaps the architect, of this arcade, almost exclusively tenanted —until very recently—by lithographers, printers, etc. The conclusion, however, would be an erroneous one. Bouginier, as far as is known, never had any property in Paris or elsewhere; least of all was he vain enough to perpetuate his own features in that manner, even if he had had an opportunity, but he had not; seeing that he was not an architect, but simply a painter, of no great talents certainly, but, withal, modest and sensible, and as such opposed to, or at any rate not sharing, the crazes of mediævalism, romanticism, and other *isms* in which the young painters of that day indulged, and which they thought fit to emphasize in public and among one another by eccentricities of costume and language, supposed to be in harmony with the periods they had adopted for illustration. This absence of enthusiasm one way or the other aroused the ire of his fellow-lodgers at the "Childebert," and one of them, whose pencil was more deft at that kind of work than those of the others, executed their vengeance, and drew Bouginier's picture on the "fag end" of a dead wall in the vicinity of the Church of St. Germain-des-Prés. The success was instantaneous and positively overwhelming, though truth compels one to state that this was the only flash of genius that illumined that young fellow's career. His name was Fourreau, and one looks in vain for his name in the biographical dictionaries or encyclopedias of artists. Fate has even been more cruel to him than to his model.

For the moment, however, the success, as I have already said, was overwhelming. In less than a fortnight there was not a single wall in Paris and its outskirts without a Bouginier on its surface. Though Paris was considerably less in area than it is now, it wanted a Herculean effort to accomplish this. No man, had he been endowed with as many arms as Briareus, would have sufficed for it. Nor would it have done to trust to more or less skilful copyists—they might have failed to catch the likeness, which was really an admirable one; so the following device was hit upon. Fourreau himself cut a number of stencil plates in brown paper, and, provided with them, an army of Childebertians started every night in various directions, Fourreau and a few undoubtedly clever youths heading the detachments, and filling in the blanks by hand.

Meanwhile summer had come, and with it the longing among the young Tintos to breathe the purer air of the country, to sniff the salt breezes of the ocean. As a matter of course, they were not all ready to start at the same time, but being determined to follow the same route, to assemble at a common goal, the contingent that was to leave a fortnight later than the first arranged to join the others wherever they might be.

"But how?" was the question of those who were left behind. "Very simply indeed," was the answer; "we'll go by the Barrière d'Italie. You'll have but to look at the walls along the road, and you'll find your waybill."

So said, so done. A fortnight after, the second division left head-quarters and made straight for the Barrière d'Italie. But when outside the gates they stood undecided. For one moment only. The next they caught sight of a magnificent Bouginier on a wall next to the excise office—of a Bouginier whose outstretched index pointed to the Fontainebleau road. After that, all went well. As far as Marseilles their Bouginier no more failed them than the clouds of smoke and fire failed the Israelites in the wilderness. At the seaport town they lost the track for a little while, rather through their want of faith in the ingenuity of their predecessors than through the latter's lack of such ingenuity. They had the Mediterranean in front of them, and even if they found a Bouginier depicted somewhere on the shore, his outstretched index could only point to the restless waves; he could do nothing more definite. Considerably depressed, they were going down the Cannebière, when they caught sight of the features of their guiding star on a panel between the windows of a shipping office. His outstretched index did not point this time; it was placed over a word, and that word spelt "Malta." They took ship as quickly as possible for the ancient habitation of the Knights-Templars. On the walls of the Customs in the island was Bouginier, with a scroll issuing from his nostrils, on which was inscribed the word "Alexandria." A similar indication met their gaze at the Pyramids, and at last the second contingent managed to come up with the first amidst the ruins of Thebes at the very moment when the word "Suez" was being traced as issuing from Bouginier's mouth.

Among the company was a young fellow of the name of Berthier, who became subsequently an architect of some note. The Passage du Caire, as I have already observed, was in those days the head-quarters of the lithographic-printing business in general, but there was one branch which flourished more than the rest, namely, that of *lettres de faire part*,* menus of restaurants and visiting-cards. The two first-named documents were, in common with most printed matter intended for circulation, subject to a stamp duty, but in the early days of the Second Empire Louis-Napoleon had it taken off. To mark their sense of the benefit conferred, the lithographic firms † determined

* The "lettre de faire part" is an intimation of a birth, marriage, or death sent to the friends, and even mere acquaintances, of a family.— EDITOR.

† The lithographers were almost the first in France to form a co-operative society, but not in the sense of the Rochdale pioneers, which

to have the arcade, which stood in sad need of repair, restored, and Berthier was selected for the task. The passage was originally built to commemorate Bonaparte's victories in Egypt, and when Berthier received the commission, he could think of no more fitting façade than the reproduction of a house at Karnac. He fondly remembered his youthful excursion to the land of Pharaohs, and at the same time the image of Bouginier uprose before him. That is why the presentment of the latter may be seen up to this day on the frieze of a building in the frowsiest part of Paris.

If I have dwelt somewhat longer on Bouginier than the importance of the subject warranted, it was mainly to convey an idea of the spirit of mischief, of the love of practical joking, that animated most of the inmates of "La Childebert." As a rule their devilries were innocent enough. The pictorial persecution of Bouginier is about the gravest thing that could be laid to their charge, and the victim, like the sensible fellow he was, rather enjoyed it than otherwise. Woe, however, to the starched bourgeois who had been decoyed into their lair, or even to the remonstrating comrade with a serious turn of mind, who wished to pursue his studies in peace! His life was made a burden to him, for the very building lent itself to all sorts of nocturnal surprises and of guerilla sorties. Elsewhere, when a man's door was shut, he might reasonably count upon a certain amount of privacy; the utmost his neighbours could do was to make a noise overhead or by his side. At the "Childebert" such privacy was out of the

dates from about the same period. The Lacrampe Association was for supplying lithographic work. It began in the Passage du Caire with ten members, and in a short time numbered two hundred workmen.—EDITOR.

question. There was not a door that held on its hinges, not a window that could be opened or shut at will, not a ceiling that did not threaten constantly to crush you beneath its weight, not a floor that was not in danger of giving way beneath you and landing you in the room below, not a staircase that did not shake under your very steps, however light they might be; in short, the place was a wonderful illustration of "how the rotten may hold together," even if it be not gently handled.

The origin of the structure, as it stood then, was wrapt in mystery. It was five or six stories high, and must have attained that altitude before the first Revolution, because the owner, a Madame Legendre, who bought it for assignats amounting in real value to about one pound sterling, when the clergy's property was sold by the nation, was known never to have spent a penny upon it either at the time of the purchase or subsequently, until she was forced by a tenant more ingenious or more desperate than the rest. That it could not have been part of the abbey and adjacent monastery built by Childebert I., who was buried there in 558, was very certain. It is equally improbable that the Cardinal de Bissy, who opened a street upon the site of the erstwhile abbey in the year of Louis XIV.'s death, would have erected so high a pile for the mere accommodation of the pensioners of the former monastery, at a time when high piles were the exception. Besides, the Nos. 1 and 3, known to have been occupied by those pensioners, all of whose rooms communicated with one another, were not more than two stories high. In short, the original intention of the builder of the house No. 9, yclept "La Childebert," has never been explained. The only tenant in the

Rue Childebert who might have thrown a light on the subject had died before the caravansary attained its fame. He was more than a hundred years old, and had married five times. His fifth wife was only eighteen when she became Madame Chanfort, and survived him for many, many years. She was a very worthy soul, a downright providence to the generally impecunious painters, whom she used to feed at prices which even then were ridiculously low. Three eggs, albeit fried in grease instead of butter, for the sum of three-halfpence, and a dinner, including wine, for sixpence, could not have left much profit; but Madame Chanfort always declared that she had enough to live upon, and that she supplied the art-students with food at cost price because she would not be without their company. At her death, in '57, two years before the "Childebert" and the street of the same name disappeared, there was a sale of her chattels, and over a hundred portraits and sketches of her, "in her habit as she lived," came under the hammer. To show that the various occupants of "La Childebert" could do more than make a noise and play practical jokes, I may state that not a single one of these productions fetched less than fifty francs—mere crayon studies; while there were several that sold for two hundred and three hundred francs, and two studies in oil brought respectively eight hundred francs and twelve hundred francs. Nearly every one of the young men who had signed these portraits had made a name for himself. The latter two were signed respectively Paul Delaroche and Tony Johannot.

Nevertheless, to those whose love of peace and quietude was stronger than their artistic instincts and watchful admiration of budding genius, the neighbourhood of "La Childebert" was a sore and grievous trial. At times the street itself, not a very long or wide one, was like Pandemonium let loose; it was when there was an "At Home" at "La Childebert," and such functions were frequent, especially at the beginning of the months. These gatherings, as a rule, partook of the nature of fancy dress *conversaziones;* for dancing, owing to the shakiness of the building, had become out of the question, even with such dare-devils as the tenants. What the latter prided themselves upon most was their strict adherence to the local colour of the periods they preferred to resuscitate. Unfortunately for the tranquillity of the neighbourhood, they pretended to carry out this revival in its smallest details, not only in their artistic productions, but in their daily lives. The actor who blacked himself all over to play Othello was as nothing to them in his attempted realism, because we may suppose that he got rid of his paint before returning to the everyday world. Not so the inmates of "La Childebert." They were minstrels, or corsairs, or proud and valiant knights from the moment they got up till the moment they went to bed, and many of them even scorned to stretch their weary limbs on so effeminate a contrivance as a modern mattress, but endeavoured to keep up the illusion by lying on a rush-bestrewn floor.

I am not sufficiently learned to trace these various and succeeding disguises to their literary and theatrical causes, for it was generally a new book or a new play that set the ball rolling in a certain direction; nor can I vouch for the chronological accuracy and completeness of my record in that respect, but I remember some phases of that ever-shifting masquerade. When I was a very little boy, I was struck more than once with the sight of young men parading the streets in doublets, trunk nose, their flowing locks adorned with velvet caps and birds' wings, their loins girded with short swords. And yet it was not carnival-time. No one seemed to take particular notice of them; the Parisians by that time had probably got used to their vagaries. Those competent in such matters have since told me that the "get-up" was inspired by "La Gaule Poétique" of M. de Marchangy, the novels of M. d'Arlincourt, and the kindred stilted literature that characterized the beginning of the Restoration. Both these gentlemen, from their very hatred of the Greeks and Romans of the first Empire, created heroes of fiction still more ridiculous than the latter, just as Metternich, through his weariness of the word "fraternity," said that if he had a brother he would call him "cousin." A few years later, the first translation of Byron's works produced its effect; and then came Defauconpret, with his very creditable French versions of Walter Scott. The influence of Paul Delaroche and his co-champions of the cause of romanticism, the revolution of July, the dramas of Alexandre Dumas and Victor Hugo, all added their quota to the prevailing confusion in the matter of style and period, and early in the forties there were at the "Childebert" several camps, fraternizing in everything save in their dress and speech, which were the visible and audible manifestation of their individual predilection for certain periods of history. For instance, it was no uncommon thing to hear the son of a concierge, whose real or fancied vocation had made him embrace the artistic profession, swear by "the faith of his ancestors," while the impoverished scion of a noble house replied by calling him "a bloated reminiscence of a feudal and superstitious age."

At the *conversaziones* which I mentioned just now, the guests of the inmates of "La Childebert" not only managed to out-Herod Herod in diction and attire, but, to heighten illusion still further, adopted as far as possible the mode of conveyance supposed to have been employed by their prototypes. The classicists, and those still addicted to the illustration of Greek and Roman mythology, though nominally in the minority at the "Childebert" itself, were, as a rule, most successful in those attempts. The ass that had borne Silenus, the steeds that had drawn the chariot of the triumphant Roman warrior, the she-goat that was supposed to have suckled Jupiter, were as familiar to the inhabitants of the Rue Childebert as the cats and mongrels of their own households. The obstructions caused by the former no longer aroused their ire; but when, one evening, Romulus and Remus made their appearance, accompanied by the legendary she-wolf, they went mad with terror. The panic was at its height when, with an utter disregard of mythological tradition, Hercules walked up the street, leading the Nemæan lion. Then the aid of the police was invoked; but neither the police nor the national guards, who came after them, dared to tackle the animals, though they might have done so safely, because the supposed wolf was a great dane, and the lion a mastiff, but so marvellously padded and painted as to deceive any but the most practised eye. The culprits, however, did not reveal the secret until they were at the commissary of police's office, enjoying the magnificent treat of setting the whole of the neighbourhood in an uproar on their journey thither, and of frightening that official on their arrival.

In fact, long before I knew them, the inmates of the "Childebert" had become a positive scourge to the neighbourhood, while the structure itself threatened ruin to everything around it. Madame Legendre absolutely refused to do any repairs. She did not deny that she had bought the place cheap, but she pointed out at the same time that the rents she charged were more than modest, and that eight times out of ten she did not get them. In the beginning of her ownership she had employed a male concierge, to prevent, as it were, the wholesale flitting which was sure to follow a more strenuous application for arrears upon which she ventured now and then in those days. That was towards the end of the Empire, when the disciples of David had been reduced to a minority in the place by those of Lethière, who sounded the first note of revolt against the unconditional classicism of the illustrious member of the Convention. If all the disciples of the Creole painter had not his genius, most of them had his courage and readiness to draw the sword on the smallest provocation,* and the various Cerberi employed by Madame Legendre to enforce her claims had to fly one after another. The rumour of the danger of the situation had spread, and at last

* Guillaume Lethière, whose real name was Guillon, was a native of Guadeloupe. He fought and seriously wounded several officers because the latter had objected to "a mere dauber wearing moustaches." He was obliged to leave Paris, but, thanks to the protection of Lucien Bonaparte, was appointed Director of the French Académie at Rome.—EDITOR.

Madame Legendre could find no man to fill it, except on monetary conditions with which she would not—perhaps could not—comply. From that day forth she employed a woman, who was safe, because she had been told to let "lawless impecuniosity" take its course, and it was recorded that pecuniarily the proprietress was the better off for this change of tactics.

I am willing to repeat that record, which, if true, did credit to the head of the landlady and the hearts of her tenants, but am compelled to supplement it by a different version. When I saw the "Childebert" in '37 or '38, no man in his senses would have paid rent for any one room in it on the two top stories; he might as well have lived in the streets. It was an absolute case of the bottomless sedan chair in which two of his fellow-porters put Pat; "but for the honour of the thing, he might have walked." Consequently the tenants there were rarely harassed for their rent; if they paid it at all, it was so much unexpected gain. It happened, however, that now and then by mistake a youngster was put there who had scruples about discharging his liabilities in that respect; and one of these was Emile Lapierre, who subsequently became a landscape-painter of note. One night, after he had taken up his quarters there, the floodgates of heaven opened over Paris. Lapierre woke up amidst a deluge. I need not say that there were no bells at the "Childebert;" nevertheless there was no fear of dying unattended, provided one could shout, for there was always a party turning night into day, or hailing the smiling morn before turning in. Lapierre's shouts found a ready echo, and in a few moments the old concierge was on the spot.

"Go and fetch a boat—go and fetch a boat!" yelled Lapierre. "I am drowning!" yelled Lapierre.

"There are none in the quarter," replied the old woman innocently, thinking he was in earnest.

"Then go and fetch Madame Legendre, to show her the pond she is letting me instead of the room for which I pay her."

"Madame would not come, not even for you, monsieur, who are the only one punctual with your rent; besides, if she did come, she would have no repairs done."

"Oh, she'll have no repairs done! We'll soon find out. I think I'll make her," screamed Lapierre; and he kept his word.

It was the only instance of Madame Legendre having had to capitulate, and I have alluded to it before; it remains for me to tell how it was done.

Lapierre, contrary to the precept, allowed the sun to go down upon his wrath, in the hope perhaps of inducing Madame Legendre to change her oft-announced decision of doing no repairs; but he rose betimes next morning, and when there was no sign of workmen, he proceeded to carry out his plan. The floors of the "Childebert" were made of brick, and he simply removed three or four squares from his, after which he went downstairs and recruited half a dozen water-carriers, and bade them empty their full pails into the opening he had made. I shall probably have some remarks to make elsewhere about the water-supply of Paris; at present it is sufficient to say that in those days there was not a single house in the capital which was not dependent upon those Auvergnats who carried the commodity round in barrels on carts drawn by hand or horse. These gentlemen, though astonished at the strange task required of them, consented. In less than ten minutes there was a string of water-carts stationed in the Rue Childebert, and in a few minutes more the lower stories were simply flooded. Aimé Millet, the sculptor, whose room was situated immediately beneath that of Lapierre, was the first victim. It was he who gave the alarm, but, as a matter of course, in the twinkling of an eye there were one or two heads at every window, and though very early, there was a stampede of very primitively clad models(?) into the street, shouting and yelling out at the top of their voices. Outside no one seemed to know exactly what had occurred; the prevailing impression was that the place was on fire. Then Madame Legendre was sent for in hot haste. By that time the truth had become known in the house. The alarm had subsided, but not the noise. When the report of Madame Legendre's coming got wind, a deputation went to the entrance of the street to welcome her. It was provided with all sorts of instruments except musical ones, and the old dame was conducted in state to Millet's room. The cause of the mischief was soon ascertained, for the water-carriers were still at work. The police had refused to interfere; in reality, they would not have been sorry to see the building come down with a crash, for it was as great a source of annoyance to them as to the peaceful burghers they were supposed to protect. A move was made to the room above, where Lapierre—without a stitch of clothing—stood directing the operations.

"What are you doing, Monsieur Lapierre?" screeched Madame Legendre.

"I am taking a bath, madame; it is very warm. You gave me one against my will the night before last; and lest I should be accused of selfishness, I am letting my neighbours partake of the pleasure."

That is how Madame Legendre was compelled to repair the roof of " La Childebert."

Such was the company amidst which I was introduced by the son of my old tutor. Many years have passed since then, during which I have been thrown into the society of the great and powerful ones of this world, rather through the force of circumstances than owing to my own merits, but I have looked in vain for the honest friendships, the disinterested actions, the genuine enthusiasm for their art, underlying their devilry, of which these young men were capable. The bourgeois vices, in the guise of civic and domestic virtues, entered the souls of Frenchmen early in the reign of Louis-Philippe, and have been gnawing since, with ever-increasing force, like a cancer, at everything that was noble and worthy of admiration in a nation. But those vices never found their way to the hearts of the inmates of " La Childebert " while they were there, and rarely in after-life. Many attained world-wide reputations; few gathered riches, even when they were as frugal as the best among them—Eugène Delacroix.

To have known these young men was absolutely a liberal education. To the Podsnap and Philistine of no matter what nationality, it seems a sad thing to have no thought for to-morrow. And these youngsters had not even a thought for the day. Their thoughts were for the future, when the world mayhap would ring with their names; but their physical or mental hearing never strained for the ring of money. They were improvident creatures, to be sure; but how much more lovable than the young painters of the present period, whose ideal is a big balance at their bankers; who would rather have their names inscribed on the registers of the public debt than in the golden book of art; whose dreamt-of Eden is a bijou villa in the Parc Monceaux or in the Avenue Villiers; whose providence is the *richard*, the parvenu, the wealthy upstart, whose features they perpetuate, regardless of the perpetuation of their own budding fame.

When I began to jot down these notes, I made up my mind to eschew comparisons and moralizing; I find I have unconsciously done both, but will endeavour not to offend again. Still, I cannot help observing how the mere "moneyed nobody" rushes nowadays to the eminent painter to have his lineaments reproduced, when a guinea photograph would serve his purpose just as well for "family use;" for I take it that no one, besides his relations and friends, cares or will care to gaze upon his features. And yet our annual picture exhibitions are crowded with the portraits of these nonentities. They advertise themselves through the painters that transfer them to canvas, and the latter are content to pocket heavy fees, like the advertising agents they are. I am certain that neither Holbein, Rubens, Van Dyck, Hals, nor Rembrandt would have lent themselves to such transactions. When they, or a Reynolds, a Lawrence, a Gainsborough, conferred the honour of their brush upon some one, it was because he or she was already distinguished from his or her fellow-creatures by beauty, social position, talents, genius, or birth; not because he or she wanted to be, or, in default of such distinction, wanted to attract the public notice at all costs. That, I fancy, was the way in which painters of other days looked upon the thing. I know it was the way in which the young fellows at the "Childebert" did; and woe to their comrade who ventured to apply in art the principle of international maritime law, that " le pavillon couvre la marchandise " (the flag covers the cargo). He was scouted and jeered at, and, moreover, rarely allowed to reap the pecuniary benefit of his artistic abasement. Hence the "patron for a portrait" seldom found his way to "La Childebert." When he did, the whole of the place conspired to make his life and that of his would-be *protégé* a misery.

To enumerate all the devices resorted to to make the sittings abortive, to "distort the features that had donned the bland smile of placid contentment" with the paralyzing fear of some impending catastrophe, would be impossible; the mention of a few must suffice. That most frequently employed, and comparatively easy of execution, was the setting alight of damp straw; the dense smoke penetrated every nook and cranny of the crazy building, and the sitter, mad with fright, rushed away. The chances were a hundred to one against his ever returning. Another was the intrusion of a male model offering his services as a Saint-Jérome, or a female one offering hers as Godiva; for, curious to relate, the devotion of the wife of Leofric of Murcia was a favourite subject with the Childebertians. As a matter of course, the applicants were in the costume, or rather lack of costume, appropriate to the character. The strait-laced bourgeois or bourgeoise was shocked, and did not repeat the visit. The cry that there was a mad dog in the house was a common one on those occasions; and at last the would-be portrait-painters had to give in, and a big placard appeared on the frontispiece: "Le commerce des portraits a été cédé aux directeur et membres de l'École des Beaux-Arts."

The most curious thing in connection with the "Childebert" was that, though the place was inexpressibly ill kept, it escaped the most terrible visitations of the cholera. I prefer not to enter into details of the absolute disregard of all sanitary conditions, but in warm weather the building became positively uninhabitable. Long before the unsavoury spectacle of "learned fleas" became a feature of the suburban fairs, Emile Signol, who is best known as a painter of religious subjects, had trained a company of performers of a different kind of nocturnal pests. He averred in his opening lecture that their ingenuity was too great to remain unknown, and cited anecdotes fully proving his words. Certain is it that they were the only enemies before which the combined forces of the Childebertians proved powerless. But even under such trying circumstances the latter never lost their buoyant spirits, and their retreats *en masse* were effected in a manner the reports of which set the whole of Paris in a roar. One Sunday morning, the faithful worshippers, going to matins at the Church of St. Germain-des-Prés, found the square occupied by a troop of Bedouins, wrapt in their burnouses, and sleeping the sleep of the just. Some had squatted in corners, calmly smoking their *chibouks*. This was in the days of the Algerian campaign, and the rumour spread like wildfire that a party of Arab prisoners of war were bivouacked round the church, where a special service would be given in the afternoon as the first step to their conversion to Christianity. It being Sunday, the whole of Paris rushed to the spot. The Bedouins had, however, disappeared, but a collection was made in their behalf by several demure-looking young men. The Parisians gave liberally. That night, and two or three nights after, the nocturnal pests' occupation was gone, for the "Childebert" was lighted *a giorno* from basement to roof, and the Childebertians held high festival. The inhabitants of the streets adjacent to the Rue Childebert spent as many sleepless nights, though their houses were perfectly wholesome and clean.

I had the honour to be a frequent guest at those gatherings, but I feel that a detailed description of them is beyond my powers. I have already said that the craziness of the structure would have rendered extremely dangerous any combined display of choregraphic art, as practised by the Childebertians and their friends, male and female, at the neighbouring Grande-Chaumière; it did, however, not prevent a lady or gentleman of the company from performing a *pas seul* now and then. This, it must be remembered, was the pre-Rigolbochian period, before Chicard with his *chahut* had been ousted from his exalted position by the more elegant and graceful evolutions of the originator of the modern cancan, the famous Brididi; when the Faubourg du Temple, the Bal du Grand Saint-Martin, and "the descent of the Courtille" were patronized by the Paris *jeunesse dorée*, and in their halcyon days, when the *habitués* of the establishment of Le Père Lahire considered it their greatest glory to imitate as closely as possible the bacchanalian gyrations of the choregraphic autocrat on the other side of the Seine. No mere description could do justice to these gyrations; only a draughtsman of the highest skill could convey an adequate idea of them. But, as a rule, the soirées at the "Childebert" were not conspicuous for such displays; their programme was a more ambitious one from an intellectual point of view, albeit that the programme was rarely, if ever, carried out. This failure of the prearranged proceedings mainly arose from the disinclination or inability of the fairer portion of the company to play the passive part of listeners and spectators during the recital of an unpublished poem of perhaps a thousand lines or so, though the reciter was no less a personage than the author. In vain did the less frivolous and male part of the audience claim "silence for the minstrel;" the interrupters could conceive no minstrel without a guitar or some kindred instrument, least of all a minstrel who merely spoke his words, and the feast of reason and flow of soul came generally to an abrupt end by the rising of a damsel more outspoken still than her companions, who proposed an adjournment to one of the adjacent taverns, or to the not far distant "Grande-Chaumière," "si on continue à nous assommer avec des vers." The threat invariably produced its effect. The "minstrel" was politely requested to "shut up," and Béranger, Desaugiers, or even M. Scribe, took the place of the Victor Hugo in embryo until the small hours of the morning; the departure of the guests being witnessed by the night-capped inhabitants of the Rue Childebert from their windows, amidst the comforting reflections that for another three weeks or so there would be peace in the festive halls of that "accursed building."

My frequent visits to "La Childebert" had developed a taste for the Bohemian attractions of the Quartier-Latin. I was not twenty, and though I caught frequent glimpses at home of some of the eminent men with whom a few years later I lived on terms of friendship, I could not aspire to their society then. It is doubtful whether I would have done so if I could. I preferred the Théâtre Bobino to the Opéra and the Comédie-Française; the Grande-Chaumière—or the Chaumière, as it was simply called—to the most brilliantly lighted and decorated ballroom; a stroll with a couple of young students in the gardens of the Luxembourg to a carriage-drive in the Bois de Boulogne; a dinner for three francs at Magny's, in the Rue Contrescarpe-Dauphine, or even one for twenty-two sous at Viot's or Bléry's, to the most sumptuous repast at the Café Riche or the Café de Paris. I preferred the buttered rolls and the bowl of milk at the Boulangerie Crétaine, in the Rue Dauphine, to the best suppers at the Café Anglais, whither I had been taken once or twice during the Carnival—in short, I was very young and very foolish; since then I have often wished that, at the risk of remaining very foolish for evermore, I could have prolonged my youth for another score of years.

For once in a way I have no need to be ashamed of my want of memory. I could not give an account of a single piece I saw during those two or three years at Bobino, but I am certain that not one of the companions of my youth could. It is not because the lapse of time has dimmed the recollection of the plots, but because there were no plots, or at any rate none that we could understand, and I doubt very much whether the actors and actresses were more enlightened in that respect than the audience. The pieces were vaudevilles, most of them, and it was sufficient for us to join in the choruses of the songs, with which they were plentifully interlarded. As for the dialogue, it might have been sparkling with wit and epigram; it was nearly always drowned by interpolations from one side of the house or the other. When the tumult became too great, the curtain was simply lowered, to be almost immediately raised, "discovering" the manager—in his dressing-gown. He seemed prouder of that piece of attire than the more modern one would be of the most faultless evening dress. He never appealed to us by invoking the laws of politeness; he never threatened to have the house cleared. He simply pointed out to us that the police would inevitably close the place at the request of the inhabitants of the Rue de Madame if the noise rose above a certain pitch, and disturbed their peaceful evening hours, spent in the bosom of their families; which remark was always followed by the audience intoning as one man Gretry's "Où peut-on être mieux qu'au sein de sa famille?" the orchestra—such an orchestra!—playing the accompaniment, and the manager himself beating time. Then he went on. "Yes, messieurs et mesdames, we are here en famille also, as much en famille as at the Grande-Chaumière; and has not M. Lahire obtained from the Government the permission de faire sa police tout seul! After all, he is providing exercise for your muscles; I am providing food for your brain."

The speech was a stereotyped one—we all knew it by

heart; it invariably produced its effect in keeping us comparatively quiet for the rest of the evening, unless a bourgeois happened to come in. Then the uproar became uncontrollable; no managerial speech could quell it until the intruder had left the theatre.

By a bourgeois was meant a man who wore broadcloth and a top hat, but especially the latter. In fact, that head-gear was rarely seen within the inner precincts of the Quartier-Latin, even during the daytime, except on the head of a professor, or on Thursdays when the collegians—the term "lycéen" was not invented—were taken for their weekly outing. The semi-military dress of the present time had not been thought of then. The collegian wore a top hat, like our Eton boys, a white necktie, a kind of black quaker coat with a stand-up collar, a very dark blue waistcoat and trousers, low shoes, and blue woollen stockings. In the summer, some of them, especially those of the Collége Rollin, had a waistcoat and trousers of a lighter texture, and drab instead of blue. They were virtually prisoners within the walls of the college all the week, for in their Thursday promenades they were little more than prisoners taking exercise under the supervision of their gaolers. They were allowed to leave on alternate Sundays, provided they had parents, relations, or friends in Paris, who could come themselves or send their servants to fetch them in the morning and take them back at night. The rule applied to all, whether they were nine or double that number of years; it prevails even now. I only set foot in a French college of those days twice to see a young friend of mine, and I thanked my stars that four or five years of that existence had been spared to me. The food and the table appointments, the bedrooms—they were more like cells with their barred windows—would have been declined by the meanest English servant, certainly by the meanest French one. I have never met with a Frenchman who looks back with fond remembrance on his school-days.

The evening was generally wound up with a supper at Dagneaux's, Pinson's, or at the rôtisseuse—that is, if the evening happened to fall within the first ten days of the month; afterwards the entertainment nearly always consisted of a meat-pie, bought at one of the charcutiers', and washed down with the bottles of wine purchased at the Hôtel de l'Empereur Joseph II., at the south-eastern angle of the Rue de Tournon, where it stands still. The legend ran that the brother of Marie Antoinette had stayed there while on a visit to Paris, but it is scarcely likely that he would have done so while his sister was within a step of the throne of France; nevertheless the Count von Falkenstein—which was the name he adopted when travelling incognito—was somewhat of a philosopher. Did not he once pay a visit to Jean-Jacques Rousseau without having apprised him of his call? Jean-Jacques was copying music as the door opened to let in the visitor, and felt flattered enough, we may be sure; not so Buffon, whom Joseph surprised under similar circumstances, and who could never forgive himself for having been caught in his dressing-gown—he who never sat down to work except in lace ruffles and frill.

If I have been unwittingly betrayed into a semi-historical disquisition, it is because almost every step in that quarter gave rise to one, even amongst those light-hearted companions of mine, to the great astonishment of the fairer portion of the company. They only took an interest in the biography of one of the inhabitants of the street, whether past or present, and that was in the biography of Mdlle. Lenormand, a well-known fortune-teller, who lived at No. 5. They had heard that the old woman, who had been the mistress of Hébert of "Père Duchesne" fame, had, during the First Revolution, predicted to Joséphine de Beauharnais that she should be empress, as some gipsy at Grenada predicted a similar elevation to Eugénie de Montyo many years afterwards. Mdlle. Lenormand had been imprisoned after Hébert's death, but the moment Napoleon became first consul she was liberated, and frequently sent for to the Luxembourg, which is but a stone's throw from the Rue de Tournon. As a matter of course her fame spread, and she made a great deal of money during the first empire. Ignorant as they were of history, the sprightly grisettes of our days had heard of that; their great ambition was to get the five francs that would open the door of Mdlle. Lenormand's to them. Mdlle. Lenormand died about the year '43. Jules Janin, who lived in the same street, in the house formerly inhabited by Théroigne de Méricourt, went to the fortune-teller's funeral. The five francs so often claimed by the *étudiante*, so rarely forthcoming from the pockets of her admirer, was an important sum in those days among the youth of the Quartier-Latin. There were few whose allowance exceeded two hundred francs per month. A great many had to do with less. Those who were in receipt of five hundred francs—perhaps not two score among the whole number—were scarcely considered as belonging to the fraternity.

They were called "ultrapontins," to distinguish them from those who from one year's end to another never crossed the river, except perhaps to go to one of the theatres, because there was not much to be seen at the Odéon during the thirties. With Harel's migration to the Porte St. Martin, the glory of the second Théâtre-Français had departed, and it was not until '41 that Lireux managed to revive some of its ancient fame. By that time I had ceased to go to the Quartier-Latin, but Lireux was a familiar figure at the Café Riche and at the divan of the Rue Le Peletier; he dined now and then at the Café de Paris. So we made it a point to attend every one of his first nights, notwithstanding the warnings in verse and in prose of every wit of Paris, Théophile Gautier included, who had written:—

'On a fait là dessus mille plaisanteries,
Je le sais; il poussait de l'herbe aux galeries;
Trente-six variétés de champignons malsains
Dans les loges tigraient la mousse des coussins.'

It was impossible to say anything very spiteful of a theatre which had remained almost empty during a gratuitous performance on the king's birthday; consequently while I frequented the Quartier-Latin the students gave it a wide berth. When they were not disporting themselves at Bobino, they were at the Chaumière, and not in the evening only. Notwithstanding the enthusiastic and glowing descriptions of it that have appeared in later days, the place was simple enough. There was a primitive shooting-gallery, a skittle-alley, and so forth, and it was open all day. The students, after having attended the lectures and taken a stroll in the gardens of the Luxembourg, repaired to the Chaumière, where, in fine weather, they were sure to find their "lady-loves" sitting at work demurely under the trees. The refreshments were cheap, and one spent one's time until the dinner hour, chatting, singing, or strolling about. The students were very clannish, and invariably remained in their own sets at the Chaumière. There were tables exclusively occupied by Bourguignons, Angevins, etc. In fact, life was altogether much simpler and more individual than it became later on.

One of our great treats was an excursion to the establishment of Le Père Bonvin, where the student of to-day would not condescend to sit down, albeit that the food he gets in more showy places is not half as good and three times as dear. Le Père Bonvin was popularly supposed to be in the country, though it was not more than a mile from the Barrière Montparnasse. The "country" was represented by one or two large but straggling plots of erstwhile grazing-land, but at that time dotted with chalk-pits, tumble-down, wooden shanties, etc. Such trees as the tract of "country" could boast were on the demesne of Père Bonvin, but they evidently felt out of their element, and looked the reverse of flourishing. The house of Père Bonvin was scarcely distinguished in colour and rickettiness from the neighbouring constructions, but it was built of stone, and had two stories. The fare was homely and genuine, the latter quality being no small recommendation in an establishment where the prolific "bunny" was the usual *plat de résistance*. For sophistication, where the rabbit was concerned, was part of the suburban traiteur's creed from time immemorial, and the fact of the former's head being visible in the dish was no guarantee as to that and the body by its side having formed one whole in the flesh. The ubiquitous collector of rags and bottles and rabbits' skins was always anxiously inquiring for their heads also, and the natural conclusion was that, thanks to the latter, stewed grimalkin passed muster as gibelotte. At Père Bonvin's no such suspicion could be entertained for one moment; the visitor was admitted to inspect his dinner while alive. Père Bonvin was essentially an honest man, and a character in his way. During the daytime he exercised the functions of garde-champêtre; at night he became the restaurateur.

In those days both his sons, François and Léon, were still at home, but the former had apparently already made up his mind not to follow in his sire's footsteps. He was a compositor by trade, but the walls of the various rooms showed plainly enough that he did not aim at the fame of an Aldine or an Elzevir, but at that of a Jan Steen or a Gerard Dow. He has fully maintained the promise given then. His pictures rank high in the modern French school; there are few of his contemporaries who have so thoroughly caught the spirit of the Dutch masters. Léon was a mere lad, but a good many among the *habitués* of Père Bonvin predicted a more glorious career for him than for his brother. The word "heaven-born musician" has been often misapplied; in Léon's instance it was fully justified. The predictions, however, were not realized. Whether from lack of confidence in his own powers, or deterred by the never-ceasing remonstrances of his father, Léon, unlike François, did not strike out for himself, but continued to assist in the business, only turning to his harmonium in his spare time, or towards the end of the evening, when all distinction between guests and hosts ceased to exist, and the whole made a very happy family. He married early. I lost sight of him altogether, until about '64 I heard of his tragic end. He had committed suicide.

CHAPTER II.

My introduction to the celebrities of the day—The Café de Paris—The old Prince Demidoff—The old man's mania—His sons—The furniture and attendance at the Café de Paris—Its high prices—A mot of Alfred de Musset—The cuisine—A rebuke of the proprietor to Balzac—A version by one of his predecessors of the cause of Vatel's suicide—Some of the *habitués*—Their intercourse with the attendants—Their courteous behaviour towards one another—Le veau à la casserole—What Alfred de Musset, Balzac, and Alexandre Dumas thought of it—A silhouette of Alfred de Musset—His brother Paul on his election as a member of the Académie—A silhouette of Balzac, between sunset and sunrise—A curious action against the publishers of an almanack—A full-length portrait of Balzac—His pecuniary embarrassments—His visions of wealth and speculations—His constant neglect of his duties as a National Guard—His troubles in consequence thereof—L'Hôtel des Haricots—Some of his fellow-prisoners—Adam, the composer of "Le Postillon de Lonjumeau"—Eugène Sue; his portrait—His dandyism—The origin of the Paris Jockey Club—Eugène Sue becomes a member—The success of "Les Mystères de Paris"—The origin of "Le Juif-Errant"—Sue makes himself objectionable to the members of the Jockey Club—His name struck off the list—His decline and disappearance.

IF these notes are ever published, the reader will gather from the foregoing that, unlike many Englishmen brought up in Paris, I was allowed from a very early age to mix with all sorts and conditions of men. As I intend to say as little as possible about myself, there is no necessity to reveal the reason of this early emancipation from all restraint, which resulted in my being on familiar terms with a great many celebrities before I had reached my twenty-first year. I had no claim on their goodwill beyond my admiration of their talents and the fact of being decently connected. The constant companion of my youth was hand and glove with some of the highest in the land, and, if the truth must be told, with a good many of the lowest; but the man who was seated at the table of Lord Palmerston at the Café de Paris at 8 p.m., could afford *de s'encanailler* at 2 a.m. next morning without jeopardizing his social status.

The Café de Paris in those days was probably not only the best restaurant in Paris, but the best in Europe. Compared to the "Frères Provençaux" Véfour and Véry, the Café de Paris was young; it was only opened on July 15, 1822, in the vast suite of apartments at the corner of the Rue Taitbout and Boulevard de Italiens, formerly occupied by Prince Demidoff, whose grandson was a prominent figure in the society of the Second Empire, and whom I knew personally. The grandfather died before I was born, or, at any rate, when I was very young; but his descendant often told me about him and his two sons, Paul and Anatole, both of whom, in addition to his vast wealth, inherited a good many of his eccentricities. The old man, like many Russian grand seigneurs, was never so happy as when he could turn his back upon his own country. He inhabited Paris and Florence in turns. In the latter place he kept in his pay a company of French actors, who were lodged in a magnificent mansion near to his own, and who enacted comedies, vaudevilles, and comic operas. The London playgoer may remember a piece in which the celebrated Ravel made a great sensation; it was entitled "Les Folies Dramatiques," and was founded upon the mania of the old man. For he was old before his time and racked with gout, scarcely able to set his feet to the ground. He had to be wheeled in a chair to his entertainments and theatre, and often fell into a dead faint in the middle of the performance or during the dinner. " It made no difference to his guests," said his grandson; "they wheeled him out as they had wheeled him in, and the play or repast went on as if nothing had happened." In fact, it would seem that the prince would have been very angry if they had acted otherwise, for his motto was that, next to enjoying himself, there was nothing so comfortable as to see others do so. Faithful to this principle, he always kept some one near, whose mission it was to enjoy himself at his expense. He was under no obligation whatsoever, except to give an account of his amusements, most frequently in the dead of the night, when he got home, because the old prince suffered from insomnia; he would have given the whole of his vast possessions for six hours' unbroken slumber.

I have an idea that the three generations of these Demidoffs were as mad as March hares, though I am bound to say, at the same time, that the form this madness took hurt no one. Personally, I only knew Prince Anatole, the second son of the old man, and Paul, the latter's nephew. Paul's father, of the same name, died almost immediately after his son's birth. He had a mania for travelling, and rarely stayed in the same spot for forty-eight hours. He was always accompanied by a numerous suite and preceded by a couple of couriers, who, nine times out of ten, had orders to engage every room in the hotel for him. Being very rich and as lavish as he was wealthy, few hotel proprietors scrupled to turn out the whole of their guests at his steward's bidding and at a moment's notice. Of course, people refused to put up with such cavalier treatment; but as remonstrance was of no avail, they often brought actions for damages, which they invariably gained, and were promptly settled by Boniface, who merely added them to Prince Paul's bill. The most comical part of the business, however, was that the prince as often as not changed his mind on arriving at the hotel, and, without as much as alighting, continued his journey. The bill was never disputed. Another of his manias was that his wife should wash her hands each time she touched a metal object. For a while Princess Demidoff humoured her husband, but she found this so terribly irksome that she at last decided to wear gloves, and continued to do so long after her widowhood.

It must be obvious to the reader that this digression has little or no *raison d'être*, even in notes that do not profess to tell a succinct story; but my purpose was to a certain extent to vindicate the character of one of the most charming women of her time, who had the misfortune to marry what was undoubtedly the most eccentric member of the family. I am referring to Princess Anatole Demidoff, *née* Bonaparte, the daughter of Jérôme, and the sister of Plon-Plon.

To return to the Café de Paris and its *habitués*. First of all, the place itself was unlike any other restaurant of that day, even unlike its neighbour and rival, the Café Hardi, at the corner of the Rue Laffitte, on the site of the present Maison d'Or. There was no undue display of white and gold; and "the epicure was not constantly reminded that, when in the act of eating, he was not much superior to the rest of humanity," as Lord Palmerston put it when commenting upon the welcome absence of mirrors. The rooms might have been transformed at a moment's notice into private apartments for a very fastidious, refined family; for, in addition to the tasteful and costly furniture, it was the only establishment of its kind in Paris that was carpeted throughout, instead of having merely sanded or even polished floors, as was the case even in some of the best Paris restaurants as late as five and six years ago (I mean in the seventies) —Bignon, the Café Foy, and the Lion d'Or, in the Rue du Helder, excepted. The attendance was in every respect in thorough keeping with the grand air of the place, and, albeit that neither of the three or four succeeding proprietors made a fortune, or anything approaching it, was never relaxed.

On looking over these notes, I am afraid that the last paragraph will be intelligible only to a small section of my readers, consequently I venture to explain. Improved communication has brought to Paris during the third quarter of the century a great many Englishmen who, not being very familiar either with French or with French customs in their better aspect, have come to look upon the stir and bustle of the ordinary Paris restaurant, upon the somewhat free-and-easy behaviour of the waiters, upon their eccentricities of diction, upon their often successful attempts at " swelling " the total of the dinner-bill as so much matter of course. The abbreviated nomenclature the waiter employs in recapitulating the bill of fare to the patron is regarded by him as merely a skilful handling of the tongue by the native; the chances are ten to one in favour of the patron trying to imitate the same in his orders to the attendant, and deriving a certain pride from being successful. The stir and bustle is attributed to the more lively temperament of our neighbours, the free-and-easy behaviour as a wish on the waiter's part to smooth the linguistically thorny path of the benighted foreigner, the attempt to multiply items as an irrepressible manifestation of French greed.

Wherever these things occur, nowadays, the patron may be certain that he is "in the wrong shop;" but in the days of which I treat, the wrong shop was legion, especially as far as the foreigner was concerned; the Café de Paris and the Café Hardi were the notable exceptions. Truly, as Alfred de Musset said of the former, "you could not open its door for less than fifteen francs;" in other words, the prices charged were very high; but they were the same for the representatives of the nations that conquered as for those who were vanquished at Waterloo. It would be more correct to say that the *personnel* of the Café, from the proprietor and manager downward, were utterly oblivious of such distinctions of nationality. Every one who honoured the establishment was considered by them a grand seigneur, for whom nothing could be too good. I remember one day in '45 or '46—for M. Martin Guépet was at the head of affairs then—Balzac announcing the advent of a Russian friend, and asking Guépet to put his best foot forward. "Assuredly, monsieur, we will do so," was the answer, "because it is simply what we are in the habit of doing every day." The retort was sharp, but absolutely justified by facts. One was never told at the Café de Paris that this or that dish "could not be recommended," that "the fish could not be guaranteed." When the quality of the latter was doubtful, it did not make its appearance on the bill of fare. À propos of fish, there was a story current in the Café de Paris which may or may not have been the invention of one of the many clever literary men who foregathered there. It was to the effect that one of Guépet's predecessors—Angilbert the younger, I believe—had cast a doubt upon the historical accuracy of the facts connected with the tragic death of Vatel, the renowned chef of the Prince de Condé. According to Angilbert, Vatel did not throw himself upon his sword because the fish for Louis XIV.'s dinner had not arrived, but because it had arrived, been cooked, and was found "not to be so fresh as it might be." The elimination of those dishes would have disturbed the whole of the economy of the *menu*, and rather than suffer such disgrace Vatel made an end of himself. "For you see, monsieur," Angilbert is supposed to have said, "one can very well arrange a perfect dinner without fish, as long as one knows beforehand; but one cannot modify a *service* that has been thought out with it, when it fails at a moment's notice. As every one of my chefs is a treasure, who would not scruple to imitate the sacrifice of his famous prototype; and as I do not wish to expose him to such a heroic, but inconvenient death, we take the certain for the uncertain, consequently doubtful fish means no fish."

Truth or fiction, the story accurately conveys the pride of the proprietors in the unsullied gastronomic traditions of the establishment, and there is no doubt that they were ably seconded in that respect by every one around them, even to the *clientèle* itself. Not a single one of the latter would have called the waiters by their names, nor would these have ventured to rehearse the names of the dishes in a kind of slang or mutilated French, which is becoming more frequent day by day, and which is at best but fit as a means of communication between waiters and scullions. Least of all, would they have numbered the clients, as is done at present. A gentleman sitting at table No. 5 was " the gentleman at table No. 5," not merely "number five." There was little need for the bellowing and shouting from one end of the room to the other, because the head waiter himself had an eye everywhere. The word "addition," which people think it good taste in the seventies and eighties to employ when asking for their bills, was never heard. People did not profess to know the nature of the arithmetical operation by which the total of their liabilities was arrived at; they left that to the cashier and the rest of the underlings.

No coal or gas was used in the Café de Paris: lamps and wood fires upstairs; charcoal, and only that of a peculiar kind, in the kitchens, which might have been a hundred miles distant, for all we knew, for neither the rattling of dishes nor the smell of preparation betrayed their vicinity. A charming, subdued hum of voices attested the presence of two or three score of human beings attending to the inner man; the idiotic giggle, the affected little shrieks of the shopgirl or housemaid promoted to be the companion of the quasi-man of the world was never heard there. The *cabinet particulier* was not made a feature of the Café de Paris, and suppers were out of the question. Now and then the frank laughter of the younger members of a family party, and that was all. As a rule, however, there were few strangers at the Café de Paris, or what are called chance customers, as distinct from periodical ones. But there were half a score of tables absolutely sacred from the invasion of no matter whom, such as those of the Marquis du Hallays, Lord Seymour, the Marquis de St. Cricq, M. Romieu, Prince Rostopchine, Prince Soltikoff, Dr. Véron, etc., etc. Lord Palmerston, when in Paris, scarcely ever dined anywhere else than at the Café de Paris—of course I mean when dining at a public establishment.

Almost every evening there was an interchange of dishes or of wines between those tables; for instance, Dr. Véron, of whom I will have a good deal to say in these notes, and who was very fond of Musigny vintage, rarely missed offering some to the Marquis du Hallays, who, in his turn, sent him of the finest dishes from his table. For all these men not only professed to eat well, but never to suffer from indigestion. Their gastronomy was really an art, but an art aided by science which was applied to the simplest dish. One of these was *veau à la casserole*, which figured at least three times a week on the bill of fare, and the like of which I have never tasted elsewhere. Its recuperative qualities were vouched for by such men as Alfred de Musset, Balzac, and Alexandre Dumas. The former partook of it whenever it was on the bill; the others often came, after a spell of hard work, to recruit their mental and bodily strength with it, and maintained that nothing set them up so effectually.

These three men were particularly interesting to me, and their names will frequently recur in these notes. I was very young, and, though perhaps not so enthusiastic about literature as I was about painting and sculpture, it would indeed have been surprising if I had remained indifferent to the fascination experienced by almost every one in their society: for let me state at once that the great poet, the great playwright and the great novelist were even something more than men of genius; they were men of the world, and gentlemen who thought it worth their while to be agreeable companions. Unlike Victor Hugo, Lamartine, Chateaubriand, and Eugène Sue, all of whom I knew about the same time, they did not deem it necessary to stand mentally aloof from ordinary mortals. Alfred de Musset and Alexandre Dumas were both very handsome, but each in a different way. With his tall, slim figure, auburn wavy hair and beard, blue eyes, and finely-shaped mouth and nose, De Musset gave one the impression of a dandy cavalry officer in mufti, rather than of a poet: the "Miss Byron" which Préault the sculptor applied to him was, perhaps, not altogether undeserved, if judged intellectually and physically at first sight. There was a feminine grace about all his movements. The "Confessions d'un Enfant du Siècle," his play, "Frédéric and Bernerette," were apt to stir the heart of women rather than that of men; but was it not perhaps because the majority of the strong sex cannot be stirred except with a pole? And the poet who was so sensitive to everything rough as to leave invariably the coppers given to him in exchange, was unlikely to take voluntarily to such an unwieldy and clumsy instrument to produce his effects.*

* This reluctance to handle coppers proved a sore grief to his more economical and less fastidious brother Paul, who watched like a

Throughout these notes, I intend to abstain carefully from literary judgments. I am not competent to enter into them; but, if I were, I should still be reluctant to do so in the case of Alfred de Musset, who, to my knowledge, never questioned the talent of any one. De Musset improved upon better acquaintance. He was apt to strike one at first as distant and supercilious. He was neither the one nor the other, simply very reserved, and at the best of times very sad, not to say melancholy. It was not affectation, as has been said so often; it was his nature. The charge of superciliousness arose from his distressing short-sightedness, which compelled him to stare very hard at people without the least intention of being offensive.

I have said that Balzac often came, after a spell of hard work, to recruit his forces with the *veau à la casserole* of the Café de Paris; I should have added that this was generally in the autumn and winter, for, at the end of the spring and during the summer, the dinner hour, seven, found Balzac still a prisoner at home. Few of his acquaintances and friends ever caught sight of him, they were often in total ignorance of his whereabouts, and such news as reached them generally came through Joseph Méry, the poet

guardian angel over his junior, whom he worshipped. It is on record that he only said a harsh word to him once in his life, namely, when they wanted to make him, Paul, a member of the Académie Française. "C'est bien assez d'un immortel dans la famille," he replied to those who counselled him to stand. Then, turning to his brother, "Je ne comprends pas pourquoi tu t'es fourré dans cette galère, si elle est assez grande pour moi, tu dois y être joliment à l'étroit." It is difficult to imagine a greater instance of brotherly pride and admiration, because Paul de Musset was by no means a nonentity, only from a very early age he had always merged his individuality in that of Alfred. To some one who once remarked upon this in my hearing, he answered, "Que voulez-vous? c'est comme cela: Alfred a eu toujours la moitié du lit, seulement la moitié était toujours prise du milieu."

and novelist, the only one who came across him during those periods of eclipse. Méry was an inveterate gambler, and spent night after night at the card-table. He rarely left it before daybreak. His way lay past the Café de Paris, and for four consecutive mornings he had met Balzac strolling leisurely up and down, dressed in a pantalon à pieds (trousers not terminating below the ankle, but with feet in them like stockings), and frock coat with velvet facings. The second morning, Méry felt surprised at the coincidence; the third, he was puzzled; the fourth, he could hold out no longer, and asked Balzac the reason of these nocturnal perambulations round about the same spot. Balzac put his hand in his pocket and produced an almanack, showing that the sun did not rise before 3.40. "I am being tracked by the officers of the Tribunal de Commerce, and obliged to hide myself during the day; but at this hour I am free, and can take a walk, for as long as the sun is not up they cannot arrest me."

I remember having read that Ouvrard, the great army contractor, had done the same for many years; nevertheless, he was arrested one day,—the authorities proved that the almanack was wrong, that the sun rose ten minutes earlier than was stated therein. He brought an action against the compiler and publishers. They had to pay him damages.

Though literary remuneration was not in those days what it became later on, it was sufficiently large to make it difficult to explain the chronic impecuniosity of Balzac, though not that of Dumas. They were not gamblers, and had not the terrible fits of idleness or drinking which left De Musset stranded every now and again. Lamartine suffered from the same complaint, I mean impecuniosity. There is proof of Balzac's industry and frugality in two extracts from his letters to his mother, dated Angoulême, July, 1832, when he himself was thirty-two years old, and had already written half a dozen masterpieces. "Several bills are due, and, if I cannot find the money for them, I will have them protested and let the law take its course. It will give me breathing time, and I can settle costs and all afterwards."

Meanwhile he works eight hours a day at "Louis Lambert," one of the best things among his numberless best things. His mother sends him a hundred francs, and, perhaps with the same pen with which he wrote those two marvellous chapters that stand out like a couple of priceless rubies from among the mass of other jewels, he thanks her and accounts for them. "For the copying of the maps, 20 frs.; for my passport, 10 frs. I owed 15 frs. for discount on one of my bills, and 15 frs. on my fare. 15 frs. for flowers as a birthday present. Lost at cards, 10 frs. Postage and servant's tips, 15 frs. Total, 100 frs."

But these ten francs have not been lost at one fell swoop; they represent his bad luck at the *gaming table* during the whole month of his stay at Angoulême, at the house of his friend and sister's schoolfellow, Madame Zulma Carraud,—hence, something like seven sous ($3\frac{1}{2}d.$) per day: for which extravagance he makes up, on his return to Paris, by plunging into work harder than ever. He goes to roost at 7 p.m., "like the fowls;" and he is called at 1 a.m., when he writes until 8 a.m. He takes another hour and a half of sleep, and, after partaking of a light meal, "gets into his collar" until four in the afternoon. After that, he receives a few friends, takes a bath, or goes out, and immediately he has swallowed his dinner he "turns in," as stated above. "I shall be compelled to lead this nigger's life for a few months without stopping, in order not to be swamped by those terrible bills that are due."

These extracts are not personal recollections. I have inserted them to make good my statement that Balzac was neither a gambler, a drunkard, nor an idler.

"How does he spend his money?" I asked Méry, when he had told us of his fourth meeting with Balzac on that very morning.

"In sops to his imagination, in balloons to the land of dreams, which balloons he constructs with his hard-won earnings and inflates with the essence of his visions, but which nevertheless will not rise three feet from the earth," he answered. Then he went on explaining: "Balzac is firmly convinced that every one of his characters has had, or has still, its counterpart in real life, notably the characters that have risen from humble beginnings to great wealth; and he thinks that, having worked out the secret of their success on paper, he can put it in practice. He embarks on the most harum-scarum speculations without the slightest practical knowledge; as, for instance, when he drew the plans for his country-house at the Jardies (Ville d'Avray), and insisted upon the builder carrying them out in every respect while he was away. When the place was finished there was not a single staircase. Of course, they had to put them outside, and he maintained that it was part of his original plan; but he had never given a thought to the means of ascent. But here is Monsieur Louis Lurine. If you would like an idea of Balzac's impracticability, let him tell you what occurred between Balzac and Kugelmann a few months ago."

Kugelmann was at that time publishing a very beautifully illustrated work, entitled, " Les Rues de Paris," which Louis Lurine was editing. We were standing outside the Café Riche, and I knew Lurine by sight. Méry introduced me to him. After a few preliminary remarks, Lurine told us the following story. Of course, many years have elapsed since, but I think I can trust to my memory in this instance.

" I had suggested," said Lurine, " that Balzac should do the Rue de Richelieu, and we sent for him. I did not want more than half a sheet, so imagine my surprise when Balzac named his conditions, viz., five thousand francs, something over six hundred francs a page of about six hundred words. Kugelmann began to yell, I simply smiled ; seeing which, Balzac said, as soberly as possible, ' You'll admit that, in order to depict a landscape faithfully, one should study its every detail. Well, how would you have me describe the Rue de Richelieu, convey an idea of its commercial aspect, unless I visit, one after the other, the various establishments it contains ? Suppose I begin by the Boulevard des Italiens : I'd be bound to take my déjeuner at the Café Cardinal, I would have to buy a couple of scores at Brandus', a gun at the gunsmith's next door, a breastpin at the next shop. Could I do less than order a coat at the tailor's, a pair of boots at the bootmaker's ? '

" I cut him short. ' Don't go any further,' I said, ' or else we'll have you in at " Compagnie des Indes," and, as both lace and Indian shawls have gone up in price, we'll be bankrupt before we know where we are.'

"Consequently," concluded Lurine, "the thing fell through, and we gave the commission to Guénot-Lacointe, who has done the thing very well and has written twice the pages Balzac was asked for, without buying as much as a pair of gloves."

When Balzac was not being harassed by the officials of the Tribunal de Commerce, he had to dodge the authorities of the National Guards, who generally had a warrant against him for neglect of duty. Unlike his great contemporary Dumas, Balzac had an invincible repugnance to play the amateur warrior—a repugnance, by-the-by, to which we owe one of the most masterly portraits in his wonderful gallery, that of the self-satisfied, bumptious, detestable bourgeois, who struts about in his uniform; I am alluding to Crével of "La Cousine Bette." But civic discipline could take no cognizance of the novelist's likes and dislikes, and, after repeated "notices" and "warnings," left at his registered domicile, his incarceration was generally decided upon. As a rule, this happened about half a dozen times in a twelvemonth.

The next thing was to catch the refractory national guard, which was not easy, seeing that, in order to avoid an enforced sojourn at the Hôtel des Haricots,* Balzac not only disappeared from his usual haunts, but left his regular domicile, and took an apartment

---

* The name of the military prison which was originally built on the site of the former College Montaigu, where the scholars were almost exclusively fed on haricot beans. Throughout its removals the prison preserved its nickname.—EDITOR.

elsewhere under an assumed name. On one occasion, at a small lodgings which he had taken near his publisher, Hippolyte Souverain, under the name of Madame Dupont, Léon Gozlan, having found him out, sent him a letter addressed to "Madame Dupont, *née* Balzac."

The sergeant-major of Balzac's company had undoubtedly a grudge against him. He happened to be a perfumer, and ever since the publication and success of " César Birotteau " the Paris perfumers bore Balzac no goodwill. That particular one had sworn by all his essences and bottles that he would lay hands on the recalcitrant private of his company in the streets, for only under such conditions could he arrest him. To watch at Balzac's ordinary domicile was of no use, and, when he had discovered his temporary residence, he had to lure him out of it, because the other was on his guard.

One morning, while the novelist was hard at work, his old housekeeper, whom he always took with him, came to tell him that there was a large van downstairs with a case addressed to him. "How did they find me out here?" exclaimed Balzac, and despatched the dame to gather further particulars. In a few moments she returned. The case contained an Etruscan vase sent from Italy, but, seeing that it had been knocking about for the last three days in every quarter of Paris in the carman's efforts to find out the consignee, the former was anxious that M. Balzac should verify the intact condition of the package before it was unloaded. Balzac fell straight into the trap. Giving himself no time even to exchange his dressing-gown, or rather his monk's frock he was in the habit of wearing, for a coat, or his slippers for a pair of boots, he rushed downstairs, watching with a benign smile the carrier handling most delicately the treasure that had come to him.

"Caught at last," said a stentorian voice behind him, and dispelling the dream as its owner laid his hand on the novelist's shoulder, while a gigantic companion planted himself in front of the street door and cut off all retreat that way.

"With a refinement of cruelty, which in the eyes of posterity will considerably diminish the glory of his victory"—I am quoting Balzac's own words as he related the scene to us at the Hôtel des Haricots—the sergeant-major perfumer would not allow his prisoner to change his clothes, and while the van with the precious Etruscan vase disappeared in the distance, Balzac was hustled into a cab to spend a week in durance vile, where on that occasion he had the company of Adolphe Adam, the composer of "Le Postillon de Lonjumeau."

However, "les jours de fête étaient passés," and had been for the last five years, ever since the Hôtel des Haricots had been transferred from the town mansion of the De Bazancourts in the Rue des Fossés-Saint-Germain to its then locale near the Orléans railway station. There were no more banquets in the refectory as there had been of yore. Each prisoner had his meals in his cell. Joseph Méry, Nestor Roqueplan, and I were admitted as the clock struck two, and had to leave exactly an hour afterwards. It was during this visit that Balzac enacted the scene for us which I have endeavoured to describe above, and reminded Méry of the last dinner he had given to Dumas, Jules

Sandeau, and several others in the former prison, which dinner cost five hundred francs. Eugène Sue, who was as unwilling as Balzac to perform his civic duties, had had three of his own servants to wait upon him there, and some of his plate and silver brought to his cell.

Seeing that the name of the celebrated author of " Les Mystères de Paris " has presented itself in the course of these notes, I may just as well have done with him, for he forms part of the least agreeable of my recollections. He was also an *habitué* of the Café de Paris. A great deal has been written about him; what has never been sufficiently insisted upon was the *inveterate snobbishness of the man.* When I first knew him, about '42–'43, he was already in the zenith of his glory, but I had often heard others mention his name before then, and never very favourably. His dandyism was offensive, mainly because it did not sit naturally upon him. It did not spring from an innate refinement, but from a love of show, although his father, who had been known to some of the son's familiars, was a worthy man, a doctor, and, it appears, a very good doctor, but somewhat brusque, like our own Abernethy; still much more of a gentleman at heart than the son. He did not like Eugène's extravagance, and when the latter, about '24, launched out into a cabriolet, he shipped him off on one of the king's vessels, as a surgeon; to which fact French literature owed the first novels of the future author of " Les Mystères de Paris " and " Le Juif-Errant."

But the father was gathered to his fathers, and Eugène, who had never taken kindly to a seafaring life, returned to Paris, to spend his inheritance and to

THE ORIGIN OF THE FRENCH JOCKEY CLUB. 53

resume his old habits, which made one of his acquaintances say that "le père and le fils had *both* entered upon a better life." It appears that, though somewhat of a *poseur* from the very beginning, he was witty and amusing, and readily found access to the circle that frequented the gardens of the Tivoli and the Café de Paris.* They, in their turn, made him a member of the Jockey Club when it was founded, which kindness they unanimously regretted, as will be seen directly.

The Tivoli gardens, though utterly forgotten at present, was in reality the birthplace of the French Jockey Club. About the year 1833 a man named Bryon, one of whose descendants keeps, at the hour I write, a large livery stables near the Grand Café, opened a pigeon-shooting gallery in the Tivoli; the pigeons, from what I have heard, mainly consisting of quails, larks, and other birds. The pigeons shot at were wooden ones, poised up high in the air, but motionless, as we still see them at the suburban fairs around Paris. Seven years before, Bryon had started a "society of amateurs of races," to whom, for a certain consideration, he let a movable stand at private meetings, for there were no others until the Society for the Encouragement of breeding French Horses started operations in 1834. But the deliberations at first took place at Bryon's place in the Tivoli gardens, and continued there until, one day, Bryon asked the fourteen or fifteen members why they should not have a locale of their own; the result was that they took

* There were two Tivoli gardens, both in the same neighbourhood, the site of the present Quartier de l'Europe. The author is alluding to the second, so often mentioned in the novels of Paul de Kock.—EDITOR.

modest quarters in the Rue du Helder, or rather amalgamated with a small club located there under the name of Le Bouge (The Den); for Lord Seymour, the Duke de Nemours, Prince Demidoff, and the rest were sufficiently clear-sighted to perceive that a Jockey Club governed on the English principle was entirely out of the question. That was the origin of the French Jockey Club, which, after various migrations, is, at the time of writing, magnificently housed in one of the palatial mansions of the Rue Scribe. As a matter of course, some of the fashionable *habitués* of the Café de Paris, though not knowing a fetlock from a pastern, were but too pleased to join an institution which, with the mania for everything English in full swing, then conferred as it were upon its members a kind of patent of "good form," and, above all, of exclusiveness, for which some, even amidst the flesh-pots of the celebrated restaurant, longed. Because, it must be remembered, though the majority of the company at the Café de Paris were very well from the point of view of birth and social position, there was no possibility of excluding those who could lay no claim to such distinctions, provided they had the money to pay their reckoning, and most of them had more than enough for that. It appears that Eugène Sue was not so objectionable as he became afterwards, when the wonderful success of his "Mystères de Paris" and the "Juif-Errant" had turned his head; he was made an original member of the club. Election on the nomination by three sponsors was not necessary then. That article was not inserted in the rules until two years after the foundation of the Paris Jockey Club.

Of the success attending Sue's two best-known works, I can speak from personal experience; for I was old enough to be impressed by it, and foolish enough to rank him, on account of it, with Balzac and Dumas, perhaps a little higher than the former. After the lapse of many years, I can only console myself for my infatuation with the thought that thousands, of far greater intellectual attainments than mine, were in the same boat, for it must not be supposed that the *furore* created by "Les Mystères de Paris" was confined to one class, and that class the worst educated one. While it appeared in serial form in the *Débats,* one had to bespeak the paper several hours beforehand, because, unless one subscribed to it, it was impossible to get it from the news-vendors. As for the reading-rooms where it was supposed to be kept, the proprietors frankly laughed in your face if you happened to ask for it, after you had paid your two sous admission. "Monsieur is joking. We have got five copies, and we let them out at ten sous each for half an hour: that's the time it takes to read M. Sue's story. We have one copy here, and if monsieur likes to take his turn he may do so, though he will probably have to wait for three or four hours."

At last the guileless demoiselle behind the counter found even a more effective way of fleecing her clients. The cabinets de lecture altered their fees, and the two sous, which until then had conferred the right of staying as long as one liked, were transformed into the price of admission for one hour. Each reader received a ticket on entering, stating the time, and the shrewd caissière made the round every ten minutes. I may say without exaggeration that the days on which the instalment of fiction was "crowded out," there was a general air of listlessness about Paris. And, after the first few weeks, this happened frequently; for by that time the Bertins had become quite as clever as their formidable rival, the proprietor and editor of the *Constitutionnel*, the famous Dr. Véron, whom I have already mentioned, but of whom I shall have occasion to speak again and again, for he was one of the most notable characters in the Paris of my early manhood. But to return for a moment to " Les Mystères de Paris " and its author.

The serial, then, was frequently interrupted for one or two days, without notice, however, to the readers; and on its resumption there was a nice little paragraph to reassure the " grandes dames de par le monde," as well as their maids, with regard to the health of M. Sue, who was supposed to have been too ill to work. The public took all this *au grand sérieux*. They either chose to forget, or were ignorant of the fact, that a novel of that kind, especially in the early days of serial feuilleton, was not delivered to the editor bit by bit. Sue, great man as he was, would not have dared to inaugurate the system only adopted somewhat later by Alexandre Dumas the Elder, namely, that of writing "from hand to mouth." These paragraphs served a dual purpose—they whetted the lady and other readers' interest in the author, and informed the indifferent ones how great that interest was. For these paragraphs were, or professed to be,—I really believe they were,—the courteous replies to hundreds of kind of inquiries which the author "could not acknowledge separately for lack of time."

But this was not all. There was really a good

excuse for Eugène Sue "se prenant au sérieux," seeing that some of the most eminent magistrates looked upon him in that light and opened a correspondence with him, submitting their ideas about reforming such criminals as "le maître d'école," and praising Prince Rodolph, or rather Eugène Sue under that name, for "his laudable efforts in the cause of humanity." In reality, Sue was in the position of Molière's "bourgeois gentilhomme" who spoke prose without being aware of it; for there was not the smallest evidence, from his former work, that he intended to inaugurate any crusade, either socialistic or philanthropic, when he began his "Mystères de Paris." He simply wanted to write a stirring novel. But, unlike M. Jourdain, he did not plead ignorance of his own good motives when congratulated upon them. On the contrary, he gravely and officially replied in the *Débats* without winking. Some of the papers, not to be outdone, gravely recounted how whole families had been converted from their evil ways by the perusal of the novel; how others, after supper, had dropped on their knees to pray for their author; how one working man had exclaimed, "You may say what you like, it would be a good thing if Providence sent many men like M. Sue in this world to take up the cudgels of the honest and struggling artisan." Thereupon Béranger, who did not like to be forgotten in this chorus of praise, paid a ceremonious visit to Sue, and between the two they assumed the protectorship of the horny-handed son of toil.

It must not be supposed that I am joking or exaggerating, and that the *engoûment* was confined to the lower classes, and to provincial and metropolitan faddists. Such men as M. de Lourdoueix, the editor of the *Gazette de France,* fell into the trap. I have pointed out elsewhere that the republicans and socialists of those days were not necessarily godless folk, and M. de Lourdoueix fitly concluded that a socialistic writer like Sue might become a powerful weapon in his hands against the Jesuits. So he went to the novelist, and gave him a commission to that effect. The latter accepted, and conceived the plot of " The Wandering Jew." When it was sketched out, he communicated it to the editor; but whether that gentleman had reconsidered the matter in the interval, or whether he felt frightened at the horribly tragic conception with scarcely any relief, he refused the novel, unless it was modified to a great extent and its blood-curdling episodes softened. The author, taking himself *au sérieux* this time as a religious reformer, declined to alter a line. Dr. Véron got wind of the affair, bought the novel as it stood, and, by dint of a system of puffing and advertising which would even make a modern American stare, obtained a success with it in the *Constitutionnel* which equalled if it did not surpass that of the *Débats* with the "Mystères."

"It is very amusing indeed," said George Sand one night, "but there are too many animals. I hope we shall soon get out of this ménagerie." Nevertheless, she frankly admitted that she would not like to miss an instalment for ever so much.

Meanwhile Sue posed and posed, not as a writer—for, like Horace Walpole, he was almost ashamed of the title—but as "a man of the world" who knew nothing about literature, but whose wish to benefit humanity had been greater than his reluctance to enter the lists with such men as Balzac and Dumas. After his dinner at the Café de Paris, he would gravely stand on the steps smoking his cigar and listen to the conversation with an air of superiority without attempting to take part in it. His mind was supposed to be far away, devising schemes for the social and moral improvement of his fellow-creatures. These philanthropic musings did not prevent him from paying a great deal of attention—too much perhaps—to his personal appearance, for even in those days of beaux, bucks, and dandies, of Counts d'Orsay and others, men could not help thinking Eugène Sue overdressed. He rarely appeared without spurs to his boots, and he would no more have done without a new pair of white kid gloves every evening than without his dinner. Other men, like Nestor de Roquoplan, Alfred de Musset, Major Fraser, all of whose names will frequently recur in these notes, did not mind having their gloves cleaned, though the process was not so perfect as it is now; Eugène Sue averred that the smell of cleaned gloves made him ill. Alfred de Musset, who could be very impertinent when he liked, but who was withal a very good fellow, said one day: "Mais enfin, mon ami, ça ne sent pas pire que les bouges que vous nous depeignez. N'y seriez vous jamais allé?"

In short, several years before the period of which I now treat, Eugène Sue had begun to be looked upon coldly at the Jockey Club on account of the "airs he gave himself;" and three years before the startling success of his work, he had altogether ceased to go there, though he was still a member, and remained so nominally until '47, when his name was removed from the list in accordance with Rule 5. Owing to momentary pecuniary embarrassments, he had failed to pay his subscription. It may safely be asserted that this was merely a pretext to get rid of him, because such stringent measures are rarely resorted to at any decent club, whether in London or Paris, and least of all at the Jockey Clubs there. The fact was, that the members did not care for a fellow-member whose taste differed so materially from their own, whose daily avocations and pursuits had nothing in common with theirs; for though Eugène Sue as early as 1835 had possessed a race-horse, named Mameluke, which managed to come in a capital last at Maisons-sur-Seine (afterwards Maisons-Lafitte); though he had ridden his *haque* every day in the Bois, and driven his cabriolet every afternoon in the Champs-Elysées, the merest observer could easily perceive that all this was done for mere show, to use the French expression, "pose." As one of the members observed, "M. Sue est toujours trop habillé, trop carossé, et surtout trop éperonné."

M. Sue was all that, and though the Jockey Club at that time was by no means the unobtrusive body of men it is to-day, its excesses and eccentricities were rarely indulged in public, except perhaps in carnival time. A M. de Chateauvillard might take it into his head to play a game of billiards on horseback, or M. de Machado might live surrounded by a couple of hundred parrots if he liked; none of these fancies attracted the public's notice: M. Sue, by his very profession, attracted too much of it, and brought a great deal of it into the club itself; hence, when he raised a violent protest against his expulsion and endeavoured to neutralize it by sending in his resignation, the committee maintained its original decision. A few years after this, Eugène Sue disappeared from the Paris horizon.

CHAPTER III.

Alexandre Dumas père—Why he made himself particularly agreeable to Englishmen—His way of silencing people—The pursuit he loved best next to literature—He has the privilege of going down to the kitchens of the Café de Paris—No one questions his literary genius, some question his culinary capacities—Dr. Véron and his cordon-bleu—Dr. Véron's reasons for dining out instead of at home—Dr. Véron's friend, the philanthropist, who does not go to the theatre because he objects to be hurried with his emotions—Dr. Véron, instigated by his cook, accuses Dumas of having collaborateurs in preparing his dishes as he was known to have collaborateurs in his literary work—Dumas's wrath—He invites us to a dinner which shall be wholly cooked by him in the presence of a delegate to be chosen by the guests—The lot falls upon me—Dr. Véron and Sophie make the *amende honorable*—A dinner-party at Véron's—A curious law-suit in connection with Weber's "Freyschutz"—Nestor Roqueplan, who became the successor of the defendant in the case, suggests a way out of it—Léon Pillet virtually adopts it and wins the day—A similar plan adopted years before by a fireman on duty at the opéra, on being tried by court-martial for having fallen asleep during the performance of "Guido et Génevra"—Firemen not bad judges of plays and operas—They were often consulted both by Meyerbeer and Dumas—Dumas at work—How he idled his time away—Dumas causes the traffic receipts of the Chemin de Fer de l'Ouest to swell during his three years' residence at Saint-Germain—M. de Montalivet advises Louis-Philippe to invite Dumas to Versailles, to see what his presence will do for the royal city—Louis-Philippe does not act upon the advice—The relations between Dumas and the d'Orleans family—After the Revolution of '48, Dumas becomes a candidate for parliament—The story of his canvass and his address to the electors at Joigny—Dumas' utter indifference to money matters—He casts his burdens upon others—Dumas and his creditors—Writs and distraints—How they are dealt with—Dumas' indiscriminate generosity—A dozen houses full of new furniture in half as many years—Dumas' frugality at table—Literary remuneration—Dumas and his son—"Leave me a hundred francs."

AMONG my most pleasant recollections of those days are those of Alexandre Dumas. To quote his own words, "whenever he met an Englishman he considered it his particular duty to make himself agreeable to him, as part of the debt he owed to Shakespeare and Walter Scott." I doubt whether Dumas ever made himself deliberately disagreeable to any one; even when provoked, he managed to disarm his adversary with an epigram, rather than wound him. One evening, a professor at one of the provincial universities had been dining at the Café de Paris, as the guest of Roger de Beauvoir. He had a magnificent cameo breast-pin. It elicited the admiration of every one, and notably that of Dumas. He said at once that it was a portrait of Julius Cæsar.

"Are you an archæologist?" asked the professor.

"I," replied Dumas, "I am absolutely nothing."

"Still," insisted the visitor, "you perceived at once that it was a portrait of Julius Cæsar."

"That is not very wonderful. Cæsar is essentially a Roman type; and, besides, I know Cæsar as well as most people, and perhaps better."

To tell a professor of history—especially a provincial one—that one knows Cæsar as well as most people and perhaps better, is naturally to provoke the question, "In what capacity?" As a matter of course the question followed immediately.

"In the capacity of Cæsar's historian," said Dumas, imperturbably.

We were getting interested, because we foresaw that the professor would, in a few minutes, get the worst of it. Dumas' eyes were twinkling with mischief.

"You have written a history of Cæsar?" asked the learned man.

"Yes; why not?"

"Well, you won't mind my being frank with you: it is because it has never been mentioned in the world of savans."

"The world of savans never mentions me."

"Still, a history of Cæsar ought to make somewhat of a sensation."

"Mine has not made any. People read it, and that was all. It is the books which it is impossible to read that make a sensation: they are like the dinners one cannot digest; the dinners one digests are not as much as thought of next morning." That was Dumas' way of putting a would-be impertinent opponent *hors de combat*, and his repartees were frequently drawn from the pursuit he loved as well, if not better than literature, namely, cooking. It may sound exaggerated, but I verily believe that Dumas took a greater pride in concocting a stew than in constructing a novel or a play. Very often, in the middle of the dinner, he would put down his knife and fork. " Ça, c'est rudement bon: il faut que je m'en procure la récette." And Guépet was sent for to authorize Dumas to descend to the lower regions and have a consultation with his chefs. He was the only one of the *habitués* who had ever been in the kitchens of the Café de Paris. As a rule these excursions were followed by an invitation to dine at Dumas' two or three days hence, when the knowledge freshly acquired would be put into practice.

There were few of us who questioned Dumas' literary genius; there were many who suspected his culinary abilities, and notably among them, Dr. Véron. The germs of this unbelief had been sown in the doctor's mind by his own cordon-bleu, Sophie. The erstwhile director of the opera lived, at that time, in a beautiful apartment on the first floor of a nice house in the Rue Taitbout, at the corner of which the Café de Paris was situated. Sophie had virtually a sinecure of it, because, with the exception of a dinner-party now and then, her master, who was a bachelor, took his dinners at the restaurant. And with regard to the déjeuner, there was not much chance of her displaying her talents, because the man, who was reputed to be a very Apicius, was frugality itself. His reasons for dining out instead of at home were perfectly logical, though they sounded paradoxical. One day, when I was remarking upon the seemingly strange habit of dining out, when he was paying "a perfect treasure" at home, he gave me these reasons. "My dear friend, depend upon it that it is man's stomach which found the aphorism, 'Qui va *piano* va *sano,* qui va *sano* va *lontano.*' In your own home the soup is on the table at a certain hour, the roast is taken off the jack, the dessert is spread out on the sideboard. Your servants, in order to get more time over their meals, hurry you up; they do not serve you, they gorge you. At the restaurant, on the contrary, they are never in a hurry, they let you wait. And, besides, I always tell the waiters not to mind me; that I like being kept a long while—that is one of the reasons why I come here.

"Another thing, at the restaurant the door is opened at every moment and something happens. A friend, a chum, or a mere acquaintance comes in; one chats and laughs: all this aids digestion. A man ought not to be like a boa-constrictor, he ought not to make digestion a business apart. He ought to dine and to digest at the same time, and nothing aids this dual function like good conversation. Perhaps the servant of Madame de Maintenon, when the latter was still Madame Scarron, was a greater philosopher than we suspect when he whispered to his mistress, 'Madame, the roast has run short; give them another story.'

"I knew a philanthropist," wound up Dr. Véron, "who objected as much to be hurried over his emotions as I object to be hurried over my meals. For that reason he never went to the theatre. When he wanted an emotional fillip, he wandered about the streets until he met some poor wretch evidently hungry and out of elbows. He took him to the nearest wine-shop, gave him something to eat and to drink, sat himself opposite to his guest, and told him to recount his misfortunes. 'But take your time over it. I am not in a hurry,' he recommended. The poor outcast began his tale; my friend listened attentively until he was thoroughly moved. If the man's story was very sad, he gave him a franc or two; if it was positively heartrending and made him cry, he gave him a five-franc piece; after which, he came to see me, saying, 'I have thoroughly enjoyed myself, and made the intervals between each sensational episode last as long as I liked, and, what is more, it has just cost me seven francs, the price of a stall at the theatre.'"

To return to Dr. Véron's scepticism with regard to Dumas' culinary accomplishments, and how he was converted. Dumas, it appears, had got the recipe for stewing carp from a German lady, and, being at that moment on very friendly terms with Dr. Véron, which was not always the case, had invited him and several others to come and taste the results of his experiments. The dish was simply splendid, and for days and days Véron, who was really a frugal eater, could talk of nothing else to his cook.

"Where did you taste it?" said Sophie, getting somewhat jealous of this praise of others; "at the Café de Paris?"

"No, at Monsieur Dumas'," was the answer.

"Well, then, I'll go to Monsieur Dumas' cook, and get the recipe."

"That's of no use," objected her master. "Monsieur Dumas prepared the dish himself."

"Well, then, I'll go to Monsieur Dumas himself and ask him to give me the recipe."

Sophie was as good as her word, and walked herself off to the Chaussée d'Antin. The great novelist felt flattered, and gave her every possible information, but somehow the dish was not like that her master had so much enjoyed at his friend's. Then Sophie grew morose, and began to throw out hints about the great man's borrowing other people's feathers in his culinary pursuits, just as he did in his literary ones. For Sophie was not altogether illiterate, and the papers at that time were frequently charging Dumas with keeping his collaborateurs too much in the background and himself too much in front. Dumas had never much difficulty in meeting such accusations, but Sophie had unconsciously hit upon the tactics of the clever solicitor who recommended the barrister to abuse the plaintiff, the defendant's case being bad, and she put it into practice. "C'est avec sa carpe comme avec ses romans, les autres les font et il y met son nom," she said one day. "Je l'ai bien vu, c'est un grand diable de vaniteux."

Now, there was no doubt about it, to those who did not know him very well, Dumas was "un grand diable de vaniteux;" and the worthy doctor sat pondering his cook's remarks until he himself felt inclined to think that Dumas had a clever chef in the background, upon whose victories he plumed himself. Meanwhile Dumas had been out of town for more than a month, but a day or so after his return he made his appearance at the Café de Paris, and, as a matter of course, inquired after the result of Sophie's efforts. The doctor was reticent at first, not caring to acknowledge Sophie's failure. He had, however, made the matter public, alleging, at the same time, Sophie's suspicions as to Dumas' hidden collaborateur, and one of the company was ill advised enough to let the cat out of the bag. During the many years of my acquaintance with Dumas, I have never seen him in such a rage as then. But he toned down in a very few minutes. "Il n'y a qu'une reponse à une accusation pareille," he said in a grandiloquent tone, which, however, had the most comical effect, seeing how trifling the matter was in reality—"il n'y qu'une reponse; vous viendrez dîner avec moi demain, vous choissirez un délégué qui viendra à partir de trois heures me voir préparer mon dîner." I was the youngest, the choice fell upon me. That is how my life-long friendship with Dumas began. At three o'clock next day I was at the Chaussée d'Antin, and was taken by the servant into the kitchen, where the great novelist stood surrounded by his utensils, some of silver, and all of them glistening like silver. With the exception of a soupe aux choux, at which, by his own confession, he had been at work since the morning, all the ingredients for the dinner were in their natural state—of course, washed and peeled, but nothing more. He was assisted by his own cook and a kitchen-maid, but he himself, with his sleeves rolled up to the elbows, a large apron round his waist, and bare chest, conducted the operations. I do not think I have ever seen anything more entertaining, though in the course of these notes I shall have to mention frequent vagaries on the part of great men. I came to the conclusion that when writers insisted upon the culinary challenges of Carême, Duglérè, and Casimir they were not indulging in mere metaphor.

At half-past six the guests began to arrive; at a quarter to seven Dumas retired to his dressing-room; at seven punctually the servant announced that "monsieur était servi." The dinner consisted of the aforenamed soupe aux choux, the carp that had led to the invitation, a ragoût de mouton à la Hongroise, rôti de faisans, and a salade Japonaise. The sweets and ices had been sent by the patissier. I never dined like that before or after, not even a week later, when Dr. Véron and Sophie made the *amende honorable* in the Rue Taitbout.

I have spent many delightful evenings with all these men; I do not remember having spent a more delightful one than on the latter occasion. Every one was in the best of humours; the dinner was very fine, albeit that, course for course, it did not come up to Dumas'; and, moreover, during the week that had elapsed between the two entertainments, one of Dr. Véron's successors at the opera, Léon Pillet, had been served with the most ludicrous citation that was ever entered on the rolls of any tribunal. For nearly nineteen years before that period there had been several attempts to mount Weber's "Freyschutz," all of which had come to nought. There had been an adaptation by Castil-Blaze, under the title of "Robin des Bois," and several others; but until '41, Weber's work, even in a mutilated state, was not known to the French opera-goer. At that time, however, M. Emilien Paccini made a very good translation; Hector Berlioz was commissioned to write the recitatives, for it must be remembered that Weber's opera contains dialogue, and that dialogue is not admissible in grand opera. Berlioz acquitted himself with a taste and reverence for the composer's original scheme that did great credit to both; he sought his themes in Weber's work itself, notably in the "Invitation à la Valse:" but notwithstanding all this, the "Freyschutz" was miserably amputated in the performance lest it should "play" longer than midnight, though a ballet was added rather than deprive the public of its so-called due. Neither Paccini nor Berlioz had set foot in the opera-house since their objections to such a course had been overruled, and they made it known to the world at large that no blame attached to them; nevertheless, this quasi "Freyschutz" met with a certain amount of success. M. Pillet was rubbing his hands with glee at his own cleverness, until a Nemesis came in the shape of a visitor from the Fatherland, who took the conceit out of the director with one fell blow, and, what was worse still, with a perfectly legal one.

The visitor was no less a personage than Count Tyszkiewicz, one of the best musical critics of the time and the editor of the foremost musical publication in the world; namely, *Die Musikalische Zeitung*, of Leipzig. The count, having been attracted by the announcement of the opera on the bills, was naturally anxious to hear how French artists would acquit themselves of a work particularly German, and, having secured a stall, anticipated an enjoyable evening. But alack and alas! in a very little while his indignation at the liberties taken with the text and the score by the singers, musicians, and conductor got the upper hand, and he rushed off to the commissary of police on duty at the theatre to claim the execution of Weber's opera in its integrity, as promised on the bills, or the restitution of his money. Failing to get satisfaction either way, he required the commissary to draw up a verbatim report of his objections and his claim, determined to bring an action. Next morning, he sent a lithographed account of the transaction to all the papers, requesting its insertion, with which request not a single one complied. Finding himself baffled at every turn, he engaged lawyer and counsel and began proceedings.

It was at that stage of the affair that the dinner at Dr. Véron's took place. As a matter of course, the coming lawsuit gave rise to a great deal of chaff on the part of the guests, although the victim of this badinage and defendant in the suit was not there. It was his successor who took up the cudgels and predicted the plaintiff's discomfiture. "The counsel," said Roqueplan, "ought to be instructed to invite the president and assessors to come and hear the work before they deliver judgment: if they like it personally, they will not decide against Pillet; if they don't, they'll fall asleep and be ashamed to own it afterwards. But should they give a verdict for the plaintiff, Pillet ought to appeal on a question of incompetence; a person with the name of Tyszkiewicz has no right to plead in the interest of harmony." *

Among such a company as that gathered round Dr. Véron's table, a single sentence frequently led to a host of recollections. Scarcely had Roqueplan's suggestion to invite the president and assessors of the court to the performance of the "Freyschutz" been broached than our host chimed in: "I can tell you a story where the expedient you recommend was really resorted to, though it did not emanate from half as clever a man as you, Roqueplan. In fact, it was only a pompier that hit upon it to get out of a terrible scrape. He was going to be brought before a court-martial for neglect of duty. It happened under the management of my immediate successor, Duponchel, at the fourth or fifth performance of Halévy's 'Guido et Génevra.' Some of the scenery caught fire, and, but for Duponchel's presence of mind, there would have been a panic and a horrible catastrophe. Nevertheless, the cause of the accident had to be ascertained, and it was found that the brigadier fireman posted at the spot where the mischief began had been asleep. He frankly admitted his fault, at the same time pleading extenuating circumstances. 'What do you mean?' asked the captain, charged with the report. 'Such a thing has never happened to me before, mon capitaine, but it is impossible for any one to keep his eyes open

---

* The latter plea was, in fact, advanced by Pillet's counsel in the first instance, on Roqueplan's advice, and perhaps influenced the court; for though it gave a verdict for the plaintiff, it was only for *seven francs* (the price of the stall), and costs. The verdict was based upon the "consideration" that the defendant had not carried out altogether the promise set forth on the programme.

during that act. You need not take my word, but perhaps you will try the effect yourself.' The captain did try; the captain sat for two or three minutes after the rise of the curtain, then he was seen to leave his place hurriedly. The brigadier and his men were severely reprimanded, but they were not tried. Out of respect for Halévy the matter was kept a secret.

"I may add," said our host, "that the pompier is by no means a bad judge of things theatrical, seeing that he is rarely away from the stage for more than three or four nights at a time. I remember perfectly well that, during the rehearsals of 'Robert le Diable,' Meyerbeer often had a chat with them. Curiously enough he now and then made little alterations after these conversations. I am not insinuating that the great composer acted upon their suggestions, but I should not at all wonder if he had done so."

Alexandre Dumas, in whose honour, it will be remembered, the dinner was given, had an excellent memory, and some years afterwards profited by the experiment. I tell the story as it was given to us subsequently by his son. Only a few friends and Alexandre the younger were present at the first of the final rehearsals of "The Three Musketeers," at the Ambigu Comique. They were not dress rehearsals proper, because there were no costumes, and the scenery merely consisted of a cloth and some wings. Behind one of the latter they had noticed, during the first six tableaux, the shining helmet of a fireman who was listening very attentively. The author had noticed him too. About the middle of the seventh tableau the helmet suddenly vanished, and the father remarked upon it to his son. When the act was finished, Dumas went in search of the pompier, who did not know him. "What made you go away?" he asked him. "Because it did not amuse me half as much as the others," was the answer. "That was enough for my father," said the younger Dumas. "There and then he went to Béraud's room, took off his coat, waistcoat, and braces, unfastened the collar of his shirt—it was the only way he could work—and sent for the prompt copy of the seventh tableau, which he tore up and flung into the fire, to the consternation of Béraud. 'What are you doing?' he exclaimed. 'You see what I am doing; I am destroying the seventh tableau. It does not amuse the pompier. I know what it wants.' And an hour and a half later, at the termination of the rehearsal, the actors were given a fresh seventh tableau to study."

I have come back by a roundabout way to the author of "Monte-Christo," because, tout chemin avec moi mène à Dumas; I repeat, he constitutes one of the happiest of my recollections. After the lapse of many years, I willingly admit that I would have cheerfully foregone the acquaintance of all the other celebrities, perhaps David d'Angers excepted, for that of Dumas père.

After the lapse of many years, the elder Dumas still represents to me all the good qualities of the French nation and few of their bad ones. It was absolutely impossible to be dull in his society, but it must not be thought that these contagious animal spirits only showed themselves periodically or when in company. It was what the French have so aptly termed "la joie de vivre," albeit that they rarely associate the phrase with any one not in the spring of life. With Dumas it was chronic until a very few months before his death. I remember calling upon him shortly after the dinner of which I spoke just now. He had taken up his quarters at Saint-Germain, and come to Paris only for a few days. "Is monsieur at home?" I said to the servant.

"He is in his study, monsieur," was the answer. "Monsieur can go in."

At that moment I heard a loud burst of laughter from the inner apartment, so I said, "I would sooner wait until monsieur's visitors are gone."

"Monsieur has no visitors; he is working," remarked the servant with a smile. "Monsieur Dumas often laughs like this at his work."

It was true enough, the novelist was alone, or rather in company with one of his characters, at whose sallies he was simply roaring.

Work, in fact, was a pleasure to him, like everything else he undertook. One day he had been out shooting, between Villers-Cotterets and Compiègne, since six in the morning, and had killed twenty-nine birds. "I am going to make up the score and a half, and then I'll have a sleep, for I feel tired," he said. When he had killed his thirtieth partridge he slowly walked back to the farm, where his son and friends found him about four hours later, toasting himself before the fire, his feet on the andirons, and twirling his thumbs.

"What are you sitting there for like that?" asked his son.

"Can't you see? I am resting."

"Did you get your sleep?"

"No, I didn't; it's impossible to sleep here. There

is an infernal noise; what with the sheep, the cows, the pigs, and the rest, there is no chance of getting a wink."

"So you have been sitting here for the last four hours, twirling your thumbs?"

"No, I have been writing a piece in one act." The piece in question was "Romulus," which he gave to Regnier to have it read at the Comédie-Française, under a pseudonym, and as the work of a young unknown author. It was accepted without a dissentient vote.

It is a well-known fact, vouched for by the accounts of the Compagnie du Chemin de Fer de l'Ouest, that during the three years Dumas lived at Saint-Germain, the receipts increased by twenty thousand francs per annum. Of course, it has been objected that railways being then in their infancy the increment would have been just the same without Dumas' presence in the royal residence, but, curiously enough, from the day he left, the passenger traffic fell to its previous state. Dumas had simply galvanized the sleepy old town into life, he had bought the theatre where the artists of the Comédie-Française, previous to supping with him, came to play "Mademoiselle de Belle-Isle" or the "Demoiselles de Saint-Cyr," for the benefit of the poor. On such occasions, there was not a room to be had at the hotels. After supper, there were twice a week fireworks on the Terrace, which could be seen from Paris and from Versailles, to the great astonishment of Louis-Philippe, who really attributed the change to the beneficence of his reign, although he failed to account for the continued dulness of the latter royal borough, where he himself resided, and whose picture-galleries he had restored and thrown open to the public, besides having the great fountains to play every first Sunday of the month.

One day the king sent for M. de Montalivet, and told him that, though gratified at the revived prosperity of Saint-Germain, he would like to see a little more gaiety at Versailles.

"You really mean it, sire?" asked the minister.

"Not only do I mean it, but I confess to you that it would give me great pleasure."

"Well, sire, Alexandre Dumas has lately been sentenced to a fortnight's imprisonment for neglecting his duty in the National Guards: make an order for him to spend that fortnight in Versailles, and I guarantee your Majesty that Versailles will be lively enough."

Louis-Philippe did not act upon the suggestion. The only member of the d'Orleans' family who was truly sympathetic to Dumas was the king's eldest son, whose untimely death shortly afterwards affected the great novelist very much, albeit that he frankly acknowledged to regretting the man and not the future ruler; for while loudly professing his republican creed, he never pretended to overlook his indebtedness to Louis-Philippe, when Duc d'Orléans, for having befriended him; nay, I am inclined to think that Dumas' gratitude was far greater than the case warranted. When, in 1847, the fancy took him to go into parliament, he naturally turned to the borough he had benefited so much by his stay there—Saint-Germain, and Saint-Germain denied him. They thought him too immoral. Dumas waited patiently for another opportunity, which did not come until the following year, when Louis-Philippe had abdicated. Addressing a meeting of electors at Joigny, he was challenged by a M. de Bonnelière to reconcile his title of republican with his title of Marquis de la Pailleterie, and the fact of his having been a secretary to the Duc d'Orléans, although he had never occupied so important a position in the Duc d'Orléans' household. His reply was simply scathing, and I give it in full as the papers of the day reproduced it. "No doubt," he said, in an off hand, bantering way, "I was formerly called the Marquis de la Pailleterie, which was my father's name, and of which I was very proud, being unable then to claim a glorious one of my own make. But at present, when I am somebody, I call myself Alexandre Dumas and nothing more; and everybody knows me, you among the rest—you, you absolute nobody, who have merely come to be able to boast to-morrow, after insulting me to-night, that you have known the great Dumas. If such was your ambition, you might have satisfied it without failing in the common courtesies of a gentleman."

When the applause which the reply provoked had subsided, Dumas went on: "There is also no doubt about my having been a secretary to the Duc d'Orléans, and that I have received all kinds of favours from his family. If you, citizen, are ignorant of the meaning of the term, 'the memory of the heart,' allow me at least to proclaim here in my loudest voice, that I am not, and that I entertain towards this royal family all the devotion an honourable man can feel."

It is, however, not my intention to sketch Alexandre Dumas as a politician, for which career I considered him singularly unfit; but the speech from which I extracted the foregoing contains a few lines which, more than thirty-five years after they were spoken, cannot fail to strike the reader with his marvellous foresight. "Geographically," he said, commenting upon the political state of Europe, "Prussia has the form of a serpent, and, like it, she seems to be asleep, and to gather her strength in order to swallow everything around her—Denmark, Holland, Belgium, and, when she shall have swallowed all that, you will find that Austria will be swallowed in its turn, and perhaps, alas, France also."

The last words, as may be imagined, provoked a storm of hisses; nevertheless, he kept his audience spellbound until midnight.

A parliamentary candidate, however eloquent, who flings his constituents into the river when they happen to annoy him, must have been a novelty even in those days, and that is what Dumas did to two brawlers after said meeting, just to show them that his "aristocratic grip" was worth their "plebeian one."

A few years later, at a dinner at Dumas', in the Rue d'Amsterdam, I met a Monsieur du Chaffault who had been an eye-witness of this, as well as of other scenes during that memorable day. Until the morning of that day, M. du Chaffault had never set eyes on the great novelist; in the evening, he was his friend for life. It only proves once more the irresistible fascination Dumas exercised over every one with whom he came in contact, because the beginning of that friendship cost M. du Chaffault six hundred francs, the expenses of that part of the electoral campaign. The story, as told by M. du Chaffault the following afternoon in the

Café Riche to Dr. Véron, myself, and Joseph Méry, is too good to be missed. I give it as near as I can remember.

"I was about twenty-four then, with nothing particular to do, and a moderate private income. They were painting and whitewashing my place, a few miles away from Sens, and I had taken up my quarters in the principal hotel in the town. The first elections under the second republic were being held. There was a good deal of excitement everywhere, and I liked it, though not taking the slightest interest in politics. This was in May, 1848; and about six, one morning while I was still in bed, the door of my room was suddenly opened without knocking, and what seemed to me a big black monster stood before me. There was a pistol lying by the side of me, and I was reaching towards it, when he spoke. 'Don't alarm yourself,' he said; 'I am Alexandre Dumas. They told me you were a good fellow, and I have come to ask you a service.'

"I had never seen Dumas in the flesh, only a portrait of him, but I recognized him immediately. 'You have often afforded me a great deal of amusement, but I confess you frightened me,' I said. 'What, in Heaven's name, do you want at this unholy hour?'

"'I have slept here,' was the answer. 'I landed here at midnight, and am starting for Joigny by-and-by, to attend a political meeting. I am putting up as a member for your department.'

"I jumped out of bed at once, Dumas handed me my trousers, and, when I got as far as my boots, he says, 'Oh, while I think of it, I have come to ask you for a pair of boots; in stepping into the carriage, one of mine has come to utter grief, and there is no shop open.'

"As you may see for yourselves, I am by no means a giant, and Dumas is one. I pointed this out to him, but he did not even answer me. He had caught sight of three or four pair of boots under the dressing-table, and, in the twinkling of an eye, chose the best pair and pulled them on, leaving me his old ones, absolutely worn out, but which I have preserved in my library at home. I always show them to my visitors as the thousand and first volume of Alexandre Dumas.*

"By the time he got the boots on we were friends, as if we had known one another for years; as for Dumas, he was 'theeing' and 'thouing' me as if we had been at school together.

"'You are going to Joigny?' I said; 'I know a good many people there.'

"'All the better, for I am going to take you along with me.'

"Having to go no further than Joigny, and being taken thither in the conveyance of my newly-made friend, I did not think it necessary to provide myself with an extra supply of funds, the more that I had between five and six hundred francs in my pocket. In a short time we were on our road, and the first stage of three hours seemed to me as many minutes. Whenever we passed a country seat, out came a lot of anecdotes and legends connected with its owners, interlarded with quaint fancies and epigrams. At that first change of horses, Dumas' secretary paid. At the second, Villevailles, Dumas says, 'Have you got

---

* Alexandre Dumas had a marvellously small foot.—EDITOR.

twenty francs change?' Without a moment's hesitation, I took out my purse, paid the money, and put down in my pocket-book, 'Alexandre Dumas, twenty francs.' I might have saved myself the trouble, as I found out in a very short time, for the moment he got out at Joigny, he rushed off in a hurry without troubling about anything. The postilion turned to me for his money, and I paid, and put down once more, 'Alexandre Dumas, thirty francs.'

"The first meeting was fixed for four, at the theatre. They applied to me for the hire of the building, for the gas. I went on paying, but I no longer put down the items, saying to myself, 'When my six hundred francs are gone, my little excursion will be at an end, and I'll go back to Sens.' The little excursion did not extend to more than one day, seeing that I had to settle the dinner bill at the Duc de Bourgogne, Dumas having invited every one he met on his way. I am only sorry for one thing, that I did not have ten thousand francs in my pocket that morning in order to prolong my excursion for a week or so. But next morning my purse was empty, and 'our defeat was certain.' I had already identified myself with Dumas' aspirations, so I returned to Sens by myself, but overjoyed at having seen and spoken to this man of genius, who is richer than all the millionnaires in the world put together, seeing that he never troubles himself about paying, and has therefore no need to worry about money. Three months afterwards, the printer at Joigny drew upon me for a hundred francs for electioneering bills, which, of course, I could not have ordered, but which draft I settled as joyfully as I had settled the rest. I have preserved the draft with the boots;

they are mementoes of my first two days' friendship with my dear friend."

At the first blush, all this sounds very much as if we were dealing with a mere Harold Skimpole, but no man was more unlike Dickens' creation than Alexandre Dumas. M. du Chaffault described him rightly when he said that he did not worry about money, not even his own. "My biographer," Dumas often said, "will not fail to point out that I was 'a panier percé,' * neglecting, as a matter of course, to mention that, as a rule, it was not I who made the holes."

The biographers have not been quite so unjust as that. Unfortunately, few of them knew Dumas intimately, and they were so intent upon sketching the playwright and the novelist that they neglected the man. They could have had the stories of Alexandre Dumas' improvidence with regard to himself and his generosity to others for the asking from his familiars. On the other hand, the latter have only told these stories in a fragmentary way; a complete collection of them would be impossible, for no one, not even Dumas himself, knew half the people whom he befriended. In that very apartment of the Rue d'Amsterdam which I mentioned just now, the board was free to any and every one who chose to come in. Not once, but a score of times have I heard Dumas ask, after this or that man had left the table, "Who is he? what's his name?" Whosoever came with, or at the tail, not of a friend, but of a simple acquaintance, especially if the acquaintance happened to wear skirts, was immediately invited to breakfast or dinner as the case might be.

---

* Literally, a basket with holes in it; figuratively, the term applied to irreclaimable spendthrifts.—EDITOR.

Count de Cherville once told me that Dumas, having taken a house at Varenne-Saint-Hilaire, his second month's bill for meat alone amounted to eleven hundred francs. Let it be remembered that his household consisted of himself, two secretaries, and three servants, and that money went a great deal further than it does at present, especially in provincial France, in some parts of which living is still very cheap. In consequence of one of those financial crises, which were absolutely periodical with Alexandre Dumas, M. de Cherville had prevailed upon him to leave Paris for a while, and to take up his quarters with him. All went comparatively well as long as he was M. de Cherville's guest; but, having taken a liking to the neighbourhood, he rented a house of his own, and furnished it from garret to cellar in the most expensive way, as if he were going to spend the remainder of his life in it. Exclusive of the furniture, he spent between fifteen thousand and eighteen thousand francs on hangings, painting, and repairs. The parasites and harpies which M. de Cherville had kept at bay came down upon him like a swarm of locusts. "And how long, think you, did Dumas stay in his new domicile? Three months, not a day more nor less. As a matter of course, the furniture did not fetch a quarter of its cost; the repairs, the decorating, etc., were so much sheer waste: for the incoming tenant refused to refund a cent for it, and Dumas, having made up his mind to go to Italy, would not wait for a more liberal or conscientious one, lest he should have the rent of the empty house on his shoulders also. Luckily, I took care that he should pocket the proceeds of the sale of the furniture."

This last sentence wants explaining. As a rule, when a man sells his sticks, he pockets the money. But the instance just mentioned was the only one in which Dumas had the disposal of his household goods. The presiding divinity invariably carried them away with her when she had to make room for a successor, and these successions generally occurred once, sometimes twice, a year. "La reine est morte, vive la reine." The new sovereign, for the first few days of her reign, had to be content with bare walls and very few material comforts; then the nest was upholstered afresh, and "il n'y avait rien de changé en la demeure, sauf le nom de la maîtresse."

Consequently, though for forty years Alexandre Dumas could not have earned less than eight thousand pounds per annum; though he neither smoked, drank, nor gambled; though, in spite of his mania for cooking, he himself was the most frugal eater—the beef from the soup of the previous day, grilled, was his favourite dish,—it rained writs and summonses around him, while he himself was frequently without a penny.

M. du Chaffault one day told me of a scene *à propos* of this which is worth reproducing. He was chatting to Dumas in his study, when a visitor was shown in. He turned out to be an Italian man of letters and refugee, on the verge of starvation. M. du Chaffault could not well make out what was said, because they were talking Italian, but all at once Dumas got up and took from the wall behind him a magnificent pistol, one of a pair. The visitor walked off with it, to M. du Chaffault's surprise. When he was gone, Dumas turned to his friend and explained: "He was utterly penniless, and so am I; so I gave him the pistol."

"Great Heavens, you surely did not recommend him to go and make an end of himself!" interrupted du Chaffault.

Dumas burst out laughing. "Of course not. I merely told him to go and sell or pawn it, and leave me the fellow one, in case some other poor wretch should want assistance while I am so terribly hard up."

And yet, in this very Rue d'Amsterdam, whether Dumas was terribly impecunious or not, the déjeuner, which generally began at about half-past eleven, was rarely finished before half-past four, because during the whole of that time fresh contingents arrived to be fed, and communication was kept up between the apartment and the butcher for corresponding fresh supplies of beefsteaks and cutlets.

Is it a wonder, then, that it rained summonses, and writs, and other law documents? But no one took much notice of these, not even one of the four secretaries, who was specially appointed to look after these things. If I remember aright, his name was Hirschler. The names of the other three secretaries were Rusconi, Viellot, and Fontaine. Unfortunately, Hirschler was as dilatory as his master, and, until the process-server claimed a personal interview, as indifferent. These "limbs of the law" were marvellously polite. I was present one day at an interview between one of these and Hirschler, for Dumas' dwelling was absolutely and literally the glass house of the ancient philosopher— with this difference, that no one threw any stones *from* it. There was no secret, no skeleton in the cupboard; the impecuniosity and the recurrent periods of plenty were both as open as the day.

The "man of law" and Hirschler began by shaking

hands, for they were old acquaintances; it would have been difficult to find a process-server in Paris who was not an old acquaintance of Dumas. After which the visitor informed Hirschler that he had come to distrain.

"To distrain? I did not know we had got as far as that," said Hirschler. "Wait a moment. I must go and see." It meant that Hirschler repaired to the kitchen, where stood a large oaken sideboard, in a capacious drawer of which all the law documents, no matter by whom received, were indiscriminately thrown, to be fished out when the "mauvais quart d'heure" came, and not until then.

"You are right," said Hirschler, but not in the least worried or excited. "I really did not know we had got as far as that. I must ask you to wait another minute. I suppose a third or a fourth of the total amount will do for the present?"

"Well, I do not know," said the process-server with most exquisite politeness. "Try what you can do. I fancy that with a third I may manage to stop proceedings for a while."

The third or fourth part of the debt was rarely in the house; messengers had to be despatched for it to Cadot, the publisher, or to the cashier of the *Moniteur, Constitutionnel,* or *Siècle.* Meanwhile the process-server was feasted in a sumptuous way, and when the messenger returned with the sum in question, Hirschler and the process-server shook hands once more, with the most cordial *au revoir* possible.

As a matter of course, the same process-server reappeared upon the scene in a few months. The comedy had often as many as a dozen representations, so that it may safely be said that a great number of Dumas' debts were paid six or seven times over. Even sixpence a line of sixty letters did not suffice to keep pace with such terrible improvidence, though the remuneration was much more frequently fourpence or fivepence. It rarely rose to sevenpence halfpenny, but in all cases a third went to Dumas' collaborateurs, another third to his creditors, and the rest to himself.

I have allowed my pen to run away with me. One more story, and then I leave Alexandre Dumas for the present. It is simply to show that he would have squandered the fortune of all the Rothschilds combined: I repeat, not on himself; he would have given it away, or allowed it to be taken. He had no notion of the value of money. About a year after I had made his acquaintance, he was ill at Saint-Germain, and I went to see him. His dog had bitten him severely in the right hand; he was in bed, and obliged to dictate. His son had just left him, and he told me, adding, "C'est un cœur d'or, cet' Alexandre." Seeing that I did not ask what had elicited the praise, he began telling me.

"This morning I received six hundred and fifty francs. Just now Alexandre was going up to Paris, and he says, 'I'll take fifty francs.'

"I did not pay attention, or must have misunderstood; at any rate I replied, 'Don't take as much as that; leave me a hundred francs.'

"'What do you mean, father?' he asked. 'I am telling you that I am going to take fifty francs.'

"'I beg your pardon,' I said. 'I understood you were going to take six hundred.'"

He would have considered it the most natural thing

in the world for his son to take six hundred and leave him fifty; just as he considered it the most natural thing to bare his arm and to have a dozen leeches put on it, because his son, when a boy of eight, having met with an accident, would not consent to blood-letting of that kind. In vain did the father tell him that the leeches did not hurt. "Well, put some on yourself, and then I will." And the giant turned up his sleeves, and did as he was told.

CHAPTER IV.

Dr. Louis Véron—The real man as distinguished from that of his own "Memoirs"—He takes the management of the Paris Opéra—How it was governed before his advent—Meyerbeer's "Robert le Diable" *underlined*—Meyerbeer and his doubts upon the merits of his work—Meyerbeer's generosity—Meyerbeer and the beggars of the Rue Le Peletier—Dr. Véron, the inventor of the modern newspaper puff—Some specimens of advertisements in their infancy—Dr. Véron takes a leaf from the book of Molière—Dr. Véron's love of money—His superstitions—His objections to travelling in railways—He quotes the Queen of England as an example—When Queen Victoria overcomes her objection, Véron holds out—"Queen Victoria has got a successor: the Véron dynasty begins and ends with me"—Thirteen at table—I make the acquaintance of Taglioni—The woman and the ballerina—Her adventure at Perth—An improvised performance of "Nathalie, la Laitière Suisse"—Another adventure in Russia—A modern Claude Du-Val—My last meeting with Taglioni—A dinner-party at De Morny's—A comedy scene between husband and wife—Flotow, the composer of "Martha"—His family—His father's objection to the composer's profession—The latter's interview with M. de Saint-Georges, the author of the libretto of Balfe's "Bohemian Girl"—M. de Saint-Georges prevails upon the father to let his son study in Paris for five years, and to provide for him during that time—The supplies are stopped on the last day of the fifth year—Flotow, at the advice of M. de Saint-Georges, stays on and lives by giving piano-lessons—His earthly possessions at his first success—"Rob Roy" at the Hôtel Castellane—Lord Granville's opinion of the music—The Hôtel Castellane and some Paris salons during Louis-Philippe's reign—The Princesse de Lieven's, M. Thiers', etc.—What Madame de Girardin's was like—Victor Hugo's—Perpetual adoration; very artistic, but nothing to eat or to drink—The salon of the ambassador of the Two Sicilies—Lord and Lady Granville at the English Embassy—The salon of Count Apponyi—A story connected with it—Furniture and entertainments—Cakes, ices, and tea; no champagne as during the Second Empire—The Hôtel de Castellane and its amateur theatricals—Rival companies—No under-studies—Lord Brougham at the Hôtel Castellane—His bad French and his would-be Don Juanism—A French rendering of Shakespeare's "There is but one step between the sublime and the ridiculous," as applied to Lord Brougham—He nearly accepts a part in a farce where his bad French is likely to produce a comic effect—His successor as a murderer of the language—M. de Saint-Georges—Like Molière, he reads his plays to his housekeeper—When the latter is not satisfied, the dinner is spoilt, however great the success of the play in public estimation—Great men and their housekeepers—Turner, Jean Jacques Rousseau, Eugène Delacroix.

NEXT to Dumas, the man who is uppermost in my recollections of that period is Dr. Louis Véron, the founder of the *Revue de Paris*, which was the precursor of the *Revue des Deux Mondes*; Dr. Véron, under whose management the Paris Opéra rose to a degree of perfection it has never attained since; Dr. Véron, who, as some one said, was as much part and parcel of the history of Paris during the first half of the nineteenth century as was Napoleon I. of the history of France; Dr. Véron, than whom there has been no more original figure in any civilized community before or since, with the exception, perhaps, of Phineas Barnum, to whom, however, he was infinitely superior in education, tact, and manners.

Dr. Véron has written his own " Memoirs" in six bulky volumes, to which he added a seventh a few years later. They are full of interesting facts from beginning to end, especially to those who did not know intimately the author or the times of which he treats. Those who did are tempted to repeat the mot of Diderot when they gave him the portrait of his father. "This is my Sunday father; I want my everyday father." The painter, in fact, had represented the worthy cutler of Langres in his best coat and wig, etc.; not as his son had been in the habit of seeing him. The Dr. Véron of the "Memoirs" is not the Dr. Véron of the Café de Paris, nor the Dr. Véron of the *avant-scène* in his own theatre, snoring a duet with Auber, and "keeping better time than the great composer himself;" he is not the Dr. Véron full of fads and superstitions and uniformly kind, "because kindness is as a rule a capital investment;" he is not the cheerful pessimist we knew; he is a grumbling optimist, as the journalists of his time have painted him; in short, in his book he is a quasi-philanthropic illusion, while in reality he was a hard-hearted, shrewd business man who did good by stealth now and then, but never blushed to find it fame.

The event which proved the starting-point of Dr. Véron's celebrity was neither of his own making nor of his own seeking. Though it happened when I was a mere lad, I have heard it discussed in after-years sufficiently often and by very good authorities to be confident of my facts. In June, 1831, Dr. Véron took the management of the Paris Opéra, which up till then had been governed on the style of the old régime, namely, by three gentlemen of the king's household with a working director under them. The royal privy purse was virtually responsible for its liabilities. Louis-Philippe shifted the burden of that responsibility on the State, and limited its extent. The three gentlemen of the king's household were replaced by a royal commissioner, and the yearly subsidy fixed at £32,500; still a pretty round sum, which has been reduced since by £500 only.

At Dr. Véron's advent, Meyerbeer's "Robert le Diable" was, what they call in theatrical parlance, "underlined," or, if not underlined, at least definitely accepted. Only one work of his had at that time been heard in Paris, "Il Crociato in Egitto."

It is difficult to determine, after so many years, whether Dr. Véron, notwithstanding his artistic instincts, was greatly smitten with the German composer's masterpiece. It has often been argued that he was not, because he insisted upon an indemnity of forty thousand francs from the Government towards the cost of its production. In the case of a man like Véron, this proves nothing at all. He may have been thoroughly convinced of the merits of "Robert le Diable," and as thoroughly confident of its success with the public, though no manager, not even the most experienced, can be; it would not have prevented him from squeezing the forty thousand francs from the minister on the plea that the performance of the work was imposed upon him by a treaty of his predecessor. To Dr. Véron's credit be it said that ho might have saved himself the hard tussle he had with the minister by simply applying for the money to Meyerbeer himself, who would have given it without a moment's hesitation, rather than see the success of "Robert le Diable" jeopardized by inefficient mounting, although up to the last Meyerbeer could never make up his mind whether magnificent scenery and gorgeous dresses were an implied compliment or the reverse to the musical value of his compositions. À propos of this there is a very characteristic story. At one of the final dress-rehearsals of "Robert le Diable," Meyerbeer felt much upset. At the sight of that beautiful set of the cloister of Sainte-Rosalie, where the nuns rise from their tombs, at the effect produced by the weird procession, Meyerbeer came up to Véron.

"My dear director," he said, "I perceive well enough

that you do not depend upon the opera itself; you are, in fact, running after a spectacular success."

"Wait till the fourth act," replied Véron, who was above all logical.

The curtain rose upon the fourth act, and what did Meyerbeer behold? Instead of the vast, grandiose apartment he had conceived for Isabella, Princess of Sicily, he found a mean, shabby set, which would have been deemed scarcely good enough for a minor theatre.

"Decidedly, my dear director," says Meyerbeer, with a bitter twinge in his features and voice, "I perceive well enough that you have no faith in my score; you did not even dare go to the expense of a new set. I would willingly have paid for it myself."

And he would willingly have paid for it, because Meyerbeer was not only very rich, but very generous.

"It is a very funny thing," said Lord ——, as he came into the Café de Paris one morning, many years afterwards; "there are certain days in the week when the Rue Le Peletier seems to be swarming with beggars, and, what is funnier still, they don't take any notice of me. I pass absolutely scot-free."

"I'll bet," remarked Roger de Beauvoir, "that they are playing 'Robert le Diable' or 'Les Huguenots' to-night, and I can assure you that I have not seen the bills."

"Now that you speak of it, they are playing 'Les Huguenots' to-night," replied Lord ——; "but what has that to do with it? I am not aware that the Paris beggars manifest a particular predilection for Meyerbeer's operas, and that they are booking their places on the days they are performed."

"It's simply this," explained De Beauvoir: "both

Rossini and Meyerbeer never fail to come of a morning to look at the bills, and when the latter finds his name on them, he is so overjoyed that he absolutely empties his pockets of all the cash they contain. Notwithstanding his many years of success, he is still afraid that the public's liking for his music is merely a passing fancy, and as every additional performance decreases this apprehension, he thinks he cannot be sufficiently thankful to Providence. His gratitude shows itself in almsgiving."

I made it my business subsequently to verify what I considered De Beauvoir's fantastical statement, and I found it substantially correct.

To return to Dr. Véron, who, there is no doubt, did the best he could for "Robert le Diable," to which and to the talent of Taglioni he owed his fortune. At the same time, it would be robbing him of part of his glory did we not state that the success of that great work might have been less signal but for him; both his predecessors and successors had and have still equally good chances without having availed themselves of them, either in the interest of lyrical art or in that of the public.

I compared Dr. Véron just now to Phineas Barnum, and the comparison was not made at random. Dr. Véron was really the inventor of the newspaper puff direct and indirect—of that personal journalism which records the slightest deed or gesture of the popular theatrical manager, and which at the present day is carried to excess. And all his subordinates and co-workers were made to share the advantages of the system, because their slightest doings also reflected glory upon him. An artist filling at a moment's notice the part of a fellow-artist who had become suddenly ill, a carpenter saving by his presence of mind the situation at a critical juncture, had not only his paragraph in next morning's papers, but a whole column, containing the salient facts of his life and career. It was the system of Frederick the Great and of the first Napoleon, acknowledging the daring deeds of their smallest as well as of their foremost aids—with this difference, that the French captain found it convenient to suppress them now and then, and that Dr. Véron never attempted to do so. When the idea of putting down these notes first entered my mind, I looked over some files of newspapers of that particular period, and there was scarcely one between 1831 and 1835 that did not contain a lengthy reference to the Grand Opéra and its director. I was irresistibly reminded of the bulletins the great Napoleon dictated on the battle-field. I have also seen a collection of posters relating to the same brilliant reign at the Opéra. Of course, compared to the eloquent effusions and ingenious attempts of the contemporary theatrical manager to bait the public, Véron's are mere child's play; still we must remember that the art of puffing was in its infancy, and, as such, some of them are worth copying. The public was not so *blasé*, and it swallowed the bait eagerly. Here they are.

"To-morrow tenth performance of . . . , which henceforth will only be played at rare intervals.

"To-morrow twentieth performance of . . . ; positively the last before the departure of M. . . .

"To-morrow seventeenth performance of . . . ; reappearance of Madame . . .

"To-morrow fifteenth performance of . . . by all the principal artists who 'created' the parts.

"To-morrow thirtieth performance of . . . The third scene of the second act will be played as on the first night.

"To-morrow twentieth performance of . . . , which can only be played for a limited number of nights.

"To-morrow sixteenth performance of . . . In the Ball-Room Scene a new pas de Châles will be introduced.

"To-morrow thirtieth performance of . . . This successful work must be momentarily suspended owing to previous arrangements."

Childish as these lines may look to the present generation, they produced a fortune of £2000 a year to Dr. Véron in four years, and, but for the outbreak of the cholera in '32, when "Robert le Diable" was in the flush of its success, would have produced another £1000 per annum. At that time Dr. Véron had already been able to put aside £24,000, and he might have easily closed his theatre during those terrible months; but, like Molière, he asked himself what would become of all those who were dependent upon him, and had not put aside anything; so he made his savings into ten parcels, intending to hold out as many months without asking help of any one. Five of the parcels went. At the beginning of the sixth month the cholera abated; by the end it had almost disappeared.

Those who would infer from this that Dr. Véron was indifferent to money, would make a great mistake. But he would not allow his love of it to get the upper hand, to come between him and his conscience, to make him commit either a dishonest or a foolish act.

By a foolish act he meant headlong speculation. When the shares of the Northern Railway were allotted, Dr. Véron owned the *Constitutionnel;* 150 shares were allotted to him, which at that moment represented a clear profit of 60,000 francs, they being 400 francs above par. Dr. Véron made up his mind to realize there and then. But it was already late; the Bourse was closed, the stockbrokers had finished business for the day. He, however, met one on the Boulevards, who gave him a cheque for 55,000 francs on the Bank of France, which could only be cashed next day. The shares were left meanwhile in Dr. Véron's possession. Three minutes after the bargain was concluded Dr. Véron went back to his office. "I must have ready money for this, or decline the transaction," he said. The stockbroker, by applying to two of his colleagues, managed to scrape together 50,000 francs. Dr. Véron gave him a receipt in full, returned home, singing as he went the French version of " A bird in the hand," etc.

Véron was exceedingly superstitious, and had fads. He could never be induced to take a railway journey. It was generally known in France at that time that, in the early days of locomotion by steam, Queen Victoria had held a similar objection. Véron, when twitted with his objection, invariably replied, "I have yet to learn that the Queen of England is less enlightened than any of you, and she will not enter a railway carriage." But one day the report spread that the queen had made a journey from Windsor to London by the "iron horse," and then Véron was sorely pressed. He had his answer ready. "The Queen of England has got a successor: the Véron dynasty begins and ends with me. I must take care to make it last as long as possible." He stuck to his text till the end of his life.

On no consideration would Véron have sat down "thirteen at table." Once or twice, when the guests and host made up that number, his coachman's son was sent for, dressed, and made presentable, and joined the party; at others he politely requested two or three of us to go and dine at the Café de Paris, and to have the bill sent to him. We drew lots as to who was to go.

It was through Dr. Véron that I became acquainted with most of the operatic celebrities — Meyerbeer, Halévy, Auber, Duprez, etc.; for though he had abdicated his directorship seven or eight years before we met, he was perhaps a greater power then in the lyrical world than at the date of his reign.

It was at Dr. Véron's that I saw Mdlle. Taglioni for the first time — off the stage. It must have been in 1844, for she had not been in Paris since 1840, when I had seen her dance at the Opéra. I had only seen her dance once before that, in '36 or '37, but I was altogether too young to judge then. I own that in 1840 I was somewhat disappointed, and my disappointment was shared by many, because some of my friends, to whom I communicated my impressions, told me that her three years' absence had made a vast difference in her art. In '44 it was still worse; her performances gave rise to many a spiteful epigram, for she herself invited comparison between her former glory and her decline, by dancing in one of her most successful creations, "L'Ombre." Those most leniently disposed towards her thought what Alfred de Muss t so gracefully expressed when requested to write some verses in her album.

> "Si vous ne voulez plus danser,
> Si vous ne faites que passer
> Sur ce grand théâtre si sombre,
> Ne courez pas après votre ombre
> Et tâchez de nous la laisser."

My disappointment with the ballerina was as nothing, however, to my disappointment with the woman. I had been able to determine for myself before then that Marie Taglioni was by no means a good-looking woman, but I did not expect her to be so plain as she was. That, after all, was not her fault; but she might have tried to make amends for her lack of personal charms by her amiability. She rarely attempted to do so, and never with Frenchmen. Her reception of them was freezing to a degree, and on the occasions—few and far between—when she thawed, it was with Russians, Englishmen, or Viennese. Any male of the Latin races she held metaphorically as well as literally at arm's length. Of the gracefulness, so apparent on the stage, even in her decline, there was not a trace to be found in private life. One of her shoulders was higher than the other; she limped slightly, and, moreover, waddled like a duck. The pinched mouth was firmly set; there was no smile on the colourless lips, and she replied to one's remarks in monosyllables.

Truly she had suffered a cruel wrong at the hands of men—of one man, bien entendu; nevertheless, the wonder to most people who knew her was not that Comte Gilbert de Voisins should have left her so soon after their marriage, but that he should have married her at all. "The fact was," said some one with whom

I discussed the marriage one day, "that De Voisins considered himself in honour bound to make that reparation, but I cannot conceive what possessed him to commit the error that made the reparation necessary." And I am bound to say that it was not the utter lack of personal attractions that made every one, men and women alike, indifferent to Taglioni. She was what the French call "une pimbêche." * "Am I not a good-natured woman?" said Mdlle. Mars one day to Hoffman, the blood-curdling novelist. "Mademoiselle, you are the most amiable creature I know between the footlights and the cloth," he replied. No one could have paid Taglioni even such a left-handed compliment, for, if all I heard was true, she was not good-tempered either on or off the stage. Dr. Véron, who was really a very loyal friend, was very reticent about her character, and would never be drawn into revelations. "You know the French proverb," he said once, when I pressed him very closely. "'On ne hérite pas de ceux que l'on tue;' and, after all, she helped me to make my fortune."

That evening I was seated next to Mdlle. Taglioni at dinner, and when she discovered my nationality she unbent a little, so that towards the dessert we were on comparatively friendly terms. She had evidently very grateful recollections of her engagements in London, for it was the only topic on which I could get her to talk on that occasion. Here is a little story I had from her own lips, and which shows the Scotch of the early thirties in quite a new light. It may have been known once, but has been probably forgotten by now, except by the "oldest inhabitant" of

* The word "shrew" is the nearest equivalent.—EDITOR.

Perth. In 1832 or 1833—I will not vouch for the exact year, seeing that it is two score of years since the story was told to me—the season in London had been a fatiguing one for Taglioni. A ballet her father had composed for her, "Nathalie, ou la Laitière Suisse," a very inane thing by all accounts, had met with great success in London. The scene, however, had, as far as I could make out, been changed from Switzerland to Scotland, but of this I will not be certain. At the termination of her engagement Taglioni wanted rest, and she bethought herself to recruit in the Highlands. After travelling hither and thither for a little while, she arrived at Perth, and, as a matter of course, put down her name in the visitors' book of the hotel, then went out to explore the sights of the town. Meanwhile the report of her arrival had spread like wildfire, and on her return to the hotel she found awaiting her a deputation from the principal inhabitants, with the request to honour them with a performance. "The request was so graciously conveyed," said Taglioni, "that I could not but accept, though I took care to point out the difficulties of performing a ballet all by myself, seeing that there was neither a corps de ballet, a male dancer, nor any one else to support me. All these objections were overruled by their promise to provide all these in the best way they could, and before I had time to consider the matter fully, I was taken off in a cab to inspect the theatre, etc. Great heavens, what a stage and scenery! Still, I had given my promise, and, seeing their anxiety, would not go back from it. I cannot tell where they got their *personnel* from. There was a director and a stage-manager, but as he did not understand French, and as my English at that time was even worse than it is now, we were obliged to communicate through an interpreter. His English must have been bewildering, to judge from the manager's blank looks when he spoke to him, and his French was even more wonderful than my English. He was a German waiter from the hotel.

"Nevertheless, thanks to him, I managed to convey the main incidents of the plot of 'Nathalie' to the manager, and during the first act, the most complicated one, all went well. But at the beginning of the second everything threatened to come to a standstill. I must tell you that my father hit upon the novel idea of introducing a kind of dummy, or lay figure, on which this idiotic Nathalie lavishes all her caresses. The young fellow, who is in love with Nathalie, contrives to take the dummy's place; consequently, in order to preserve some semblance of truth, and not to make Nathalie appear more idiotic than she is already, there ought to be a kind of likeness between the dummy and the lover. I know not whether the interpreter had been at fault, or whether in the hurry-scurry I had forgotten all about the dummy, but a few minutes before the rise of the curtain I discovered that there was no dummy. 'You must do the dummy,' I said to Pierre, my servant, 'and I'll pretend to carry you on.' Pierre nodded a silent assent, and immediately began to don the costume, seeing which I had the curtain rung up, and went on to the stage. I was not very comfortable, though, for I heard a violent altercation going on behind the scenes, the cause of which I failed to guess. I kept dancing and dancing, getting near to the wings every now and then, to ask whether Pierre was ready. He seemed to me inordinately long in changing his dress, but the delay was owing to something far more serious than his careful preparation for the part. Pierre had a pair of magnificent whiskers, and the young fellow who enacted the lover had not a hair on his face. Pierre was ready to go on, when the manager noticed the difference. 'Stop!' he shouted; 'that won't do. You must have your whiskers taken off.' Pierre indignantly refused. The manager endeavoured to persuade him to make the sacrifice, but in vain, until at last he had him held down on a chair by two stalwart Scotchmen while the barber did his work.

"All this had taken time, but the public did not grow impatient. They would have been very difficult to please indeed had they behaved otherwise, for I never danced to any audience as I did to them. One of the few pleasant recollections in my life is that evening at Perth; and, curiously enough, Pierre, who is still with me, refers to it with great enthusiasm, notwithstanding the cavalier treatment inflicted upon him. It was his first and last appearance on any stage."

Here is another story Taglioni told me on a subsequent occasion. I have often wondered since whether Macaulay would not have been pleased with it even more than I was.

"The St. Petersburg theatrical season of '24-'25 had been particularly brilliant, and nowhere more so than at the Italian Opera. I came away laden with presents, among others one from the Czar—a magnificent necklet of very fine pearls. When the theatre closed at Lent, I was very anxious to get away, in spite of the inclement season, and notwithstanding the frequent warnings that the roads were not safe. Whenever the conversation turned on that topic, the name of Trischka was sure to crop up; he, in fact, was the leader of a formidable band of highwaymen, compared with whose exploits those of all the others seemed to sink into insignificance. Trischka had been steward to Prince Paskiwiecz, and was spoken of as a very intelligent fellow. Nearly every one with whom I came in contact had seen him while he was still at St. Petersburg, and had a good word to say for him. His manners were reported to be perfect; he spoke French and German very fairly; and, most curious of all, he was an excellent dancer. Some went even as far as to say that if he had adopted that profession, instead of scouring the highways, he would have made a fortune. By all accounts he never molested poor people, and the rich, whom he laid under contribution, had never to complain of violent treatment either in words or deeds—nay, more, he never took all they possessed from his victims; he was content to share and share alike. But papa n'écoutait pas de cet' oreille là; papa était très peu partageur; and, truth to tell, I was taking away a great deal of money from St. Petersburg—which was perhaps another reason why papa did not see the necessity of paying tithes to Trischka. If we had followed papa's advice, we should have either applied to the Czar for an armed escort, or else delayed our departure till the middle of the summer, though he failed to see that the loss of my engagements elsewhere would have amounted to a serious item also. But papa had got it into his head not to part with any of the splendid presents I had received; they were mostly jewels, and people who do not know papa can form no idea what they meant to him. However, as we were plainly told that Trischka conducted his operations all the year round, that we were as likely to be attacked by him in summer as in winter, papa reluctantly made up his mind to go in the beginning of April. Papa provided himself with a pair of large pistols that would not have hurt a cat, and were the laughing-stock of all those who accompanied us for the first dozen miles on our journey; for I had made many friends, and they insisted on doing this. We had two very roomy carriages. My father, my maid, two German violinists, and myself were in the first; the second contained our luggage.

"At the first change of horses after Pskoff, the postmaster told us that Trischka and his band had been seen a few days previously on the road to Dunabourg; at the same time, he seemed to think very lightly of the matter, and, addressing himself particularly to me, opined that, with a little diplomacy on my part and a good deal of *sang-froid*, I might be let off very cheaply. All went well until the middle of next night, when all of a sudden, in the thick of a dense forest, our road was barred by a couple of horsemen, while a third opened the door of our carriage. It was Trischka himself. 'Mademoiselle Taglioni?' he said in very good German, lifting his hat. 'I am Mademoiselle Taglioni,' I replied in French. 'I know,' he answered, with a deeper bow than before. 'I was told you were coming this way. I am sorry, mademoiselle, that I could not come to St. Petersburg to see you dance, but as chance has befriended me, I hope you will do me the honour to dance before me here.' 'How can I dance here, in this road, monsieur?' I said beseechingly. 'Alas, mademoiselle, I have no drawing-room to offer you,' he replied, still as polite as ever. 'Nevertheless,' he continued, 'if you think it cannot be done, I shall be under the painful necessity of confiscating your carriages and luggage, and of sending you back on foot to the nearest post-town.' 'But, monsieur,' I protested, 'the road is ankle-deep in mud.' 'Truly,' he laughed, showing a beautiful set of teeth, 'but your weight won't make any difference; besides, I dare say you have some rugs and cloths with you in the other carriage, and my men will only be too pleased to spread them on the ground.'

"Seeing that all my remonstrance would be in vain, I jumped out of the carriage. While the rugs were being laid down, my two companions, the violinists, tuned their instruments, and even papa was prevailed upon to come out, though he was sulky and never spoke a word.

"I danced for about a quarter of an hour, and I honestly believe that I never had such an appreciative audience either before or afterwards. Then Trischka led me back to the carriage, and, simply lifting his hat, bade me adieu. 'I keep the rugs, mademoiselle. I will never part with them,' he said. The last I saw of him, when our carriages were turning a bend in the road, was a truly picturesque figure on horseback, waving his hand."

More than eight years elapsed before I met Taglioni again, and then she looked absolutely like an old woman, though she was under fifty. It was at the Comte (afterwards Duc) de Morny's, in '52, and, if I remember rightly, almost immediately after his resignation as Minister of the Interior. Taglioni and

Mdlle. Rachel were the only women present. Just as we were sitting down to dinner, Count Gilbert De Voisins came in, and took the next seat but one on my left which had been reserved for him. We were on friendly, though not on very intimate, terms. He was evidently not aware of the presence of his wife, for after a few minutes he asked his neighbour, pointing to her, "Who is this governess-looking old maid?" He told him. He showed neither surprise nor emotion; but, if an artist could have been found to sketch his face there, its perfect blank would have been more amusing than either. He seemed, as it were, to consult his recollections; then he said, "Is it? It may be, after all;" and went on eating his dinner. His wife acted less diplomatically. She recognized him at once, and made a remark to her host in a sufficiently loud voice to be overheard, which was not in good taste, the more that De Morny, notwithstanding his many faults, was not the man to have invited both for the mere pleasure of playing a practical joke. In fact, I have always credited De Morny with the good intention of bringing about a reconciliation between the two; but the affair was hopeless from the very beginning, after Taglioni's exhibition of temper. I am far from saying that Count Gilbert would have been more tractable if it had not occurred, but his spouse shut the door at once upon every further attempt in that direction. Nevertheless, whether out of sheer devilry or from a wish to be polite, he went up to her after dinner, accompanied by a friend, who introduced him as formally as if he and she had never seen one another. It was at a moment when the Comte de Morny was out of the room, because I feel certain that he was already sorry then for what he had endeavoured to do, and had washed his hands of the whole affair. Taglioni made a stately bow. "I am under the impression," she said, "that I have had the honour of meeting you before, about the year 1832." With this she turned away. Let any playwright reproduce that scene in a farcical or comedy form, and I am sure that three-fourths of his audience would scout it as too exaggerated, and yet every incident of it is absolutely true.

Among my most pleasant recollections of those days is that connected with Von Flotow, the future composer of "Martha." In appearance he was altogether unlike the traditional musician; he looked more like a stalwart officer of dragoons. Though of noble origin, and with a very wealthy father, there was a time when he had a hard struggle for existence. Count von Flotow, his father, and an old officer of Blucher, was nearly as much opposed to his son becoming a musician as Frederick the Great's. Nevertheless, at the instance of Flotow's mother, he was sent to Paris at the age of sixteen, and entered the Conservatoire, then under the direction of Reicha. His term of apprenticeship was not to extend beyond two years, "for," said the count, "it does not take longer for the rawest recruit to become a good soldier." "That will give you a fair idea," remarked Von Flotow to me afterwards, "how much he understood about it. He had an ill-disguised contempt for any music which did not come up to his ideal. His ideal was that performed by the drum, the fife, and the bugle. And the very fact of Germany ringing a few years later with the names of Meyerbeer and Halévy made matters worse instead of mending them. His feudal pride would not allow of his son's entering a profession the foremost ranks of which were occupied by Jews. 'Music,' he said, 'was good enough for bankers' sons and the like,' and he considered that Weber had cast a slur upon his family by adopting it."

The two years grudgingly allowed by Count von Flotow for his son's musical education were interrupted by the revolution of 1830, and the young fellow had to return home before he was eighteen, because, in his father's opinion, "he had not given a sign of becoming a great musician;" in other words, he had not written an opera or anything else which had attracted public notice. However, towards the beginning of 1831, the count took his son to Paris once more; "and though Meyerbeer nor Halévy were not so famous then as they were destined to become within the next three years, their names were already sufficiently well known to have made an introduction valuable. It would not have been difficult to obtain such. My father would not hear of it. 'I will not have my son indebted for anything to a Jew,' he said; and I am only quoting this instance of prejudice to you because it was not an individual but a typical one among my father's social equals. The remark about 'his son's entering a profession in which two Jews had carried off the highest prizes' is of a much later date. Consequently we landed in Paris, provided with letters of introduction to M. de Saint-Georges.* Clever, accomplished, refined as was M. de Saint-Georges, he was scarcely the authority a

---

* Jules-Henri de Saint-Georges, one of the most fertile librettists of the time, the principal collaborateur of Scribe, and best known in England as the author of the book of Balfe's "Bohemian Girl."—EDITOR.

father with serious intentions about his son's musical career would have consulted; he was a charming, skilful librettist and dramatist, a thorough man of the world in the best sense of the word, but absolutely incapable of judging the higher qualities of the composer. Nevertheless, I owe him much; but for him I should have been dragged back to Germany there and then; but for him I should have been compelled to go back to Germany five years later, or starved in the streets of Paris.

"My father's interview with M. de Saint-Georges, and my first introduction to him," said Flotow on another occasion, "were perhaps the most comical scenes ever enacted off the stage. You know my old friend, and have been to his rooms, so I need not describe him nor his surroundings to you. You have never seen my father; but, to give you an idea of what he was like, I may tell you that he was an enlarged edition of myself. A bold rider, a soldier and a sportsman, fairly well educated, but upon the whole a very rough diamond, and, I am afraid, with a corresponding contempt for the elegant and artistic side of Paris life. You may, therefore, picture to yourself the difference between the two men—M. de Saint-Georges in a beautiful silk dressing-gown and red morocco slippers, sipping chocolate from a dainty porcelain cup; my father, who, contrary to German custom, had always refused to don that comfortable garment, and who, to my knowledge, had never in his life tasted chocolate. For the moment I thought that everything was lost. I was mistaken.

"'Monsieur,' said my father in French, which absolutely creaked with the rust of age, I have come to ask your advice and a favour besides. My son desires to become a musician. Is it possible?'

"'There is no reason why he should not be,' replied M. de Saint-Georges, 'provided he has a vocation.'

"'Vocation may mean obstinacy,' remarked my father. 'But let us suppose the reverse—that obstinacy means vocation: how long would it take him to prove that he has talent?'

"'It is difficult to say—five years at least.'

"'And two he has already spent at the Conservatoire will make seven. I hope he will not be like Jacob, who, after that period of waiting, found that they had given him the wrong goddess!' growled my father, who could be grimly humorous when he liked. 'Five years more be it, then, but not a single day longer. If by that time he has not made his mark, I withdraw his allowance. I thank you for your advice; and now I will ask a favour. Will you kindly supply my place—that is, keep an eye upon him, and do the best you can for him? Remember, he is but twenty. It is hard enough that I cannot make a soldier of him; from what I have heard and from what I can see, you will prevent him from becoming less than a gentleman.'

"M. de Saint-Georges was visibly moved. 'Let me hear what he can do,' he said, 'and then I will tell you.'

"I sat down to the piano for more than an hour.

"'I will see that your son becomes a good musician, M. le Comte,' said M. de Sainte-Georges.

"Next morning my father went back to Germany. Nothing would induce him to stay a single day. He said the atmosphere of Paris was vitiated.

"I need not tell you that M. de Saint-Georges kept his word as far as he was able; he kept it even more rigorously than my father had bargained for, because when, exactly on the last day of the stipulated five years, I received a letter demanding my immediate return, and informing me that my father's banker had instructions to stop all further supplies, M. de Saint-Georges bade me stay.

"'I promised to make a musician of you, and I have kept my word. But between a musician and an acknowledged musician there is a difference. I say stay!' he exclaimed.

"'How am I to stay without money?'

"'You'll earn some.'

"'How?'

"'By giving piano-lessons, like many a poor artist has done before you.'

"I followed his advice, and am none the worse for the few years of hardships. The contrast between my own poverty and my wealthy surroundings was sufficiently curious during that time, and never more so than on the night when my name really became known to the general public. I am alluding to the first performance of 'Le Duc de Guise,' which, as you may remember, was given in aid of the distressed Poles, and sung throughout by amateurs. The receipts amounted to thirty thousand francs, and the ladies of the chorus had something between ten and twelve millions of francs of diamonds in their hair and round their throats. All my earthly possessions in money consisted of six francs thirty-five centimes."

I was not at the Théâtre de la Renaissance that night, but two or three years previously I had heard the first opera Flotow ever wrote, at the Hôtel Castellane. I never heard " Rob Roy " since; and, curiously enough, many years afterwards I inquired of Lord Granville, who sat next to me on that evening in 1838, whether he had. He shook his head negatively. "It is a great pity," he said, " for the music is very beautiful." And I believe that Lord Granville is a very good judge.

The Hôtel Castellane, or " La Maison du Mouleur," as it was called by the general public on account of the great number of scantily attired mythological deities with which its façade was decorated, was one of the few houses where, during the reign of Louis-Philippe, the discussion of political and dynastic differences was absolutely left in abeyance. The scent of party strife—I had almost said miasma—hung over all the other salons, notably those of the Princesse de Lieven, Madame Thiers, and Madame de Girardin, and even those of Madame Le Hon and Victor Hugo were not free from it. Men like myself, and especially young men, who instinctively guessed the hollowness of all this—who, moreover, had not the genius to become political leaders and not sufficient enthusiasm to become followers—avoided them; consequently their description will find little or no place in these notes. The little I saw of Princesse de Lieven at the Tuileries and elsewhere produced no wish to see more. Thiers was more interesting from a social and artistic point of view, but it was only on very rare occasions that he consented to doff his political armour, albeit that he did not wear the latter with unchanging dignity. Madame Thiers was an uninteresting woman, and only the "feeder" to her husband, to use a theatrical phrase. Madame Le Hon was exceedingly beautiful, exceedingly selfish, and, if anything, too amiable. The absence of all serious mental qualities was cleverly disguised by the mask of a grande dame; but I doubt whether it was anything else but a mask. Madame Delphine de Girardin, on the other hand, was endowed with uncommon literary, poetical, and intellectual gifts; but I have always considered it doubtful whether even the Nine Muses, rolled into one, would be bearable for any length of time. As for Victor Hugo, no man not blessed with an extraordinary bump of veneration would have gone more than once to his soirées. The permanent entertainment there consisted of a modern version of the "perpetual adoration," and of nothing else, because, to judge by my few experiences, his guests were never offered anything to eat or to drink. As a set-off, the furniture and appointments of his apartments were more artistic than those of most of his contemporaries; but Becky Sharp has left it on record that "mouton aux navets," dished up in priceless china and crested silver, is after all but "mouton aux navets," and at Hugo's even that homely fare was wanting.

Among the few really good salons were those of the ambassadors of the Two Sicilies, of England, and of Austria. The former two were in the Faubourg Saint-Honoré, the latter in the Faubourg Saint-Germain. The soirées of the Duc de Serra-Cabriola were very animated; there was a great deal of dancing. I cannot say the same of those of Lord and Lady Granville, albeit that both the host and hostess did the honours with charming and truly patrician grace and hospitality. But the English guests would not throw off their habitual reserve, and the French in the end imitated the manner of the latter, in deference, probably, to Lord and Lady Granville, who were not at all pleased at this sincerest form of French flattery of their countrymen.

There was no such restraint at Count Apponyi's, in the Faubourg Saint-Germain, the only house where the old French noblesse mustered in force. The latter virtually felt themselves on their own ground, for the host was known to have not much sympathy with parvenus, even titled ones, though the titles had been gained on the battle-field. Had he not during the preceding reign ruthlessly stripped Soult and Marmont, and half a dozen other dukes of the first empire, by giving instructions to his servants to announce them by their family names? Consequently, flirtation à la Marivaux, courtly *galanterie* à la Louis XV., sprightly and witty conversation, "minuetting" à la Watteau, was the order of the day as well as of the night there, for the déjeuner dansant was a frequent feature of the entertainment. No one was afraid of being mistaken for a financier anobli; the only one admitted on a footing of intimacy bore the simple name of Hope.

Nevertheless, it must not be thought that the entertainments, even at the three embassies, partook of anything like the splendour so noticeable during the second empire. The refreshments elsewhere partook of a simple character; ices and cake, and lukewarm but by no means strong tea, formed the staple of them. Of course there were exceptions, such as, for instance, at the above-named houses, and at Mrs. Tudor's, Mrs. Locke's, and at Countess Lamoyloff's; but the era of flowing rivers of champagne, snacks that were like banquets, and banquets that were not unlike orgies, had not as yet dawned. And, worse than all, in a great many salons the era of mahogany and Utrecht velvet was in full swing, while the era of white-and-gold walls, which were frequently neither white nor gold, was dying a very lingering death.

The Hôtel Castellane was a welcome exception to this, and politics were rigorously tabooed, the reading of long-winded poems was interdicted. Politicians were simply reminded that the adjacent Elysée-Bourbon, or even the Hôtel Pontalba, might still contain sufficiently lively ghosts to discuss such all-important matters with them;* poets who fancied they had something to say worth hearing, were invited to have it said for them from behind the footlights by rival companies of amateurs, each of which in many respects need not have feared comparison with the professional one of the Comédie-Française. Amateur theatricals were, therefore, the principal feature of the entertainments at the Hôtel Castellane; but there were " off nights" to the full as brilliant as the others. There was neither acting nor dancing on such occasions, the latter amusement being rarely indulged in, except at the grand balls which often followed one another in rapid succession.

I have said rival companies, but only the two

---

* The Elysée-Bourbon, which was the official residence of Louis-Napoleon during his presidency of the second republic, was almost untenanted during the reign of Louis-Philippe.

The Hôtel Pontalba was partly built on the site of the former mansion of M. de Morfontaine, a staunch royalist, who, curiously enough, had married the daughter of Le Peletier de Saint-Fargeau, the member of the Convention who had voted the death of Louis XVI., and who himself fell by the hand of an assassin. Mdlle. le Peletier Saint-Fargeau was called " La Fille de la Nation."—EDITOR.

permanent ones came under that denomination; the others were what we should term "scratch companies," got together for one or two performances of a special work, generally a musical one, as in the case of Flotow's "Rob Roy" and "Alice." They vied in talent with the regular troupes presided over respectively by Madame Sophie Gay, the mother of Madame Emile de Girardin, and the Duchesse d'Abrantès. Each confined itself to the interpretation of the works of its manageress, who on such evening did the honours, or of those whom the manageress favoured with her protection. The heavens might fall rather than that an actor or actress of Madame Gay's company should act with Madame d'Abrantès, and *vice versâ*. Seeing that neither manageress had introduced the system of "under-studies," disappointments were frequent, for unless a member of the Comédie-Française could be found to take up the part at a moment's notice, the performance had necessarily to be postponed, the amateurs refusing to act with any but the best. Such pretensions may at the first blush seem exaggerated; they were justified in this instance, the amateurs being acknowledged to be the equals of the professionals by every unbiassed critic. In fact, several ladies among the amateurs "took eventually to the stage," notably Mdlles. Davenay and Mdlle. de Lagrange. The latter became a very bright star in the operatic firmament, though she was hidden to the musical world at large by her permanent stay in Russia. St. Petersburg has ever been a formidable competitor of Paris for securing the best histrionic and lyrical talent. Madame Arnould-Plessy, Bressant, Dupuis, and later on M. Worms, deserted their native scenes for the more remunerative, though perhaps really less artistic, triumphs of the theatre Saint-Michel; and when they returned, the delicate bloom that had made their art so delightful was virtually gone. "C'était de l'art Français à la sauce Tartare," said some one who was no mean judge.

The Comte Jules de Castellane, though fully equal, and in many respects superior, in birth to those who professed to sneer at the younger branch of the Bourbons, declined to be guided by these opponents of the new dynasty in their social crusade against the adherents to the latter; consequently the company was perhaps not always so select as it might have been, and many amusing incidents and *piquantes* adventures were the result. He put a stop to these, however, when he discovered that his hospitality was being abused, and that invitations given to strangers, at the request of some of his familiars, had been paid for in kind, if not in coin.

As a rule, though, the company was far less addicted to scandal-mongering and causing scandal than similarly composed "sets" during the subsequent reign. They were not averse to playing practical jokes, especially upon those who made themselves somewhat too conspicuous by their eccentricities. Lord Brougham, who was an assiduous guest at the Hôtel Castellane during his frequent visits to Paris, was often selected as their victim. He, as it were, provoked the tricks played upon him by his would-be Don-Juanesque behaviour, and by the many opportunities he lost of holding his tongue—in French. He absolutely murdered the language of Molière. His worthy successor in that respect was Lady Normanby, who, as some one said, "not only murdered the tongue, but tortured it besides." The latter, however, never lost her dignity amidst the most mirth-compelling blunders on her part, while the English statesman was often very near enacting the buffoon, and was once almost induced to accept a rôle in a vaudeville, in which his execrable French would no doubt have been highly diverting to the audience, but would scarcely have been in keeping with the position he occupied on the other side of the Channel. "Quant à Lord Brougham," said a very witty Frenchman, quoting Shakespeare in French, "il n'y a pour lui qu'un pas entre le sublime et le ridicule. C'est le pas de Calais, et il le traverse trop souvent."

In 1842, when the Comte Jules de Castellane married Mdlle. de Villontroys, whose mother had married General Rapp and been divorced from him, a certain change came over the spirit of the house; the entertainments were as brilliant as ever, but the two rival manageresses had to abdicate their sway, and the social status of the guests was subjected to a severer test. The new dispensation did not ostracize the purely artistic element, but, as the comtesse tersely put it, "dorénavant, je ne recevrai que ceux qui ont de l'art ou des armoiries." She strictly kept her word, even during the first years of the Second Empire, when pedigrees were a ticklish thing to inquire into.

I have unwittingly drifted away from M. de Saint-Georges, who, to say the least, was a curious figure in artistic and literary Paris during the reigns of Louis-Philippe and his successor. He was quite as fertile as Scribe, and many of his plots are as ingeniously conceived and worked out as the latter's, but he suffered both in reputation and purse from the restless activity and pushing character of the librettist of "Robert le Diable." Like those of Rivarol,* M. Saint-Georges' claims to be of noble descent were somewhat contested, albeit that, unlike the eighteenth-century pamphleteer, he never obtruded them; but there could be no doubt about his being a gentleman. He was utterly different in every respect from his rival. Scribe was not only eaten up with vanity, but grasping to a degree; he had dramatic instinct, but not the least vestige of literary refinement. M. de Saint-Georges, on the contrary, was exceedingly modest, very indifferent to money matters, charitable and obliging in a quiet way, and though perhaps not inferior in stage-craft, very elegant in his diction. When he liked, he could write verses and dialogue which often reminded one of Molière. It was not the only trait he had in common with the great playwright. Molière is said to have consulted his housekeeper, Laforêt, with regard to his productions; M. de Saint-Georges was known to do the same—with this difference, however, that he did not always attend to Marguérite's suggestions, in which case Marguérite grew wroth, especially if the piece turned out to be a success, in spite of her predictions of failure. On such occasions the popular approval scarcely compensated M. de Saint-Georges for his discomforts at home; for though Marguérite was an admirable manager at all times—when she liked, though there was no bachelor more carefully looked after than the author of "La Fille du Régiment," he had now and then to bear the brunt of Marguérite's

* One of the great wits of the Revolution.—EDITOR.

temper when the public's verdict did not agree with hers.

If under such circumstances M. de Saint-Georges ventured to give a dinner, the viands were sure to be cold, the Bordeaux iced, and the Champagne lukewarm. M. de Saint-Georges, who, notwithstanding his courtly manners, was candour itself, never failed to state the reasons of his discomfiture as a host to his guests. "Que voulez vous, mes amis, la pièce n'a pas plu à Marguérite et le dîner s'en ressent. Si je lui faisais une observation, elle me repondrait comme elle m'a repondu déjà maintes fois. Le diner était mauvais, vous dîtes? C'est possible, il était assez bien pour ceux qui ont eu le bon goût d'applaudir votre pièce hier-au-soir." Because Mdlle. Marguérite had a seat in the upper boxes reserved for her at all the first representations of her master's pieces. She did not always avail herself of the privilege at the Opéra, but she never missed a first night at the Opéra-Comique. I have quoted textually the words of M. de Saint-Georges on the morrow of the *première* of "Giselle," a ballet in two acts, written in collaboration with Théophile Gautier. "'Giselle' had been a great success; Marguérite had predicted a failure; hence we had a remarkably bad dinner."

I had had many opportunities of seeing Marguérite, and often wondered at the secret of the tyranny she exercised. She was not handsome—scarcely comely; she was not even as smart in her appearance as dozens of servants I have seen, and her mental attainments, as far as I could judge, were not above those of her own class. One can understand a Turner, a Jean Jacques Rousseau, submitting to the influence of such a low-born companion, because, after all, they, though men of genius, sprang from the people, and may have felt awkward, ill at ease, in the society of well-bred men and women, especially of women. Béranger sometimes gave me that idea. But, as I have already said, no one could mistake M. de Saint-Georges for anything but a well-bred man. Notwithstanding his little affectations, his inordinate love of scents, his somewhat effeminate surroundings, good breeding was patent at every sentence, at every movement. He was not a genius, certainly not, but the above remarks hold good of a man who *was* a genius, and who sprang, moreover, from the higher bourgeoisie of the eighteenth century—I am alluding to Eugène Delacroix.

CHAPTER V.

The Boulevards in the forties—The Chinese Baths—A favourite tobacconist of Alfred de Musset—The price of cigars—The diligence still the usual mode of travelling—Provincials in Paris—Parliamentary see-saw between M. Thiers and M. Guizot—Amenities of editors—An advocate of universal suffrage—Distribution of gratuitous sausages to the working man on the king's birthday—The rendezvous of actors in search of an engagement—Frédérick Lemaître on the eve of appearing in a new part—The Legitimists begin to leave their seclusion and to mingle with the bourgeoisie—Alexandre Dumas and Scribe—The latter's fertility as a playwright—The National Guards go shooting, in uniform and in companies, on the Plaine Saint-Denis—Vidocq's private inquiry office in the Rue Vivienne—No river-side resorts—The plaster elephant on the Place de la Bastille—The sentimental romances of Loïsa Puget—The songs of the working classes—Cheap bread and wine—How they enjoyed themselves on Sundays and holidays—Théophile Gautier's pony-carriage—The hatred of the bourgeoisie—Nestor Roqueplan's expression of it—Gavarni's—M. Thiers' sister keeps a restaurant at the corner of the Rue Drouot—When he is in power, the members of the Opposition go and dine there, and publish facetious accounts of the entertainment—All appearances to the contrary, people like Guizot better than Thiers—But few entries for the race for wealth in those days—The Rothschilds still live in the Rue Lafitte—Favourite lounges—The Boulevards, the Rue Le Peletier, and the Passage de l'Opéra—The Opéra—The Rue Le Peletier and its attractions—The Restaurant of Paolo Broggi—The Estaminet du Divan—Literary waiters and Boniface—Major Fraser—The mystery surrounding his origin—Another mysterious personage—The Passage de l'Opéra is invaded by the stockjobbers, and loses its prestige as a promenade—Bernard Latte's, the publisher of Donizetti's operas, becomes deserted—Tortoni's—Louis-Blanc—His scruples as an editor—A few words about duelling—Two tragic meetings—Lola Montès—Her adventurous career—A celebrated trial—My first meeting with Gustave Flaubert, the author of "Madame Bovary" and "Salambô"—Emile de Girardin—His opinion of duelling—My decision with regard to it—The original of "La Dame aux Camélias"—Her parentage—Alexandre Dumas gives the diagnosis of her character in connection with his son's play—L'Homme au Camellia—M. Lautour-Mézerai, the inventor of children's periodical literature in France—Auguste Lireux—He takes the management of the Odéon—Balzac again—His schemes, his greed—Lireux more fortunate with other authors—Anglophobia on the French stage—Gallophobia on the English stage.

EVEN in those days "the Boulevards" meant to most of us nothing more than the space between the present opera and the Rue Drouot. But the Crédit Lyonnais and other palatial buildings which have been erected since were not as much as dreamt of; if I remember rightly, the site of that bank was occupied by two or three "Chinese Baths." I suppose the process of steaming and cleansing the human body was something analogous to that practised in our Turkish baths, but I am unable to say from experience, having never been inside, and, curious to relate, most of my familiars were in a similar state of ignorance. We rarely crossed to that side of the boulevard except to go and dine at the Café Anglais. At the corner of the Rue Lafitte, opposite the Maison d'Or, was our favourite tobacconist's, and the cigars we used to get there were vastly superior to those we get at present in Paris at five times the cost. The assistant who served us was a splendid creature. Alfred de Musset became so enamoured of her that at one time his familiars apprehended an "imprudence on his part." Of course, they were afraid he would marry her.

In those days most of our journeys in the interior of France had still to be made by the mails of Lafitte-Caillard, and the people these conveyances brought up from the provinces were almost as great objects of curiosity to us as we must have been to them. It was the third lustre of Louis-Philippe's reign. "God," according to the coinage, "protected France," and when the Almighty seemed somewhat tired of the task, Thiers and Guizot alternately stepped in to do the safeguarding. Parliament resounded with the eloquence of orators who are almost forgotten by now, except by students of history; M. de Genoude was clamouring for universal suffrage; M. de Cormenin, under the *nom de plume* of "Timon," was the fashionable pamphleteer; the papers indulged in vituperation against one another, compared to which the amenities of the rival Eatanswill editors were compliments. Grocers and drapers objected to the participation of M. de Lamartine in the affairs of State. The *Figaro* of those days went by the title of *Corsaire-Satan*, and, though extensively read, had the greatest difficulty in making both ends meet. In order to improve the lot of the working man, there was a gratuitous distribution of sausages once a year on the king's fête-day. The ordinary rendezvous of provincial and metropolitan actors out of an engagement was not at the Café de Suède on the Boulevard Montmartre, but under the trees at the Palais-Royal. Frédérick Lemaître went to confession and to mass every time he " created " a new rôle. The Legitimists consented to leave their aristocratic seclusion, and to breathe the same air with the bourgeoisie and proletarians of the Boulevard du Crime, to see him play. The Government altered the title of Sue and Goubeaux's drama " Les Pontons Anglais " into " Les Pontons," short, and made the authors change the scene from England to Spain. Alexandre Dumas chaffed Scribe, and flung his money right and left; while the other saved it, bought country estates, and produced as many as twenty plays a year (eight more than he had contracted for). The National Guards went in uniform and in companies to shoot hares and rabbits on the Plaine Saint-Denis, and swaggered about on the Boulevards, ogling the women. Vidocq kept a private inquiry office in the Passage Vivienne, and made more money by blackmailing or catching unfaithful husbands than by catching thieves. Bougival, Asnières and Joinville-le-Pont had not become riparian resorts. The plaster elephant on the Place de la Bastille was crumbling to pieces. The sentimental romances of Madame Loïsa Puget proved the delight of every bourgeoise family, while the chorus to every popular song was " Larifla, larifla, fla, fla, fla."

Best of all, from the working man's point of view, was the low price of bread and wine; the latter could be had at four sous the litre in the wine-shops. He, the working man, still made excursions with his wife and children to the Artesian well at Grenelle; and if stranded perchance in the Champs-Elysées, stood lost in admiration at the tiny carriage with ponies to match, driven by Théophile Gautier, who had left off wearing the crimson waistcoats wherewith in former days he hoped to annoy the bourgeois, though he ceased not to rail at him by word of mouth and with his pen. He was not singular in that respect. Among his set, the hatred of the bourgeois was ingrained; it found constant vent in small things. Nestor Roqueplan wore jackboots at home instead of slippers, because the latter chaussure was preferred by the shopkeeper. Gavarni published the most biting pictorial satires against him. Here is one. A dissipated-looking loafer is leaning against a lamp-post, contemptuously staring at the spruce, trim bourgeois out for his Sunday walk with his wife. The loafer is smoking a short clay pipe, and some of the fumes of the tobacco come between the wind and the bourgeois' respectability. "Voyou!" says the latter contemptuously. "Voyou tant que vous voulez, pas épicier," is the answer.

In those days, when M. Thiers happened to be in power, many members of the Opposition and their journalistic champions made it a point of organizing little gatherings to the table-d'hôte kept by Mdlle. Thiers, the sister of the Prime Minister of France. Her establishment was at the entrance of the present Rue Drouot, and a sign-board informed the passer-by to that effect. There was invariably an account of these little gatherings in next day's papers—of course, with comments. Thiers was known to be the most wretched shot that ever worried a gamekeeper, and yet he was very fond of blazing away. "We asked Mdlle. Thiers," wrote the commentators, "whether those delicious pheasants she gave us were of her illustrious brother's bagging. The lady shook her head. 'Non, monsieur; le Président du Conseil n'a pas l'honneur de fournir mon établissement; à quoi bon, je peux les acheter à meilleur marché que lui et au même endroit. S'il m'en envoyait, il me ferait payer un bénéfice, parcequ'il ne fait jamais rien pour rien. C'est un peu le défaut de notre famille.'" I have got a notion that, mercurial as was M. Thiers up to the last hour of his life, and even more so at that period, and sedate as was M. Guizot, the French liked the latter better than the former.

M. Guizot had said, "Enrichissez vous," and was known to be poor; M. Thiers had scoffed at the advice, and was known to be hoarding while compelling his sister to earn her own living. It must be remembered that at the time the gangrene of greed had not entered the souls of all classes of Frenchmen so deeply as it has now, that the race for wealth had as yet comparatively few votaries, and that not every stockjobber and speculator aspired to emulate the vast financial transactions of the Rothschilds. The latter lived, in those days, in the Rue Lafitte, where they had three separate mansions, all of which since then have been thrown into one, and are at present exclusively devoted to business purposes. The Rue Lafitte was, however, a comparatively quiet street. The favourite lounges, in addition to the strip of Boulevards I have already mentioned, were the Rue Le Peletier and the galleries of the Passage de l'Opéra. Both owed the preference over the other thoroughfares to the immediate vicinity of the Opéra, which had its frontage in the last-named street, but was by no means striking or monumental. Its architect, Debret, had to run the gauntlet of every kind of satire for many a year after its erection; the bitterest and most scathing of all was that, perhaps, of a journalist, who wrote one day that, a provincial having asked him the way to the grand opéra, he had been obliged to answer, "Turn down the street, and it is the first large gateway on your right."

But if the building itself was unimposing, the company gathered around its entrance consisted generally of half a dozen men whose names were then already household words in the musical world—Auber, Halévy, Rossini and Meyerbeer, St. Georges, Adam. Now and then, though rarely together, all of these names will frequently reappear in these notes. The chief attractions, though, of the Rue Le Peletier were the famous Italian restaurant of Paolo Broggi, patronized by a great many singers, the favourite haunt of Mario, in the beginning of his career, and l'Estaminet du Divan, which from being a very simple café indeed, developed into a kind of politico-literary club under the auspices of a number of budding men of letters, journalists, and the like, whose modest purses were not equal to the charges of the Café Riche and Tortoni, and who had gradually driven all more prosaic customers away. I believe I was one of the few habitués who had no literary aspirations, who did not cast longing looks to the inner portals of the offices of the *National*, the bigwigs of which—Armand Marrast, Baron Dornés, Gérard de Nerval, and others—sometimes made their appearance there, though their restaurant in ordinary was the Café Hardi. The Estaminet du Divan, however, pretended to a much more literary atmosphere than the magnificent establishment on the boulevard itself. It is a positive fact that the waiters in the former would ask, in the most respectful way imaginable, "Does monsieur want Sue's or Dumas' feuilleton with his café?" Not once but a dozen times I have heard the proprietor draw attention to a remarkable article. Major Fraser, though he never dined there, spent an hour or two daily in the Estaminet du Divan to read the papers. He was a great favourite with every one, though none of us knew anything about his antecedents. In spite of his English name, he was decidedly not English, though he spoke the language. He was one of the best-dressed men of the period, and by a well-dressed man I do not mean one like Sue. He generally wore a tight-fitting, short-skirted, blue frock-coat, grey trousers, of a shape which since then we have defined as "pegtops," but the fashion of which was borrowed from the Cossacks.

They are still worn by some French officers in cavalry regiments, notably crack cavalry regiments.

Major Fraser might have fitly borrowed Piron's epitaph for himself: "Je ne suis rien, pas même Académicien." He was a bachelor. He never alluded to his parentage. He lived by himself, in an entresol at the corner of the Rue Lafitte and the Boulevard des Italiens. He was always flush of money, though the sources of his income were a mystery to every one. He certainly did not live by gambling, as has been suggested since; for those who knew him best did not remember having seen him touch a card.

I have always had an idea, though I can give no reason for it, that Major Fraser was the illegitimate son of some exalted personage, and that the solution of the mystery surrounding him might be found in the records of the scandals and intrigues at the courts of Charles IV. and Ferdinand VII. of Spain. The foreign "soldiers of fortune" who rose to high posts, though not to the highest like Richards and O'Reilly, were not all of Irish origin. But the man himself was so pleasant in his intercourse, so uniformly gentle and ready to oblige, that no one cared to lift a veil which he was so evidently anxious not to have disturbed. I only remember his getting out of temper once, namely, when Léon Gozlan, in a comedy of his, introduced a major who had three crosses. The first had been given to him because he had not one, the second because he had already one, and the third because all good things consist of three. Then Major Fraser sent his seconds to the playwright; the former effected a reconciliation, the more that Gozlan pledged his word that an allusion to the major was farthest from his thoughts. It afterwards leaked out that our irrepressible Alexandre Dumas had been the involuntary cause of all the mischief. One day, while he was talking to Gozlan, one of his secretaries came in and told him that a particular bugbear of his, and a great nonentity to boot, had got the Cross of the Legion of Honour.

"Grand Dieu," exclaimed Gozlan, "pourquoi lui a-t-on donné cette croix?"

"Vous ne savez pas?" said Alexandre, looking very wise, as if he had some important state secret to reveal.

"Assurément, je ne le sais pas," quoth Gozlan, "ni vous non plus."

"Ah, par exemple, moi, je le sais."

"Hé bien, dites alors."

"On lui a donné la croix parceque il n'en avait pas."

It was the most childish of all tricks, but Gozlan laughed at it, and, when he wrote his piece, remembered it. He amplified the very small joke, and, on the first night of his play, the house went into convulsions over it.

Major Fraser's kindness and gentleness extended to all men—except to professional politicians, and those, from the highest to the lowest, he detested and despised. He rarely spoke on the subject of politics, but when he did every one sat listening with the raptest attention; for he was a perfect mine of facts, which he marshalled with consummate ability in order to show that government by party was of all idiotic institutions the most idiotic. But his knowledge of political history was as nothing to his familiarity with the social institutions of every civilized country and of every period. Curiously enough, the whole of his library in his own apartment did not exceed two or three scores of volumes. His memory was something prodigious, and even men like Dumas and Balzac confessed themselves his inferiors in that respect. The mere mention of the most trifling subject sufficed to set it in motion, and the listeners were treated to a "magazine article worth fifty centimes la ligne au moins," as Dumas put it. But the major could never be induced to write one. Strange to say, he often used to hint that his was no mere book-knowledge. "Of course, it is perfectly ridiculous," he remarked with a strange smile, "but every now and again I feel as if all this did not come to me through reading, but from personal experience. At times I become almost convinced that I lived with Nero, that I knew Dante personally, and so forth."

When Major Fraser died, not a single letter was found in his apartment giving a clue to his antecedents. Merely a file of receipts, and a scrap of paper attached to one—the receipt of the funeral company for his grave, and expenses of his burial. The memorandum gave instructions to advertise his demise for a week in the *Journal des Débâts*, the money for which would be found in the drawer of his dressing-table. His clothes and furniture were to be sold, and the proceeds to be given to the Paris poor. "I do not charge any one with this particular duty," the document went on; "I have so many friends, every one of whom will be ready to carry out my last wishes."

Another "mystery," though far less interesting than Major Fraser, was the Persian gentleman whom one met everywhere, at the Opéra, at the Bois de Boulogne, at the concerts of the Conservatoire, etc. Though invariably polite and smiling, he never spoke to any one. For ten years, the occupant of the stall next to his at the Opéra had never heard him utter a syllable. He always wore a long white silk petticoat, a splendidly embroidered coat over that, and a conical Astrakan cap. He was always alone; and though every one knew where he lived, in the Passage de l'Opéra, no one had ever set foot in his apartment. As a matter of course, all sorts of legends were current about him. According to some, he had occupied a high position in his own country, from which he had voluntarily exiled himself, owing to his detestation of Eastern habits; according to others, he was simply a dealer in Indian shawls, who had made a fortune. A third group, the spiteful ones, maintained that he sold dates and pastilles, and that the reason why he did not speak was because he was dumb, though not deaf. He died during the Second Empire, very much respected in the neighbourhood, for he had been very charitable.

Towards the middle of the forties the Passage de l'Opéra began to lose some of its prestige as a lounge. The outside stockjobbers, whom the police had driven from the Boulevards and the steps of Tortoni, migrated thither, and the galleries that had resounded with the sweet warblings—in a very low key—of the clients of Bernard Latte, the publisher of Donizetti's operas, were made hideous and unbearable with the jostling and bellowing of the money-spinners. Bernard Latte himself was at last compelled to migrate.

In the house the ground-floor of which was occupied by Tortoni, and which was far different in aspect from what it is now, lived Louis Blanc. Towards nine in the morning he came down for his cup of café au lait.

It was the first cup of coffee of the day served in the establishment. I was never on terms of intimacy with Blanc, and least of all then, for I shared with Major Fraser a dislike to politic-mongers, and, rightly or wrongly, I have always considered the author of "L'Histoire de Dix Ans" as such. Though Louis Blanc was three or four and thirty then, he looked like a boy of seventeen—a fact not altogether owing to his diminutive stature, though he was one of the smallest men, if not the smallest man, I ever saw. Of course I mean a man not absolutely a dwarf. I have been assured, however, that he was a giant compared to Don Martinoz Garay, Duke of Altamira, and Marquis of Astorga, a Spanish statesman, who died about the early part of the twenties. These notes do not extend beyond the fall of the Commune, and it was only after that event that I met M. Blanc once or twice in his old haunts. Hence my few recollections of him had better be jotted down here. They are not important. The man, though but sixty, and apparently not in bad health, looked *désillusioné*. They were, no doubt, the most trying years to the Third Republic, but M. Blanc must have perceived well enough that, granting all the existing difficulties, the men at the head of affairs were not the Republicans of his dreams. He had, moreover, suffered severe losses; all his important documents, such as the correspondence between him and George Sand and Louis-Napoleon while the latter was at Ham, and other equally valuable matter, had been destroyed at the fire of the Northern Goods Station at La Villette, a fire kindled by the Communists. He was dressed almost in the fashion of the forties, a wide-skirted, long, brown frockcoat, a shirt innocent of starch, and a broad-brimmed hat. A few years later, he founded a paper, *L'Homme-Libre,* the offices of which were in the Rue Grange-Batelière. The concern was financed by a Polish gentleman. Blanc gave his readers to understand that he would speak out plainly about persons and things, whether past or present; that he would advance nothing except on documentary proofs; but that, whether he did or not, he would not be badgered into giving or accepting challenges in defence of his writings. "I am, first of all, too old," he said; "but if I were young again, I should not repeat my folly of '47, when I wanted to fight with Eugène Pelletan on account of a woman whose virtue, provided she had any, could make no difference to either of us. It does not matter to me that we were not the only preux chevaliers of that period, ready to do battle for or against the charms of a woman whose remains had crumbled to dust by then." *

* M. Eugène Pelletan, the father of M. Camille Pelletan, the editor of *La Justice,* and first lieutenant to M. Clemenceau, having severely criticized some passages in M. Blanc's "Histoire de la Révolution," relating to Marie-Antoinette, the author quoted a passage of Madame Campan's "Mémoires" in support of his writings. The critic refused to admit the conclusiveness of the proof, whereupon M. Blanc appealed to the Société des Gens de Lettres, which, on the summing up of M. Taxile Delord, gave a verdict in his favour. M. Pelletan declined to submit to the verdict, as he had refused to admit the jurisdiction, of the tribunal. M. Blanc, who had at first scouted all idea of a duel, considered himself obliged to resort to this means of obtaining satisfaction, seeing that M. Pelletan stoutly maintained his opinion. A meeting had been arranged when the Revolution of '48 broke out. The opponents having both gone to the Hôtel-de-Ville, met by accident at the entrance, and fell into one another's arms. "Thank Heaven!" exclaimed Thiers, when he heard of it. "If Pelletan had killed Blanc, I should have been the smallest man in France."

M. Blanc's allusion to other "preux chevaliers" aimed particularly at M. Cousin, who, having become a minister against his will, resumed with a sigh of relief his studies under the Second Empire. He was

M. Blanc's boast that he would advance nothing except on proof positive was not an idle one, as his contributors found out to their cost. Every afternoon, at three, he arrived at the office to read the paper in proof from the first line to the last. Not the slightest inaccuracy was allowed to pass. Kind as he was, his reporters' lives became a burden. One of the latter told me a story which, though it illustrates the ridiculousness of M. Blanc's scruples when carried too far, is none the less valuable. A dog had been run over on the Boulevards, and the reporter, with a hankering after the realistic method, had endeavoured to reproduce onomatopœically the sounds uttered by the animal in pain.

"Are you quite sure, monsieur, about your sounds?" asked Blanc.

"Of course, I am as sure as a non-scientific man can be," was the answer.

"Then strike them out; one ought to be scientifically sure. By-the-by, I see you have made use of the word 'howl' (*hurler*). Unless I am mistaken, a dog when in pain yelps (*glapit*). Please alter it."

On another occasion, on going through the advertisements, he found a new one relating to a cough mixture, setting forth its virtues in the most glowing terms.

especially fond of the seventeenth century, and all at once he, who had scarcely ever noticed a pretty woman, became violently smitten with the Duchesse de Longueville, who had been in her grave for nearly two centuries. He positively invested her with every perfection, moral and mental; unfortunately, he could not invest her with a shapely bust, the evidence being too overwhelmingly against her having been adorned that way. One day some one showed him a portrait of the sister of the "grand Condé," in which she was amply provided with the charms the absence of which M. Cousin regretted. He wrote a special chapter on the subject, and was well-nigh challenging all his contradictors.—EDITOR.

Immediately the advertisement canvasser was sent for, M. Blanc having refused to farm out that department to an agency, as is frequently done in Paris, in order to retain the absolute control over it.

"Monsieur, I see that you have a new advertisement, and it seems to me a profitable one; still, before inserting it, I should like to be certain that the medicine does all it professes to do. Can you personally vouch for its efficiency?"

"Mon Dieu, monsieur, I believe it does all it professes to do, but you can scarcely expect me to run the risk of bronchitis in order to test it upon myself!"

"Heaven forbid that I should be so exacting and indifferent to other people's health, but until you can bring me some one who has been cured, we will not insert it."

Let me come back for a moment to that sentence of Louis Blanc, about the practice of duelling, in connection with one of the most tragic affairs of that kind within my recollection. I am alluding to the Dujarrier-Beauvallon duel. I have been in the habit for years, whenever an important meeting took place in France, to read every shade of English opinion on the subject; and while recognizing the elevated sentiments of the writers, I have no hesitation in saying that not a single one knew what he was writing about. They could not grasp the fact that for a man of social standing to refuse a challenge or to refrain from sending one, save under very exceptional circumstances, was tantamount to courting social death. They knew not that every door would henceforth be closed against him; that his wife's best friends would cease to call upon her, by direction of their husbands; that his children at school would be shunned by their comrades; that no young man of equal position to his, were he ever so much in love with his daughter, would ask her to become his wife, that no parents would allow their daughter to marry his son. That is what backing out of a duel meant years ago; that is what it still means to-day—of course, I repeat, with certain classes. Is it surprising, then, that with such a prospect facing him, a man should risk death rather than become a pariah? Would the English leader-writer, if he be a man of worth, like to enter his club-room without a hand held out to welcome him from those with whom he was but a few weeks ago on the most friendly footing, without a voice to give him the time of day? I think not; and that is what would happen if he were a Frenchman who neglected to ask satisfaction for even an imaginary insult.

I knew M. Dujarrier, the general manager of *La Presse*, and feel convinced that he was not a bit more quarrelsome or eager "to go out" than Louis Blanc. It is, moreover, certain that he felt his inferiority, both as a swordsman and as a marksman, to such a practised shot and fencer as M. de Beauvallon; and well he might, seeing that subsequent evidence proved that he, Dujarrier, had never handled either weapon. Yet he not only strenuously opposed all attempts on the part of his friends to effect a reconciliation, but would not afford a hint to his adversary of his want of skill, lest the latter should make him a present of his life. The present would not have been worth accepting. It would have been a Nessus-shirt, and caused the moral death of the recipient. Consequently, Dujarrier literally went like a lamb to the slaughter rather than be branded as a coward, and he made no secret of his contemplated sacrifice. "I have no alternative but to fight," he said, two days before the meeting, to Alexandre Dumas, who taxed all his own ingenuity, and that of his son, to prevent, at any rate, a fatal issue. The only way to effect this, according to the very logical reasoning of the two Dumases, was to induce Dujarrier, who, as the offended party, had the choice of weapons, to choose the sword. They counted upon the generosity of Beauvallon, who, as a gentleman, on discovering his adversary's utter lack of skill, would disarm, or inflict a slight wound on him. Unfortunately, young Dumas, with the best intentions, unburthened himself to that effect among those most interested in the affair, namely, the staffs of *La Presse* and *Le Globe*. These two journals were literally at daggers drawn, and some writers connected with the latter went hinting, if not saying openly, that Dujarrier was already showing the white feather. Whether Dujarrier heard of the comments in that shape, or whether he instinctively guessed what they would be, has never been clearly made out, but it is certain that from that moment he insisted upon the use of pistols. "I do not intend my adversary to show me the slightest favour, either by disarming me or by wounding me in the arm or leg. I mean to have a serious encounter," he said. Young Dumas, frightened perhaps at his want of reticence in the matter, begged his father to go and see Grisier,* and claim his intervention. Alexandre Dumas, than whom no stauncher friend ever existed, who would have

* The great fencing-master, whom Dumas immortalized in his "Maître d'Armes."— EDITOR.

willingly risked his own life to save that of Dujarrier, had to decline the mission suggested by his son. "I cannot do it," he said; "the first and foremost thing is to safeguard Dujarrier's reputation, which is the more precious because it is his first duel."

"His first duel," — here is the key-note to the whole of the proceedings as far as Dujarrier and his personal friends were concerned. Had Dujarrier been in the position of the editor of his paper, Emile de Girardin,—had he been out before and killed or severely wounded his man, as the latter killed Armand Carrel nine years before,—he might have openly announced his determination "never to go out again" under no matter what provocation. Unfortunately, Dujarrier was not in that position; in fact, it is no exaggeration to say that Dujarrier paid the penalty of M. de Girardin's decision. A great deal of mawkish sentiment has been wasted upon the tragic fate of Armand Carrel; in reality, he had what he deserved, albeit that no one more than M. de Girardin himself regretted his untimely end. Most writers will tell one that Carrel fell a victim to his political opinions; nothing is farther from the truth. Armand Carrel fell a victim to a "question of shop" of which he allowed himself, though perhaps not deliberately, to become the champion. After many attempts, more or less successful, in the way of popular journalism, M. de Girardin, in 1836, started *La Presse,* a serious journal of the same size as the then existing ones, but at half the subscription of the latter, all of which absolutely banded at once against him. Armand Carrel, who was a soldier, and a valiant soldier, a writer of talent, and a gentleman to boot, ought to have stood aloof from that kind of polemics. Emile de Girardin was not the likely man to submit to open or implied insult. His best, albeit his least-known, book, "Emile," which is as it were an autobiography, had given the measure of his thoughts on the subject of duelling. "Emile" goes into society as a soldier would go into an enemy's country. Not that he is by nature cruel or bloodthirsty, but he knows that, to hold his own, he must be always ready, not only for defence, but for attack.

"The secret one is bound to preserve with regard to the preparations for a meeting, and those preparations themselves are simply horrible. The care, the precautions to be taken, the secret which is not to leak out, all these are very like the preparations for a crime," he says. "Nevertheless," he goes on, "the horror of all this disappears, when the man, impelled by hatred or resentment, is thirsting for revenge; but when the heart is absolutely without gall, and when the imagination is still subject to all the softer emotions, then, in order not to recoil with fear at the ever horrible idea of a duel, a man must be imbued with all the force of a prejudice which resists the very laws that condemn it."

It was under the latter circumstances that M. de Girardin confronted his adversary. The two men had probably never exchanged a word with one another, they felt no personal animosity; nay, more, the duel was not an *inevitable* one; and yet it cost one man his life, and burthened the other with lifelong regrets.

Had the issue been different, *La Presse* would probably have disappeared, and all recrimination ceased. As it was, unable to goad M. de Girardin into a reversal of his decision "never to go out again," and that in spite of nine years of direct insult from a so-called political party, of every kind of quasi-legal vexation, M. de Beauvallon constituted himself a second Armand Carrel, selecting Dujarrier as his victim, the chief not being available. But here all resemblance to Armand Carrel ceased, and the law itself was anxious to mark the difference. In the one case it had been set at nought by two men of undoubted courage and undoubted honour, meeting upon equal terms; in the other, it was proved that, not content with Dujarrier's well-known inferiority, De Beauvallon's pistols had been tried before the encounter. The court could take no cognizance of this, but it marked its disapproval by sentencing Beauvallon to eight years', and one of his seconds, M. d'Ecquevilley, to ten years' imprisonment for perjury. Both had declared on oath that the pistols had not been tried. The Dujarrier duel caused a deep and painful sensation. I have dwelt upon it at greater length than was absolutely necessary, because it inspired me with a resolution from which I have never departed since. I was twenty-seven at the time, and, owing to circumstances which I need not relate here, foresaw that the greater part of my life would be spent in France. I am neither more courageous nor more cowardly than most persons, but I objected to be shot down like a mad dog on the most futile pretext because some one happened to have a grudge against me. To have declined "to go out" on the score of my nationality would not have met the case in the conditions in which I was living, so from that moment I became an assiduous client at Gosset's shooting-gallery, and took fencing lessons of Grisier. I do not know that I became very formidable with either weapon, only sufficiently skilled not to be altogether defenceless. I took care at the same time to let it go forth that a duel to me not only meant one or both parties so severely wounded as not to be able to continue the struggle, but the resumption of the combat, when he or they had recovered, until one was killed. Of course, it implied that I would only go out for a sufficiently weighty reason, but that, if compelled to do so for a trifling one, I would still adhere to my original resolution. Only once, more than twelve years afterwards, I had a quarrel fastened upon me, arising out of the excitement consequent upon the attempt of Orsini. I was the offended party, and, as such, could dictate the conditions of the meeting. I declined to modify in the least the rules I had laid down for my own guidance, and stated as much to those who were to act for me—General Fleury and Alexandre Dumas. My adversary's friends refused to accept the terms. I was never molested afterwards, though an Englishman had not always a pleasant life of it, even under the Second Empire.

In connection with Dujarrier's duel, I may say a few words here of that quasi-wonderful woman, Lola Montès. I say "quasi," because really there was nothing wonderful about her, except perhaps her beauty and her consummate impudence. She had not a scrap of talent of any kind; education she had none, for, whether she spoke in English, French, or Spanish, grammatical errors abounded, and her expressions were always those of a pretentious housemaid, unless they were those of an excited fishwife.

She told me that she had been at a boarding school in Bath, and that she was a native of Limerick, but that when quite a child she was taken to Seville by her parents. Her father, according to her account, was a Spaniard, her mother a Creole. "But I scandalized every one at school, and would not learn." I could quite believe that; what I could not believe was that a girl of her quick powers—for she undoubtedly possessed those—could have spent, however short a time in the society of decent girls of her own age, let alone of presumedly refined schoolmistresses, without having acquired some elementary notions of manner and address. Her gait and carriage were those of a duchess, for she was naturally graceful, but the moment she opened her lips, the illusion vanished—at least to me; for I am bound to admit that men of far higher intellectual attainments than mine, and familiar with very good society, raved and kept raving about her, though all those defects could not have failed to strike them as they had struck me. I take it that it must have been her beauty, for, though not devoid of wit, her wit was that of the pot-house, which would not have been tolerated in the smoking-room of a club in the small hours.

When Dujarrier was carried home dying to the Rue Lafitte, a woman flung herself on the body and covered his face with kisses. That woman was Lola Montès. In his will he left her eighteen shares in the Palais-Royal Theatre, amounting in value to about 20,000 francs. She insisted afterwards in appearing as a witness at the trial at Rouen, although her evidence threw not the slightest light upon the matter. She wanted to create a sensation; and she accomplished her aim. I was there, and though the court was crowded with men occupying the foremost ranks in literature, art, and Paris society, no one attracted the attention she did. Even the sober president and assessors sat staring at her open-mouthed when she took her stand behind the little rail which does duty for a witness-box in France. She was dressed in mourning—not the deepest, but soft masses of silk and lace—and when she lifted her veil and took off her glove to take the prescribed oath, a murmur of admiration ran through the court. That is why she had undertaken the journey to Rouen, and verily she had her reward.

It was on that occasion that I became acquainted, though quite by accident, with the young man who, ten or eleven years later, was to leap into fame all of a sudden with one novel. I have already said that the court was very crowded, and next to me was standing a tall, strapping fellow, somewhat younger than myself, whom, at the first glance, one would have taken to be an English country gentleman or well-to-do farmer's son. Such mistakes are easily made in Normandy. When Lola Montès came forward to give her evidence, some one on the other side of him remarked that she looked like the heroine of a novel.

"Yes," he replied; "but the heroines of the real novels enacted in everyday life do not always look like that."

Then he turned to me, having seen me speak to several people from Paris and in company of Alexandre Dumas and Berryer, whom everybody knew. He asked me some particulars about Lola Montès, which I gave him. I found him exceedingly well-informed. We chatted for a while. When he left he handed me his card, and hoped that we should see one another again. The card bore the simple superscription of "Gustave Flaubert." I was told during the evening that he was the son of a local physician of note. Twelve years later the whole of France rang with his name. He had written "Madame Bovary," and laid the foundation of what subsequently became the ultra-realistic school of French fiction.

To return for a moment to Lola Montès. The trial was really the starting-point of her notoriety, for, in spite of her beauty, she had been at one time reduced to sing in the streets in Brussels. That was after she had fled from Calcutta, whither her first husband, a captain or lieutenant James, in the service of the East India Company, had taken her. She landed at Southampton, and, during her journey to London, managed to ingratiate herself with an English nobleman, by pretending that she was the wife of a Spanish soldier who had been shot by the Carlists. She told me all this herself, because she was not in the least reticent about her scheming, especially after her scheming had failed. She would, however, not divulge the name of her travelling companion, who tried to befriend her by introducing her to some of his acquaintances, with the view of obtaining singing lessons for her. "But I did not make my expenses, because you English are so very moral and my patron was suspected of not giving himself all that trouble for nothing. Besides, they managed to ferret out that I was not the widow of a Spanish officer, but the wife of an English one; and then, as you may imagine, it was all up. I got, however, an engagement at the Opera House in the ballet, but not for long; of course,

I could not dance much, but I could dance as well as half your wooden ugly women that were there. But they told tales about me, and the manager dismissed me.*

* The English nobleman must have been Lord Malmesbury, who alludes to her as follows: "This was a most remarkable woman, and may be said by her conduct at Munich to have set fire to the magazine of revolution, which was ready to burst forth all over Europe, and which made the year 1848 memorable. I made her acquaintance by accident, as I was going up to London from Heron Court, in the railway. The Consul at Southampton asked me to take charge of a Spanish lady who had been recommended to his care, and who had just landed. I consented to do this, and was introduced by him to a remarkably handsome person, who was in deep mourning, and who appeared to be in great distress. As we were alone in the carriage, she, of her own accord, informed me, in bad English, that she was the widow of Don Diego Leon, who had lately been shot by the Carlists after he was taken prisoner, and that she was going to London to sell some Spanish property that she possessed, and give lessons in singing, as she was very poor. On arriving in London she took some lodgings, and came to my house to a little concert which I gave, and sang some Spanish ballads. Her accent was foreign, and she had all the appearance of being what she pretended to be. She sold different things, such as veils, etc., to the party present, and received a good deal of patronage. Eventually she took an engagement for the ballet at the Opera House, but her dancing was very inferior. At last she was recognized as an impostor, her real name being Mrs. James, and Irish by extraction, and had married an officer in India. Her engagement at the Opera was cancelled, she left the country, and retired to Munich. She was a very violent woman, and actually struck one of the Bavarian generals as he was reviewing the troops. The king became perfectly infatuated with her beauty and cleverness, and gave her large sums of money, with a title, which she afterwards bore when she returned to England." ("Memoirs of an Ex-minister," by the Earl of Malmesbury.)

Lord Malmesbury is wrong in nearly every particular which he has got from hearsay. Lola Montès did not retire to Munich after her engagement at the Opera House had been cancelled, but to Brussels, and from there to Warsaw. Nor did she play the all-important part in the Bavarian riots or revolution he ascribes to her. The author of these notes has most of the particulars of Lola Montès' career previous to her appearance in Munich from her own lips, and, as he has already said, she was not in the least reticent about her scheming, especially when her scheming had failed. For the story of the events at Munich, I gather inferentially from his notes that he is indebted to Karl von Abel, King Ludwig's ultramontane minister, who came afterwards to Paris, and who, if I mistake not, was the father or the uncle of Herr von Abel, the Berlin correspondent of the *Times*, some fourteen or fifteen years ago.—EDITOR.

She fostered no illusions with regard to her choregraphic talents; in fact, she fostered no illusions about anything, and her candour was the best trait in her character. She had failed as a dancer in Warsaw, whither she had gone from London, by way of Brussels. In the Belgian capital, according to her own story, she had been obliged to sing in the streets to keep from starvation. I asked her why she had not come from London to Paris, "where, for a woman of her attractions, and not hampered by many scruples," as I pointed out to her, "there were many more resources than elsewhere." The answer was so characteristic of the daring adventuress, who, notwithstanding her impecuniosity, flew at the highest game to be had, that I transcribe it in full. I am often reluctant to trust to my memory: in this instance I may; I remember every word of it. This almost illiterate schemer, who probably had not the remotest notion of geography, of history, had pretty well "the Almanach de Gotha" by heart, and seemed to guess instinctively at things which said Almanach carefully abstained from mentioning, namely, the good understanding or the reverse between the married royal couples of Europe, etc.

"Why did not I come to Paris!" she replied. "What was the good of coming to Paris where there was a king, bourgeois to his finger-nails, tight-fisted besides, and notoriously the most moral and best father all the world over; with princes who were nearly as much married as their dad, and with those who were single far away? What was the good of coming to a town where you could not bear the title of 'la maîtresse du prince' without the risk of being taken to the frontier between two gendarmes, where you could not have squeezed a thousand louis out of any of the royal sons for the life of you? What was the good of trying to get a count, where the wife of a grocer or a shoemaker might have objected to your presence at a ball, on the ground of your being an immoral person? No, I really meant to make my way to the Hague. I had heard that William II. whacked his wife like any drunken labourer, so that his sons had to interfere every now and then. I had heard this in Calcutta, and from folk who were likely to know. But as I thought that I might have the succession of the whacks, as well as of the lord, I wanted to try my chance at Brussels first; besides, I hadn't much money."

"But King Leopold is married, and lives very happily with his wife," I interrupted.

"Of course he does—they all do," was the answer; "mais ça n'empêche pas les sentiments, does it? I am very ignorant, and haven't a bit of memory, but I once heard a story about a Danish or Swedish king —I do not know the difference—who married an adventuress like myself, though the queen and the mother of his heir was alive. He committed bigamy, but kings and queens may do things we mayn't. One day, he and his lawful wife were at one of their country seats, and, leaning out of the window, when a carriage passed with a good-looking woman in it, 'Who is this lady?' asked the queen. 'That's my wife,' replied the king. 'Your wife! what am I, then?' said the queen. 'You? well, you are my queen.'*

"Never mind, whatever my intentions on Leopold's

* Lola Montès was perfectly correct. It was Frederick IV. of Denmark, only the woman was not an adventuress like herself, but the Countess Reventlow, whom he had abducted.—EDITOR.

money or affections may have been, they came to nothing; for before I could get as much as a peep at him, my money had all been spent, and I was obliged to part with my clothes first, and then to sing in the streets to get food. I was taken from Brussels to Warsaw by a man whom I believe to be a German. He spoke many languages, but he was not very well off himself. However, he was very kind, and, when we got to Warsaw, managed to get me an engagement at the Opera. After two or three days, the director told me that I couldn't dance a bit. I stared him full in the face, and asked him whether he thought that, if I could dance, I would have come to such a hole as his theatre. Thereupon he laughed, and said I was a clever girl for all that, and that he would keep me on for ornament. I didn't give him the chance for long. I left after about two months, with a Polish gentleman, who brought me to Paris. The moment I get a nice round lump sum of money, I am going to carry out my original plan; that is, trying to hook a prince. I am sick of being told that I can't dance. They told me so in London, they told me in Warsaw, they told me at the Porte Saint-Martin where they hissed me. I don't think the men, if left to themselves, would hiss me; their wives and their daughters put them up to it: a woman like myself spoils their trade of honest women. I am only waiting my chance here; for though you are all very nice and generous and all that kind of thing, it is not what I want."

Shortly after this conversation, the death of Dujarrier and his legacy to her gave her the chance she had been looking for. She left for London, I heard, with an Englishman; but I never saw him, so I cannot say for certain. But, it appears, she did not stay long, because, a little while after, several Parisians, on their return from Germany, reported that they had met her at Wiesbaden, at Homburg, and elsewhere, punting in a small way, not settling down anywhere, and almost deliberately avoiding both Frenchmen and Englishmen. The rumour went that her husband was on her track, and that her anxiety to avoid him had caused her to leave London hurriedly. In spite of her chequered career, in spite of the shortcomings at Brussels, Lola Montès was by no means anxious for the "sweet yoke of domesticity." In another six months, her name was almost forgotten by all of us, except by Alexandre Dumas, who now and then alluded to her. Though far from superstitious, Dumas, who had been as much smitten with her as most of her admirers, avowed that he was glad she had disappeared. "She has 'the evil eye,'" he said; "and sure to bring bad luck to any one who closely links his destiny with hers, for however short a time. You see what has occurred to Dujarrier. If ever she is heard of again, it will be in connection with some terrible calamity that has befallen a lover of hers." We all laughed at him, except Dr. Véron, who could have given odds to Solomon Eagle himself at prophesying. Fortunately he was generally afraid to open his lips, for he was thoroughly sincere in his belief that he could prevent the event by not predicting it—at any rate aloud. For once in a way, however, Alexandre Dumas proved correct. When we did hear again of Lola Montès, it was in connection with the disturbances that had broken out at Munich, and the abdication of her royal lover, Louis I. of Bavaria, in favour of his eldest son, Maximilian.

The substance of the following notes relating to said disturbances was communicated to me by a political personage who played a not inconsiderable part in the events themselves. As a rule it is not very safe to take interested evidence of that kind, " but in this instance," as my informant put it, " there was really no political reputation to preserve, as far as he was concerned." Lola Montès had simply tried to overthrow him as Madame Dubarry overthrew the Duc de Choiseul, because he would not become her creature; and she had kept on repeating the tactics with every succeeding ministry, even that of her own making. But it should be remembered that revolution was in the air in the year '48, and that if Lola Montès had been the most retiring of favourites, or Louis I. the most moral of kings, the uprising would have happened just the same, though the upshot might have been different with regard to Louis himself.

Here is a portrait of him, which, in my literary ignorance, I think sufficiently interesting to reproduce.

"Louis was a chip of the old Wittelsbach block; that is, a Lovelace, with a touch of the *minnesinger* about him. Age had not damped his ardour; for, though he was sixty-one when Lola Montès took up her quarters at Munich, any and every " beauty" that came to him was sure of an enthusiastic welcome. And Heaven alone knows how many had come to him during his reign; they seemed really directed to him from every quarter of the globe. The new arrival had her portrait painted almost immediately; it was added to the collection for which a special gallery had been set apart, and whither Louis went to meditate by himself at least once a day. He averred that he went thither for poetic inspiration, for he took himself au sérieux as a poet, and, above all, as a classical poet, modelling his verse upon those of ancient times. He had published a volume of poems, entitled 'Walhalla's Genossen;'* but his principal study of antiquity was mainly confined to the rites connected with the worship of Venus. He was very good-natured and pleasant in his dealings with every one; he had not an ounce of gall in the whole of his body. He was, moreover, very religious in his own way, and consequently the tool of the Jesuits, who really governed the kingdom, but who endeavoured to make his own life sweet and pleasant to him. They liked him to take part in the religious processions, as any burgher of devout tendencies might, but being aware of his tendency to be attracted by the first pretty face he caught sight of, they took care to relegate all the handsome maidens and matrons to the first and second floors. In that way Louis's eyes were always lifted heavenwards, and religious appearances were preserved.

"Under such conditions, it was not difficult for a woman of Lola Montès' attractions and daring to gain her ends. She was not altogether without means when she came to Munich, though the sum in her possession was far from a hundred thousand francs, as she afterwards alleged it was. At any rate, she was not the penniless adventuress she had formerly been, and when, in her beautiful dresses, she applied to the director of the Hof-Theatre for an engagement, the latter was fairly dazzled, and granted her request without a murmur. She did, however, not want to dance, and, before her first appearance, she managed to set tongues

* "Companions in Walhalla."—EDITOR.

wagging about her beauty, and, as a matter of course, the rumours reached the king's ears. I am afraid I shall have to prefer a grave charge, but I am not doing so without foundation. It is almost certain by now that the Jesuits, seeing in her a tool for the further subjugation of the superannuated royal troubadour, countenanced, if they did not assist her in her schemes; they, the Jesuits, did many things of which a Catholic, like myself, however firm in his allegiance to Rome, could not but disapprove. At any rate, three or four days after the king's first meeting with her, Lola Montès was presented at court, and introduced to the royal family and corps diplomatique by the sovereign himself, as 'his best friend.' Events proceeded apace. In August, '47, the king granted her patents of 'special naturalization,' created her Baroness von Rosenthal, and, almost immediately afterwards, Countess von Landsfeld. She received an annuity of twenty thousand florins, and had a magnificent mansion built for her. At the instance of the king, the queen was compelled to confer the order of St. Thérèse upon her. I, and many others, had strenuously opposed all this, though not unaware that, up till then, the Jesuits were on her side, rather than on ours. We paid the penalty of our opposition with our dismissal from office, and then Lola Montès confronted the Jesuits by herself. She was absolutely mad to invade Wurtemberg, not for any political reason; she could no more have accounted for any such than the merest hind, but simply because, a few months before her appearance at Munich, she had been, in her opinion, slighted by the old king. The fact was, old William, sincerely attached to Amalia

Stubenrauch, the actress, had not fallen a victim to Lola Montès' charms, and had taken little or no notice of her. The contemplated invasion of Wurtemberg was an act of private revenge. But mad as she was, there was some one more mad still—King Louis I. of Bavaria.

"The most ill-advised thing she did, perhaps, was to change her supporters. Like the ignorant, overbearing woman she was, she would not consent to share her power over the king with the Jesuits; she tried to form an opposition against them among the students at the University, and she succeeded to a certain extent. These adherents constituted the nucleus of a corps which soon became known under the title of 'Allemanen.' But the more noble-minded and patriotic youths at the Munich University virtually ostracized the latter, and several minor disturbances had already broken out in consequence of this, when, in the beginning of February, '48, a more than usually serious manifestation against 'Lola's creatures,' as they were called, took place. The woman did not lack pluck, and she insisted upon defying the rioters by herself. But they proved too much for her; and, after all, she was a woman. She endeavoured to escape from their violence, but every house was shut against her; the Swiss on guard at the Austrian Embassy refused her shelter. A most painful scene happened; the king himself, the moment the news reached him, rushed to her rescue, and, having elbowed his way through the threatening, yelling crowd, offered her his arm, and conducted her to the church of the Theatines, hard by. As a matter of course, several officers had joined him, and all might have been well, if she had taken the lesson to heart. But her violent, domineering, vindictive temper got the better of her. No sooner did she find herself in comparative safety, than, emboldened by the presence of the officers, she snatched a pistol from one of them, and, armed with it, leapt out of the building, confronting the crowd, and threatening to fire. Heaven alone knows what would have been the result of this mad act, but for the timely arrival of a squadron of cuirassiers, who covered her retreat.

"The excitement might have died out in a week or a fortnight, though the year '48 was scarcely a propitious one for a display of such quasi-feudal defiance, if she had merely been content to forego the revenge for the insults she herself had provoked; but on the 10th of February she prevailed upon the king to issue a decree, closing the University for a twelvemonth. The smouldering fire of resentment against her constant interference in the affairs of the country blazed forth once more, and this time with greater violence than ever. The working men, nay, the commercial middle classes, hitherto indifferent to the king's vagaries, which, after all, brought grist to their mill, espoused the students' cause. Barricades were erected; the cry was not 'Long live the Constitution,' or 'Long live the Republic,' but 'Down with the concubine.' It was impossible to mistake the drift of that insurrection, but, in order to leave no doubt about it in the sovereign's mind, a deputation of the municipal council and one of the Upper House waited upon Louis, and insisted upon the dismissal of Lola Montès, who, in less than an hour, left Munich, escorted by a troop of gendarmes, who, however, had all their work to do to prevent her from being torn to pieces by the mob. Her departure was the signal for the pillaging of her mansion, at which the king looked on—as he thought—incognito. It is difficult to determine what prompted him to commit so rash an act. Was it a feeling of relief at having got rid of her—for there was a good deal of cynicism about that semi-philosophical, semi-mystical troubadour—or a desire to chew the cud of his vanished happiness? Whatever may have been the reason, he paid dearly for it, for some one smashed a looking-glass over his head, and he was carried back to the palace, unconscious, and bleeding profusely. It was never ascertained who inflicted the wounds, though there is no doubt that the assailant knew his victim. Meanwhile Lola Montès had succeeded in slipping away from her escort, and three hours later she re-entered Munich disguised, and endeavoured to make her way to the palace. But the latter was carefully guarded, and for the next month all her attempts in that direction proved fruitless, though, audacious as she was, she did not dare stop for a single night in the capital itself. Besides, I do not believe that a single inhabitant would have given her shelter. Unlike a good many royal favourites of the past, she had no personal adherents, no faithful servants who would have stood by her through thick and thin, because she never treated any one kindly in the days of her prosperity: she could only bribe; she was incapable of inspiring disinterested affection among those who were insensible to the spell of her marvellous beauty."

So far the narrative of my informant. The rest is pretty well known by everybody. A few years later, she committed bigamy with another English officer, named Heald, who was drowned at Lisbon about the same time that her real husband died. Alexandre

Dumas was right—she brought ill-luck to those who attached themselves to her for any length of time, whether in the guise of lovers or husbands.

These notes about Lola Montès remind me of another woman whom public opinion would place in the same category, though she vastly differed in character. I am alluding to Alphonsine Plessis, better known to the world at large as "La Dame aux Camélias." I frequently met her in the society of some of my friends between '43 and '47, the year of her death. Her name was as I have written it, and not Marie or Marguérite Duplessis, as has been written since.

The world at large, and especially the English, have always made very serious mistakes, both with regard to the heroine of the younger Dumas' novel and play, and the author himself. They have taxed him with having chosen an unworthy subject, and, by idealizing it, taught a lesson of vice instead of virtue; they have taken it for granted that Alphonsine Plessis was no better than her kind. She was much better than that, though probably not sufficiently good to take a housemaid's place and be obedient to her pastors and masters, to slave from morn till night for a mere pittance, in addition to her virtue, which was ultimately to prove its own reward—the latter to consist of a home of her own, with a lot of squalling brats about her, where she would have had to slave as she had slaved before, without the monthly pittances hitherto doled out to her. She was not sufficiently good to see her marvellously beautiful face, her matchless graceful figure set off by a cambric cap and a calico gown, instead of having the first enhanced by the gleam of priceless jewels in her hair and the second wrapped in soft laces and velvets and satins; but, for all that, she was not the common courtesan the goody-goody people have thought fit to proclaim her—the common courtesan, who, according to these goody-goody people, would have descended to her grave forgotten, but for the misplaced enthusiasm of a poetical young man, who was himself corrupted by the atmosphere in which he was born and lived afterwards.

The sober fact is that Dumas *fils* did not idealize anything at all, and, least of all, Alphonsine Plessis' character. Though very young at the time of her death, he was then already much more of a philosopher than a poet. He had not seen half as much of Alphonsine Duplessis during her life as is commonly supposed, and the first idea of the novel was probably suggested to him, not by his acquaintance with her, but by the sensation her death caused among the Paris public, the female part of which—almost without distinction—went to look at her apartment, to appraise her jewels and dresses, etc. "They would probably like to have had them on the same terms," said a terrible cynic. The remark must have struck young Dumas, in whose hearing it was said, or who, at any rate, had it reported to him; for if we carefully look at *all* his earlier plays, we find the spirit of that remark largely pervading them.

Alphonsine Plessis had probably learned even less in her girlhood than Lola Montès, but she had a natural tact, and an instinctive refinement which no education could have enhanced. She never made grammatical mistakes, no coarse expression ever passed her lips. Lola Montès could not make friends;

Alphonsine Plessis could not make enemies. She never became riotous like the other, not even boisterous; for amidst the most animated scenes she was haunted by the sure knowledge that she would die young, and life, but for that knowledge, would have been very sweet to her. Amidst these scenes, she would often sit and chat to me: she liked me, because I never paid her many compliments, although I was but six years older than the most courted woman of her time. The story of her being provided for by a foreign nobleman because she was so like his deceased daughter, was not a piece of fiction on Dumas' part; it was a positive fact. Alphonsine Plessis, after this provision was made for her, might have led the most retired existence; she might, like so many demi-mondaines have done since, bought herself a country-house, re-entered "the paths of respectability," have had a pew in the parish church, been in constant communication with the vicar, prolonged her life by several years, and died in the odour of sanctity: but, notwithstanding her desperate desire to live, her very nature revolted at such self-exile. When Alexandre Dumas read the "Dame aux Camélias" to his father, the latter wept like a baby, but his tears did not drown the critical faculty. "At the beginning of the third act," he said afterwards, "I was wondering how Alexandre would get his Marguérite back to town without lowering her in the estimation of the spectator. Because, if such a woman as he depicted was to remain true to nature—to her nature—and consequently able to stand the test of psychological analysis, she could not have borne more than two or three months of such retirement. This does not mean that she would have severed her connection with Armand Duval, but he would have become 'un plat dans le menu' after a little while, nothing more. The way Alexandre got out of the difficulty proves that he is my son every inch of him, and that, at the very outset of his career, he is a better dramatist than I am ever likely to be. But depend upon it, that if, in real life and with such a woman, le père Duval had not interfered, la belle Marguérite would have taken the 'key of the street' on some pretext—and that, notwithstanding the sale of her carriages, the pledging of her diamonds and her furs—in order not to worry the man she loved, for the time being, with money matters. Honestly speaking, it wanted my son's cleverness to make a piece out of Alphonsine Plessis' life. True, he was fortunate in that she died, which left him free to ascribe that death to any cause but the right one, namely, consumption. I know that he made use of it, but he took care to show the malady aggravated by Armand Duval's desertion of her, and this is the only liberty he took with the psychological, consequently scientific and logical, development of the play. People have compared his Marguérite Gautier to Manon Lescaut, to Marion Delorme, and so forth: it just shows what they know about it. They might just as well compare Thiers to Cromwell. Manon Lescaut, Marion Delorme, Cromwell, knew what they wanted: Marguérite Gautier and Thiers do not; both are always in search of *l'inconnu*, the one in experimental politics, the other in experimental love-making. Still, my son has been true to Nature; but he has taken an episode showing her at her best. He was not bound to let the public know that the frequent recurrence of these love episodes, but always with a different partner, constitutes a disease which is as well known to specialists as the disease of drunkenness, and for which it is impossible to find a cure. Messalina, Catherine II., and thousands of women have suffered from it. When they happen to be born in such exalted stations as these two, they buy men; when they happen to be born in a lowly station and are attractive, they sell themselves; when they are ugly and repulsive they sink to the lowest depths of degradation, or end in the padded cells of a madhouse, where no man dares come near them. Nine times out of ten the malady is hereditary, and I am certain that if we could trace the genealogy of Alphonsine Plessis, we should find the taint either on the father's side or on the mother's, probably on the former's, but more probably still on both." *

* The following is virtually a summary of an article by Count G. de Contades, in a French bibliographical periodical, Le Livre (Dec. 10, 1885), and shows how near Alexandre Dumas was to the truth. I have given it at great length. My excuse for so doing is the extraordinary popularity of Dumas' play with all classes of playgoers. As a consequence, there is not a single modern play, with the exception of those of Shakespeare, the genesis of which has been so much commented upon. It is no exaggeration to say that most educated playgoers, not to mention professional students of the drama, have at some time or other expressed a wish to know something more of the real Marguérite Gautier's parentage and antecedents than is shown by Dumas, either in his play or in his novel, or than what they could gather from the partly apocryphal details given by her contemporaries. Dumas himself, in his preface to the play, says that she was a farm servant. He probably knew no more than that, nor did Alphonsine Plessis herself. In after-years, the eminent dramatist had neither the time nor the inclination to search musty parish registers; Count de Contades has done so for him. Here are the results, as briefly as possible, of his researches. Alphonsine Plessis' paternal grandmother, "moitié mendiante et moitié prostituée," inhabited, a little less than a century ago, the small parish of Longé-sur-Maire, which has since become simply Longé in the canton of Briouze, arrondissement of Argentan (about thirty miles from Alençon). She had been nicknamed " La Guénuchetonne," a rustic version of the archaic French word guénippe (slattern). Louis Descours, a kind of country clod who had entered the priesthood

There were few of us who, during Alphonsine Plessis' lifetime, were so interested in her as to have gone to without the least vocation, and just because his people wished him to do so, becomes enamoured of "La Guénuchetonne," and early in January, 1790, the curé Philippe christens a male child, which is registered as Marin Plessis, mother Louis-Renée Plessis, father unknown. That the father was known well enough is proved by the Christian name bestowed upon the babe, Marin, which was that of Louis Descours' father. This gallant adventure of the country priest was an open secret for miles around.

Marin Plessis grew into a handsome fellow, and when about twenty took to travelling in the adjacent provinces of lower and upper Normandy with a pack of smallwares. Handsome and amiable besides, he was a welcome guest everywhere, and soon became a great favourite with the female part of the Normandy peasantry. For a little while he flitted from one rustic beauty to another, until he was fairly caught by one more handsome than the rest, Marie Deshayes. She was not, perhaps, immaculately virtuous, but, apart from her extraordinary personal attractions, she was something more than an ordinary peasant girl.

Some sixty years before Marin Plessis' union with Marie Deshayes, there lived in the neighbourhood of Evreux a spinster lady of good descent, though not very well provided with worldly goods. She was comely and sweet-tempered enough, but then, as now, comeliness and a sweet temper do not count for much in the French matrimonial market, and least of all in the provincial one. Owing to the modesty of her marriage portion, she had no suitors for her hand, and, being of an exceedingly amorous disposition, she bestowed her affection where she could, "without regret, and without false shame," as the old French chronicler has it.

The annals of the village—for, curiously enough, these annals do exist, though only in manuscripts—are commendably reticent about the exact number and names of her lovers. It would seem that the author, a contemporary of Mdlle. Anne du Mesnil d'Argentelles and the great-grandfather of the present possessor of the notes, a gentleman near Bernay, was divided between the wish of not being too hard upon his neighbour, who was, after all, a gentlewoman, and the desire to leave a record of a peculiar phase of the country manners of those days to posterity. Be this as it may, Mdlle. d'Argentelles' swains, previous to the very last one, have been doomed to anonymous obscurity. But with the advent of Etienne Deshayes, the annalist becomes less reticent, he is considered worthy of being mentioned in full, perhaps as a reward for having finally "made an honest woman" of his inamorata. For that is the final upshot of the love-story between him and Mdlle. d'Argentelles, which, in its earlier stages, bears a certain resemblance to that between Jean-Jacques Rousseau and Madame de Warens, with this difference—that the Normand Jean-Jacques is considerably older than his mistress.

The children born of this marriage were very numerous. One of the length of such a psychological analysis of her pedigree. Nevertheless, most men were agreed that she was no ordinary girl. Her candour about her early want of education increased the interest. "Twenty or twenty-five years ago," said Dr. Véron, one day, after Alphonsine Plessis had left the dinner table, "a woman of her refinement would not have been phenomenal in her position, because at that period the grisette, promoted to the rank of femme entretenue, had not made her appearance. The expression 'femme entretenue' was not even known. Men chose their companions, outside marriage, from a different class; they were generally women of education and often of good family who had made a faux pas, and, as such, forfeited the society and countenance of their equals who had not stumbled in that way, at any rate not in the sight of the world. I confess, Alphonsine Plessis interests me very much. She is, first of all, the best-dressed woman in Paris; secondly, she neither flaunts nor hides her vices; thirdly, she is not always talking or hinting about money; in short, she is a wonderful courtesan."

The result of all this admiration was very favourable to Alexandre Dumas *fils* when he brought out his book about eighteen months after her death. It was in

them, Louis-Deshayes, married a handsome peasant girl, Marie-Madeleine Marra, who appears to have been somewhat too intimate with a neighbouring squire, but who gave birth a few years after to a daughter, of whose paternity there could not be the smallest doubt, seeing that she grew up into a speaking likeness of her maternal grandmother, the erstwhile Mdlle. Anne du Mesnil d'Argentelles. Fate ought to have had a better lot in store for beautiful Marie Deshayes than a marriage with a poor pedlar like Marin Plessis; but the latter was very handsome, and, notwithstanding the opposition of the family, she became his wife. On the 15th of January, 1824, the child which was to be immortalized as "La Dame aux Camélias" saw the light, in a small village in Lower Normandy.—EDITOR.

every one's hands, and the press kept whetting the curiosity of those who had not read it as yet with personal anecdotes about the heroine. In addition to this, the title was a very taking one, and, moreover, absolutely new; for, though it was obvious enough from Alphonsine Plessis' habit of wearing white camellias the greater part of the year, no one had ever thought of applying it to her while she was alive; hence, the credit of its invention belongs decidedly to Dumas *fils*.

I may return to the subject of "La Dame aux Camélias" in connection with the play; meanwhile, I will say a few words of the only man among our set who objected to the title, "because it injures my own," as he put it; namely, M. Lautour-Mézerai, who had been surnamed "L'Homme au Caméllia;" in the singular, from his habit of never appearing in public without that flower in his button-hole. And be it remembered that in those days, the flower was much more rare than it is at present, and consequently very expensive. The plagiarist, if there was one, must have been Alphonsine Plessis, for Dr. Véron, who was one of his oldest friends, did not remember having even seen him *minus* the camellia, and their friendship dated from the year 1831. It is computed that during the nineteen years Mézerai was in Paris, previous to his departure for the South of France and afterwards for Algeria, in both of which provinces he fulfilled the functions of prefect, he must have spent no less than fifty thousand francs on his favourite floral ornament, for he frequently changed it twice a day, and its price, especially in the thirties and earlier part of the forties, was not less than five francs. It is, therefore, not surprising that he resented the usurpation of his title. M. Lautour-Mézerai was one of the most elegant men I knew. He not only belonged to a very good provincial stock, but his family on both sides counted some eminent names in literature.* He was a most charming companion, exceedingly generous; but he would not have parted with the flower in his buttonhole for any consideration, not even to oblige his greatest friend, male or female. It was more than an ornament to him, he looked upon it as a talisman. He always occupied the same place at the Opéra, in the balcony, or what we call the "dress-circle," and many a covetous glance from the brightest eyes was cast at the dazzling white camellia, standing out in bold relief against the dark blue coat, but neither glances nor direct requests had any effect upon him. He became absolutely savage in his refusal when too hardly pressed, because, by his own admission, he was superstitious enough to believe that, if he went home without it, something terrible would happen to him during the night.

M. Lautour-Mézerai was, however, something more than a mere man of fashion. To him belongs the credit of having founded—at any rate in France—the children's periodical. For the comparatively small subscription of six francs per annum, thousands of little ones received every month a number of the *Journal des Enfants*, stitched in blue paper, and with their own name on the wrapper. It flattered their pride to be treated like their elders by having their literature despatched to them in that way, and there is

---

* Curiously enough, he belonged to the same department, and died almost on the very spot where Marin Plessis was born.—EDITOR.

no doubt that this ingenious device contributed, to a certain extent, to the primary and enormous success of the undertaking. But M. Lautour-Mézerai was too refined a littérateur to depend upon such a mere trick, and a look at even the earlier numbers of the *Journal des Enfants,* would prove conclusively that, in the way of amusing children while instructing them a little, nothing better has been done since, whether in France, England, or Germany. The editor and manager succeeded in grouping around him such men as Paul Lacroix (*le bibliophile Jacob*) and Charles Nodier, both of whom have never been surpassed in making history attractive to young minds. Emile Souvestre, Léon Gozlan, Eugène Sue, and even Alexandre Dumas told them the most wonderful stories. The men who positively kept the adult population of France spellbound by their stirring romances seemed to take a delight in competing with women like Virginie Ancelot, the Duchesse d'Abrantès, and others on the latter's ground. As a consequence, it became the fashion to present the young ones on New Year's Day with a receipt for a twelvemonth's subscription, made out in their names, instead of the everlasting bag of sweets. At one time the circulation of *Le Journal des Enfants* was computed at 60,000, and M. Lautour-Mézerai was said to make 100,000 francs per annum out of it.

In a former note, I incidentally mentioned Auguste Lireux. He is scarcely remembered by the present generation of Frenchmen; I doubt whether there are a hundred students of French literature in England who know his name, let alone his writings: yet he is worthy of being remembered by both. He had—what a great many French writers of talent, far greater than his own, essentially lack—humour. True, the latter was not subtle; but it was rarely, if ever, coarse. The nearest approach to him among the journalists of the present day is M. Francisque Sarcey; but the eminent dramatic critic has had a better education. Nevertheless, if Lireux had finished as he began, he would not be so entirely forgotten. Unfortunately for his fame, if not for his material welfare, he took it into his head to become a millionnaire, and he almost succeeded; at any rate, he died very well off, in a beautiful villa at Bougival.

I remember meeting with Lireux almost immediately after he landed in Paris, at the end of '40 or the beginning of '41. He came, I believe, from Rouen; though, but for his accent, he might have come from Marseilles. Tall, well-built, with brown hair and beard and ruddy complexion, a pair of bright eyes behind a pair of golden spectacles, very badly dressed, though his clothes were almost new, very loud and very restless, his broad-brimmed hat cocked on one side, he gave one the impression of what in Paris we used to call a "departemental oracle." He was that to a certain extent, still he was not really pompous, and the feeling of discomfort one experienced at first soon wore off. He was not altogether unknown among the better class of journalists in the capital, for it appears that he frequently contributed to the Paris papers from the provinces. He had a fair knowledge of the French drama theoretically, for he had never written a piece, and openly stated his intention never to do so. But in virtue of his dramatic criticisms in several periodicals—which, in spite of the difference in education between the two men, read uncommonly like the articles of M. Sarcey in the *Temps*—and his unwavering faith in his lucky star, he considered himself destined not only to lift the Odéon from the slough in which it had sunk, but to make it a formidable rival to the house in the Rue de Richelieu. He had no ambition beyond that. The Odéon was really at its lowest depth. Harel had enjoyed a subsidy of 130,000 francs, M. d'Epagny eleven years later had to content himself with less than half, and yet the authorities were fully cognizant of the necessity of a second Théâtre-Français. Whether from incapacity or ill-luck, M. d'Epagny did not succeed in bringing back the public to the old house. The direction was offered then to M. Hippolyte Lucas, the dramatic critic of *Le Siècle*, and one of the best English scholars I have ever met with among the French, and, on his declining the responsibility, given to Lireux, who for the sake of making a point, exclaimed, "Directeur! . . . au refus d'Hippolyte Lucas!"*

It was a piece of bad taste on Lireux's part, because M. Lucas was his superior in every respect, though he would probably have failed where the other succeeded—at least for a while. Save for this mania of saying smart things in and out of season, Lireux was really a good-natured fellow, and we were all glad that he had realized his ambition. The venture looked promising enough at the start. He got an excellent company together, comprising Bocage, Monrose, Gil-Pères, Maubant, Mdlles. Georges and Araldi, Madame Dorval, etc.; and if, like young Bonaparte's

---

* An imitation of the line of Don Carlos in Hugo's "Hernani;" "Empereur! . . . au refus de Frédéric-le-Sage!"—Editor.

troops, they were badly paid and wanted for everything, they worked with a will, because, like Bonaparte, Lireux inspired them with confidence. He, on the other hand, knew their value, and on no pretext would allow them to be ousted from the positions they had honourably won by their talents and hard work. Presumptuous mediocrity, backed either by influence or intrigue, found him a stern adversary; the intriguer got his answer in such a way as to prevent him from returning to the charge. One day an actor of reputed incapacity, Machanette, claimed the title-rôle in Molière's "Misanthrope."

"You have no one else to play Alceste," he said.

"Yes, I have. I have got one of the checktakers," replied Lireux.

Auguste Lireux was one of those managers the race of which began with Harel at the Porte Saint-Martin and Dr. Véron at the Opéra. Duponchel, at the latter house, Montigny at the Gymnase, Buloz and Arsène Houssaye at the Comédie-Française, endeavoured as far as possible to follow their traditions of liberality towards the public and their artists, and encouragement given to untried dramatists. It was not Lireux's fault that he did not succeed for any length of time. Of course, there is a ridiculous side to everything. During the terrible cholera visitation of 1832, Harel published a kind of statistics, showing that not a single one of the spectators had been attacked by the plague; but all this cannot blind us to the support given to the struggling playwright, Dumas, in the early part of his career. During the winter of 1841-42, which was a severe one, Lireux sent foot-warmers to the rare audience that patronized him on a bitterly cold night, "when tragedy still further chills the house;" the little bit of charlatanism cannot disturb the fact of his having given one of the foremost dramatists of the day a chance with "La Cigue." I am alluding to the first piece of Emile Augier.

This kind of thing tells with a general public, more so still with a public composed of generous-minded, albeit somewhat riotous youths like those of the Quartier-Latin in the early forties. Gradually the latter found their way to the Odéon, "sinon pour voir la pièce, alors pour entendre Lireux, qui est toujours amusant;" which, in plain language, meant that come what may they would endeavour to provoke Lireux into giving them a speech.

Flattering as was this resolve on their part to Lireux's eloquence, the means they employed to encompass their end would have made the existence of an ordinary manager a burden to him. But Lireux was not an ordinary manager; he possessed "the gift of the gab" to a marvellous degree: consequently he made it known that he would be happy at any time to address MM. les étudiants without putting them to the expense of apples and eggs on the evening of the performance, and voice-lozenges the next day, if they, MM. les étudiants, would in return respect his furniture and the dresses of his actors. The arrangement worked exceedingly well, and for four years the management and the student part of the audience lived in the most perfect harmony.

Lireux did more than that, he forestalled their possible objections to a doubtful episode in a play. I remember the first night of "Jeanne de Naples." The piece had dragged fearfully. Lireux had made three different speeches during the evening, but he foresaw a riot at the end of the piece which no eloquence on his part would be able to quell. It appears—for we only found this out the next day—that the condemned woman, previous to being led to execution, had to deliver a monologue of at least a hundred and fifty or two hundred lines. The unhappy queen had scarcely begun, when a herculean soldier rushed on the stage, took her into his arms and carried her off by main force, notwithstanding her struggles. It was a truly sensational ending, and the curtain fell amidst deafening applause. It redeemed the piece!

Next day Lireux made his appearance at Tortoni's in the afternoon, and, as matter of course, the production of the previous evening was discussed.

"I cannot understand," said Roger de Beauvoir, "how a man with such evident knowledge of stagecraft as the author displayed in that dénoûment, could have perpetrated such an enormity as the whole of the previous acts."

Lireux was fairly convulsed with laughter. "Do you really think that was his own invention?" he asked.

"Of course I do," was the reply.

"Well, it is not. His dénoûment was a speech which would have taken about twenty minutes, at the end of which the queen is tamely led off between the soldiers. I know what would have been the result: the students would have simply torn up the benches and Heaven knows what else. You know that if the gas is left burning, if only a moment, after twelve, there is an extra charge irrespective of the quantity consumed. I looked at my watch when she began to speak her lines. It was exactly thirteen minutes to twelve; she might have managed to get to the end by twelve, but it was doubtful. What was not doubtful was the row that would have ensued, and the time it would have taken me to cope with it. My mind was made up there and then. I selected the biggest of the supers, told him to go and fetch her, and you know the rest."

There were few theatrical managers in those days who escaped the vigilance of Balzac. Among the many schemes he was for ever hatching for benefiting mankind and making his own fortune, there was one which cannot be more fitly described than in the American term of "making a corner;" only that particular "corner" was to be one in plays.

About two years before the advent of Lireux, and when the house at Ville d'Avray, of which I have spoken elsewhere, was completed, a party of literary men received an invitation to spend the Sunday there. It was not an ordinary invitation, but a kind of circular-letter, the postscriptum to which contained the following words, " M. de Balzac will make an important communication." Léon Gozlan, Jules Sandeau, Louis Desnoyers, Henri Monnier, and those familiar with Balzac's schemes, knew pretty well what to expect; and when Lassailly, one of the four men whose nose vied with the legendary one of Bouginier, confirmed their apprehensions that it was a question of making their fortunes, they resigned themselves to their fate. Jules Sandeau, who was gentleness itself, merely observed with a sigh that it was the fifteenth time Balzac had proposed to make him a millionnaire; Henri Monnier offered to sell his share of the prospective profits for 7 francs, 50 centimes; Léon Gozlan suggested that their host might have discovered a diamond mine, whereupon Balzac, who had just entered the room, declared that a diamond mine was nothing to it. He was simply going to monopolize the whole of the Paris theatres. He exposed the plan in a magnificent speech of two hours' duration, and would have continued for two hours more had not one of the guests reminded him that it was time for dinner.

"Dinner," exclaimed Balzac; "why, I never thought of it."

Luckily there was a restaurant near, and the future millionaires and their would-be benefactor were enabled to sit down to "a banquet quite in keeping, not only with the magnificent prospects just disclosed to them, but with the splendour actually surrounding them," as Méry expressed it.

For it should be added that the sumptuous dwelling which was to be, was at that moment absolutely bare of furniture, save a few deal chairs and tables. The garden was a wilderness, intersected by devious paths, sloping so suddenly as to make it impossible to keep one's balance without the aid of an Alpenstock or the large stones imbedded in the soil, but only temporarily, by the considerate owner. One day, Dutacq, the publisher, having missed his footing, rolled as far as the wall inclosing the domain, without his friends being able to stop him.

The garden, like everything else connected with the schemes of Balzac, was eventually to become a gold-mine. Part of it was to be built upon, and converted into a dairy; another part was to be devoted to the culture of the pine-apple and the Malaga grape, all of which would yield an income of 30,000 francs annually "at least"—to borrow Balzac's own words.

The apartments had been furnished in the same grandiose way—theoretically. The walls were, as I have already remarked, absolutely bare, but on their plaster, scarcely dry, were magnificent inscriptions of what was to be. They were mapped out regardless of expense. On that facing the north there was a splendid piece of thirteenth-century Flemish tapestry —in writing, of course, flanked by two equally priceless pictures by Raphael and Titian. Facing these, one by Rembrandt, and, underneath, a couch, a couple of arm-chairs, and six ordinary ones, Louis XV., and upholstered in Aubusson tapestry—subjects, Lafontaine's Fables. Opposite again, a monumental mantelpiece in malachite (a present of Czar Nicholas, who had expressed his admiration of Balzac's novels), with bronzes and clock by De Gouttières. The place on the ceiling was marked for a chandelier of Venetian glass, and in the dining-room a square was drawn on the carpetless floor for the capacious sideboard, whereon would be displayed "the magnificent family plate."

Pending the arrival of the furniture, the building of the dairy, hothouses, and vineries, the guests had to sit on hard wooden chairs, to eat a vile dinner, supplemented, however, by an excellent dessert. Balzac was very fond of fruit, and especially of pears, of which he always ate an enormous quantity. The wine was, as a rule, very inferior, but on that particular occasion Balzac's guests discovered that their host's imagination could even play him more cruel tricks in the selection of his vintages than it played him in his pursuit of financial schemes and the furnishing of his house.

When the fruit was placed upon the table, Balzac assumed a most solemn air. "Gentlemen," he said, "I am going to give you some Château-Lafitte, such as you have never tasted—such as it has been given to few mortals to taste. I wish you to sip it carefully—I might almost say reverently, because the opportunity may not repeat itself in our lives."

Wherewith the guests' glasses were filled; all of them made horrible faces, for it was abominable stuff, but one more outspoken than the rest gave his opinion there and then—

"This may be 'Château de la Rue Lafitte,' but it is enough to give one the colic."

Any one else but Balzac would have been horribly disconcerted; he, on the contrary, did not budge. "Yes," he said proudly, "you are right in one respect; this ambrosial nectar comes in a straight line from the Rue Lafitte, for it is Baron James de Rothschild who made me a present of two barrels, for which I am profoundly grateful. Drink, gentlemen, drink, and be thankful also."

Those who would consider this a piece of clever acting on Balzac's part, would be greatly mistaken. His imagination at times affected his palate as well as his other organs, and at that moment he was under the distinct impression that he was offering his guests one of the rarest vintages on record.

I have endeavoured hitherto to digress as little as possible in my recollections, though their very nature made it difficult. In this instance, digression was absolutely necessary to convey an idea of the shock which would naturally result from the contact of two such brains as those of Balzac and Lireux; for it was not long after the young manager's advent to the Odéon that Balzac found his way to his sanctum. The play he offered him was "Les Ressources de Quinola." Strange as it may seem to us, even as late as '42, Balzac's name as a novelist did not rank first in the list with the general public, still it is very doubtful whether any young manager would have refused a stage play by him; consequently, Lireux accepted "Les Ressources de Quinola" almost without fear. It is not to the purpose to say that it was a bad play, and that he ought to have known better; it has been amply proved by now that the most experienced manager is not infallible; but it is a moot point whether the greatest masterpiece would have succeeded with the tactics adopted by Balzac to insure its success. The following may appear like a scene from a farcical comedy; I can vouch for the truth of every word of it, because I had it from the lips of Lireux himself, who, after all, was the heaviest sufferer by Balzac's incurable greed, or, to put it as leniently as one can, by his constant chase after a capital stroke of business. His resolve to pack the house on the first night was not due to a desire to secure a favourable reception from a friendly audience, but to the determination to secure "a lump sum," let come what might. In Balzac are found the two contradictory traits of the money-grubber and the spendthrift.

The scene alluded to just now, took place when the rehearsals were far advanced; the author and the manager were discussing the invitations to be sent out, etc. All at once Balzac declared that he would have none but Knights of the Order of Saint-Louis in the pit. "I am agreeable," replied Lireux; "provided you ferret them out."*

"I'll see to that," said Balzac. "Pray go on. What is the next part of the house?"

"Orchestra stalls."

"Nothing but peers of France there."

"But the orchestra stalls will not hold them all, Monsieur de Balzac."

"Those who cannot find room in the house will have to stand in the lobbies," said Balzac, imperturbably.

"Stage boxes?" continued Lireux.

"They will be reserved for the Court."

"Stage boxes on the first tier?"

"For the ambassadors and plenipotentiaries."

"The open boxes on the ground floor?"

"For the wives and families of the ambassadors."

"Upper circle?" enumerated Lireux, not a muscle of his face moving.

"For the deputies and grand officers of State."

"Third circle?" enumerated Lireux.

"The heads of the great banking and financial establishments."

* It shows that Lireux was not very familiar with the royal edicts affecting that order, and that Balzac himself exaggerated the social and monetary importance of its wearers. For, though Louis-Philippe at his accession suppressed the order, not less than twelve thousand new knights had been created by his two immediate predecessors. They, the recently created knights, were allowed to retain their honours and pensions; but, even before the fall of the Bourbons, the distinction had lost much of its prestige. After the Battle of Navarino, Admiral de Rigny, soliciting rewards for his officers who had distinguished themselves, tacitly ignored the order of Saint-Louis in favour of that of the Legion of Honour. The order, as founded by Louis XIV. in 1693, was only available to officers and Catholics. Several modifications were introduced afterwards in its statutes. The Order of Saint-Louis and that of "Military Merit" were the only two recognized by the Constituent Assembly of 1789; but the Convention suppressed the former, only leaving the latter.—EDITOR.

"The galleries and amphitheatre?"

"A carefully selected, but varied, bourgeoisie," wound up Balzac.

Lireux, who was a capital mimic, re-enacted the scene for us four and twenty hours after it had been enacted in his own room, and while he was still under the impression that it was merely a huge joke on Balzac's part. He soon discovered, however, that the latter was terribly in earnest, when, a few days later, Balzac claimed the whole of the seats for the first three nights, on the penalty of withdrawing his piece there and then. Lireux foolishly submitted, the box office was closed; every one applying for tickets was referred to Balzac himself, or, rather, to the shady individual who had egged him on to this speculation. The latter, at the first application, had run up the prices; the public felt disgusted, and, when the curtain rose upon "Les Ressources de Quinola," the house was almost empty. Thereupon a batch of nondescripts was sent into the streets to dispose of the tickets at any price; the bait was indignantly rejected, and the curtain fell amidst violent hisses. I repeat, a masterpiece would have failed under such circumstances; but the short run of the revival, almost a quarter of a century later at the Vaudeville, proved that the piece was not even an ordinary money-drawing one. It only kept the bills for about nine or ten days.

Lireux was more fortunate with several other pieces, notably with that of Léon Gozlan, known to students of the French drama as "La Main Droite et la Main Gauche," but which originally bore the title of "Il était une Fois un Roi et une Reine." There could be no doubt about its tendency in its original form; it was nothing less than an indictment for bigamy both against Queen Victoria and her Consort; and the authorities had to insist not only upon the change of title and the names of the *dramatis personæ*, but upon the action being shifted from London to Stockholm. The author and manager had to comply; but the public, who had got wind of the affair, crowded the house every night in order to read between the lines.

One of my great sources of amusement for many years has been the perusal of political after-dinner speeches, and political leaders in the English papers, especially when the speakers and writers have endeavoured to lay stress upon the cordial relations between the French and the English, upon the friendly feelings guiding their actions on both sides. I am putting together these notes nearly fourteen years after the conclusion of the Franco-German War, nearly three quarters of a century after Waterloo. There is not a single Frenchman, however Chauvinistic, who ever thinks, let alone talks, of avenging Napoleon's defeat by Wellington; while, on the other hand, there is not a single Frenchman, however unpatriotic, who does not dream now and then of wiping out the humiliation suffered at Sedan. Well, in spite of the almost entire oblivion of the one disaster, and the poignant recollection of the other, the French of to-day hate the English more than the Germans; or—let me put it more correctly—they hate the Germans, they despise us. Nothing that we can do will ever remove this dislike of us.

It has been thus as long as I can remember; no royal visits, no exchange of so-called international courtesies will alter the feeling. It is ready to burst forth, the smallest provocation or fancied one will set it ablaze. During the forties there were a good many real or imaginary provocations on the part of England, and, as a consequence, the hostile feeling against her broke forth where it is almost always sure to break forth first in France—on the stage and in song. After "La Main Droite et la Main Gauche," came Halévy's opera of "Charles VI." It is but fair to say that the Government did all it could to stem the tide, but, notwithstanding its positive orders to modify the chorus of the famous war song in the first act, the song was henceforth regarded as a patriotic hymn. Nor did the visit of the Queen to Louis-Philippe at Eu, in 1843, effect much improvement in this state of things; and, as a matter of course, we on the English side of the Channel retaliated the skits, etc., though I do not think we took them au grand sérieux. When, in January, '44, I went to London for a few days, I found the Christmas pantomime of "King Pippin" in full swing at Drury Lane. I well remember a scene of it, laid in the shop of a dealer in plaster figures. Two of these represented respectively the King of France and the Queen of Great Britain and Ireland. At a given moment, the two statues became animated, drew close to one another, and exchanged the most profuse salutations. But meanwhile, at the back of the stage, the Gallic cock and the British lion (or leopard) assumed a threatening attitude, and at each mark of affection between the two royal personages, shook their heads violently and seemed to want desperately to come to close quarters. The audience applauded vociferously, and it was very evident to me that neither in Paris nor in London the two nations shared the entente cordiale of their rulers.

CHAPTER VI.

Rachel and some of her fellow-actors—Rachel's true character—Her greediness and spitefulness—Her vanity and her wit—Her powers of fascination — The cost of being fascinated by her — Her manner of levying toll—Some of her victims, Comte Duchâtel and Dr. Véron—The story of her guitar—A little transaction between her and M. Fould—Her supposed charity and generosity—Ten tickets for a charity concert—How she made them into twenty—How she could have made them into a hundred—Baron Taylor puzzled—Her manner of giving presents—Beauvallet's precaution with regard to one of her gifts—Alexandre Dumas the younger, wiser or perhaps not so wise in his generation—Rachel as a raconteuse—The story of her *début* at the Gymnase—What Rachel would have been as an actor instead of an actress—Her comic genius—Rachel's mother—What became of Rachel's money—Mama Félix as a pawnbroker—Rachel's trinkets—Two curious bracelets—Her first appearance before Nicholas I.—A dramatic recital in the open air—Rachel's opinion of the handsomest man in Europe—Rachel and Samson—Her obligations to him—How she repays them—How she goes to Berryer to be coached in the fable of "The Two Pigeons"—An anecdote of Berryer—Rachel's fear of a "warm reception" on the first night of "Adrienne Lecouvreur"—How she averts the danger—Samson as a man and as an actor—Petticoat-revolts at the Comédie-Française—Samson and Régnier as buffers—Their different ways of pouring oil upon the troubled waters—Mdlle. Sylvanie Plessy—A parallel between her and Sarah Bernhardt—Samson and Régnier's pride in their profession—The different character of that pride—"Apollo with a bad tailor, and who dresses without a looking-glass"—Samson gives a lesson in declamation to a procureur-impérial—The secret of Régnier's greatness as an actor—A lesson at the Conservatoire—Régnier on "make-up"—Régnier's opinion of genius on the stage—A mot of Augustine Brohan—Giovanni, the wigmaker of the Comédie-Française—His pride in his profession—M. Ancessy, the musical director, and his three wigs.

THERE were few authors of my time who came in contact with Rachel without writing about her; there were absolutely none who have represented her in her true character. Either her genius blinded them to her faults, or else they were content to perpetuate the popular belief in her amiability, good nature, generosity, etc. The fact is, that Rachel off the stage was made of very ordinary clay. She had few of the good qualities of her race, and a good many of the bad ones; she was greedy to a degree, and could be very spiteful. All these drawbacks, in the eyes of most of her biographers, were redeemed by her marvellous tragic abilities on the stage, by a wonderful "gift of the gab," by a "happy-go-lucky," "hail-fellow, well-met" manner off the stage to those whom she liked to propitiate. Nevertheless, there were times when she had not a single friend at the Comédie-Française, and though her champions attributed this hostility to jealousy of her great gifts, a moment's consideration would show us that such a feeling could scarcely have influenced the men who to a great extent shared her histrionic triumphs, viz. Beauvallet, Régnier, Provost, Samson, and least of all the latter. Still, all these would have willingly kept her out of the Comédie-Française after she had left it in a huff. She was difficult to get on with; her modesty, assumed in everyday life, was a sham, for woe to the host who, deceived by it, did not at once make her the queen of the entertainment! And, in reality, nothing in her warranted such a temporary elevation. She was witty in her way and after her kind—that is, she had the quick-wittedness of the French woman who is not an absolute fool, and who has for many years rubbed elbows with everything distinguished in art and literature. Notwithstanding this intimacy, I am doubtful whether she had ever read, let alone appreciated, any of the masterpieces by the writers of her own days that did not directly bear upon her profession. I exclude fiction—I mean narrative fiction, and especially that of a sensational kind, of which she was probably as fond as the meanest concierge and most romantic milliner-girl.

Nevertheless, provided one did not attempt to analyze it, the power of fascinating the coldest interlocutor was there. To their honour be it said, her contemporaries, especially the men, rarely made such an attempt at analysis. They applauded all she said (off and on the stage), they tolerated all she did, albeit that they paid the cost of many of her so-called "amiable tricks," which were mainly so many instances of greed and nothing else. One evening she was dining at Comte Duchâtel's, the minister of Louis-Philippe. The table was positively laden with flowers, but Rachel did not care much about them; what she wanted was the splendid silver centre-piece. But she was too clever to unmask her batteries at once, so she began by admiring the contents, then at last she came to the principal point. The host was either in one of his generous or foolish moods, and made her a present of it there and then. Rachel knew, though, that even with a grand seigneur like Comte Duchâtel, there are "les lendemains de l'enthousiasme," especially when he is a married man, whose wife does not willingly submit to have her home stripped of its art-treasures. The tragédienne came in a hackney cab; the comte offered to send her back in his carriage. She struck the iron while it was hot. "Yes, that will do admirably; there will be no fear of my being robbed of your present, which I had better take with me." "Perfectly, mademoiselle," replied the comte; "but you will send me back my carriage, won't you?"

Dr. Véron was despoiled with even less ceremony. Having taken a fancy to some silver saucers or cups in which the proprietor of the *Constitutionnel* offered ices to his visitors, she began by pocketing one, and never rested until she had the whole of the set. In short, everything was fish to her net. She made her friends give her bibelots and knickknacks of no particular value, to which she attached some particular legend—absolute inventions for the greatest part—in order to sell them for a thousand times their original cost. One day she noticed a guitar at the studio of one of her familiars. "Give me that guitar; people will think it is the one with which I earned my living on the Place Royale and on the Place de la Bastille." And as such it was sold by her to M. Achille Fould for a thousand louis. The great financier nearly fell into a fit when the truth was told to him at Rachel's death; he, in his turn, having wanted to "do a bit of business." In this instance no Christian suffered, because buyer and vendor belonged to the same race. Of course the panegyrists of Rachel, when the story came to their ears, maintained that the thousand louis were employed for some charitable purpose, without, however, revealing the particular quarter whither they went; but those who judged Rachel dispassionately could not even aver that her charity began at home, because, though she never ceased complaining of her brother's and her sisters' extravagance, both brother and sisters could have told very curious tales about the difficulty of making her loosen her purse-strings for even the smallest sums. As for Rachel's doing good by stealth and blushing to find it fame, it was all so much fudge. Contrary to the majority of her fellow-professionals, in the past as well as the present, she even grudged her services for a concert or a performance in aid of a deserving object, although she was not above swelling her own hoard by such entertainments.

The following instance, for the absolute truth of which I can vouch, is a proof of what I say. One day the celebrated Baron Taylor, who had been the director of the Comédie-Française, came to solicit her aid for a charity concert; I am not certain of the object, but believe it was in aid of the Christians in Persia or China. The tickets were to be a hundred francs each. Sontag, Alboni, Rosine Stoltz, Mario, Lablache, Vieuxtemps, and I do not know how many more celebrated artists had promised their services.

It was in 1850 when M. Arsène Houssaye was her director, and I am particular about giving the year, because Rachel refused on the pretext that her director would never give her leave to appear on any other stage. Now, it so happened that no woman ever had a more devoted friend and chivalrous champion than Rachel had in Arsène Houssaye. His friendship for her was simply idolatry, and I verily believe that if she had asked him to stand on his head to please her, he would have done so, at the risk of making himself supremely ridiculous—he who feared ridicule above everything, who was one of the most sensible men of his time, who was and is the incarnation of good-nature, to whom no one in distress or difficulties ever appealed in vain.

Baron Taylor argued all this, but Rachel remained inflexible. "I am very sorry," he said at last, rising to go, "because I am positive that your name on the bill would have made a difference of several thousand francs in the receipts."

"Oh, if you only want my name," was the answer, "you may have it; you can make an apology at the eleventh hour for my absence on the score of sudden indisposition—the public at charity concerts are used to that sort of thing; besides, you will have so many celebrities that it will make very little difference. By-the-by"—as he was at the door—"I think my name is worth ten or twenty tickets." Taylor knew Rachel too well to be in the least surprised at the demand, and left ten tickets on the mantelpiece.

That same afternoon he met Count Walewski, and as a matter of course asked him to take some tickets.

"Very sorry, cher baron, but I have got ten already. You see, poor Rachel did not know very well how to get rid of the two hundred you burdened her with as a lady patroness; so she wanted me to have twenty, but I settled the matter with ten. As it is, it cost me a thousand francs."

Taylor did not say another word—he probably could not; he was struck dumb with astonishment at the quickness with which Rachel had converted the tickets into money. But what puzzled him still more was the fact of her having offered Walewski double the quantity of tickets he had given her. Where had she got the others from? He was coming to the conclusion that she had offered twenty in order to place ten, when he ran against Comte Le Hon, the husband of the celebrated Mdlle. Musselmans, the erstwhile Belgian ambassador to the court of Louis-Philippe, who averred frankly that he was the father of a family, though he had no children of his own.

Taylor thought he would try another chance, and was met with the reply, "Cher baron, I am very sorry, but I have just taken five tickets from Mdlle. Rachel. It appears that she is a lady patroness, and that they burdened her with two hundred; fortunately, she told me, people were exceedingly anxious to get them, and these were the last five."

"Then she had two hundred tickets after all," said Baron Taylor to himself, making up his mind to find out who had been before him with Rachel. But no one had been before him. The five tickets sold to Comte Le Hon were five of the ten she had sold to Comte Walewski. When the latter had paid her, she made him give her five tickets for herself and family, or rather for her four sisters and herself. Of Comte Le Hon she only took toll of one, which, wonderful to relate, she did not sell. That was Rachel's way of bestirring herself in the cause of charity.

"Look at the presents she made to every one," say the panegyrists. They forget to mention that an hour afterwards she regretted her generosity, and from that moment she never left off scheming how to get the thing back. Every one knew this. Beauvallet, to whom she gave a magnificent sword one day, instead of thanking her, said, "I'll have a chain put to it, mademoiselle, so as to fasten it to the wall of my dressing-room. In that way I shall be sure that it will not disappear during my absence." Alexandre Dumas the younger, to whom she made a present of a ring, bowed low and placed it back on her finger at once. "Allow me to present it to you in my turn, mademoiselle, so as to prevent you asking for it." She did not say nay, but carried the matter with one of her fascinating smiles. "It is most natural to take back what one has given, because what one has given was dear to us," she replied.

Between '46 and '53 I saw a great deal of Rachel, generally in the green-room of the Comédie-Française, which was by no means the comfortable or beautiful apartment people imagine, albeit that even in those days the Comédie had a collection of interesting pictures, busts, and statues worthy of being housed in a small museum. The chief ornament of the room was a large glass between the two windows, but if the apartment had been as bare as a barn, the conversation of Rachel would have been sufficient to make one forget all about its want of decoration; for, with the exception of the elder Dumas, I have never met any one, either man or woman, who exercised the personal charm she did. I have been told since that Bismarck has the same gift. I was never sufficiently intimate with the great statesman to be able to judge, having only met him three or four times, and under conditions that did not admit of fairly testing his powers in that respect, but I have an idea that the charm of both lay in their utter indifference to the effect produced, or else in their absolute confidence of the result of their simplicity of diction. Rachel's art of telling a story, if art it was, reminded one of that of the chroniclers of the *Niebelungen;* for notwithstanding her familiarity with Racine and Corneille, her vocabulary was exceedingly limited, and her syntax, if not her grammar, off the stage, not always free from reproach.

I do not pretend, after the lapse of so many years, to give these stories in her own language, or all of them; there are a few, however,' worth the telling, apart from the fascination with which she invested them.

One evening she said to me, "Do you know Poirson?"

I had known Poirson when he was director of the Gymnase. He afterwards always invited me to his soirées, one of which, curiously enough, was given on the Sunday before the Revolution of '48. So I said, "Yes, I know Poirson."

"Has he ever told you why he did not re-engage me?"

"Never."

"I'll tell you. People said it was because I did not succeed in 'La Vendéenne' of Paul Duport; but that was not the cause. It was something much more ridiculous; and now that I come to think of it, I am not sure that I ought to tell you, for you are an Englishman, and you will be shocked."

I was not shocked, I was simply convulsed with laughter, for Rachel, not content with telling the story, got up, and, gradually drawing to the middle of the room, enacted it. It was one of those ludicrous incidents that happen sometimes on the stage, which no amount of foresight on the part of the most skilful and conscientious manager or actor can prevent, but which almost invariably ruins the greatest masterpiece. There were about eight or nine actors and actresses in the room—Régnier, Samson, Beauvallet, etc. It was probably the most critical audience in Europe, but every one shook, and Mdlle. Anaïs Aubert went into a dead faint. Régnier often averred that if Rachel had been a man, she would have been the greatest comic actor that ever lived; and it is not generally known that she once played Dorine in "Tartuffe," and set the whole of the house into a perfect roar; but on that evening I became convinced that Rachel, in addition to her tragic gifts, was the spirit of Aristophanesque comedy personified. I am afraid, however, that I cannot tell the story, or even hint at it, beyond mentioning that Poirson is reported to have said that Rachel did not want a stage-manager, but a nurse to take care of her. The criticism was a cruel one, though justified by appearances. It was Mama Félix, and not her daughter, who was to blame. The child—she was scarcely more than that—had hurt herself severely, and instead of keeping her at home, she sent her to the theatre, "poulticed all over," as Rachel expressed it afterwards.

Mama Félix was the only one who was a match for her famous daughter in money matters. What the latter did with the enormous sums of money she earned has always been a mystery. As I have already said, they were not spent in charity. Nowadays, whatever other theatres may do, the Comédie-Française dresses its pensionnaires as well as its sociétaires from head to foot; it pays the bootmaker's as well as the wigmaker's bill, and the laundress's also. Speaking of the beginning of her career, which coincided with the end of Rachel's, Madeleine Brohan, whose language was often more forcible than elegant, remarked, "Dans ma jeunesse, on nous mettait toutes nues sur la scène; nous étions assez jolies pour cela." But Rachel's costumes varied so little throughout her career as to have required but a small outlay on her part. Nor could her ordinary dresses and furniture, which I happened to see in April, 1858, when they were sold by public auction at her apartments in the Place Royale, have made a considerable inroad on her earnings. The furniture was commonplace to a degree; such pictures and knickknacks as were of value had been given to her, or acquired in the manner I have already described; the laces and trinkets were, undoubtedly, not purchased with her own money. It is said that her brother Raphael was a spendthrift. He may have been, but he did not spend his celebrated sister's money; of that I feel certain. Then what became of it? I am inclined to think that Mdlle. Rachel dabbled considerably in stocks, and that, notwithstanding her shrewdness and sources of information, she was the victim of people cleverer than she was. At any rate, one thing is certain—she was nearly always hard up; and, after having exhausted the good will of all her male acquaintances and friends, compelled to appeal to her mother, who had made a considerable hoard for her other four sisters, and perhaps also for her scapegrace son; for, curiously enough, with Mama Félix every one of her children was a goddess or god, except *the goddess*. This want of appreciation on the mother's part reminds me of a story told to me by Meisonnier. His granddaughter, on her fifteenth or sixteenth birthday, had a very nice fan given to her. The sticks were exquisitely carved in ivory, and must have cost a pretty tidy sum, but the fan itself, of black gauze, was absolutely plain. The donor probably intended the grandfather's art to enhance the value of the present, and the latter was about to do so, when the young lady stopped him with the cry, "Voilà qu'il va me gâter mon éventail avec ses mannequins!" The irony of non-appreciation by one's nearest and dearest could no further go.

Mama Félix, then, was very close-fisted, and would never lend her daughter any money, except on very good security, namely, on her jewels. In addition to this, she made her sign an undertaking that if not redeemed at a certain date they would be forfeited; and forfeited they were, if the loan and interest were not forthcoming at the stipulated time, notwithstanding the ravings of Rachel. This would probably account for the comparatively small quantity of valuable jewellery found after her death.

Some of the ornaments I have seen her wear had an artistic value utterly apart from their cost, others were so commonplace and such evident imitations as to have been declined by the merest grisette. One day I noticed round her wrist a peculiar bracelet. It was composed of a great number of rings, some almost priceless, others less valuable but still very artistic, others again possessing no value whatsoever, either artistically or otherwise. I asked her to take it off, and found it to be very heavy, so heavy that I remarked upon it. "Yes," she replied, "I cannot wear two of the same weight, so I am obliged to wear the other in my pocket." And out came the second, composed of nearly double the number of rings of the first. I was wondering where all those rings came from, but I refrained from asking questions. I was enabled to form my own conclusions a little while afterwards, in the following way.

While we were still admiring the bracelet, Rachel took from her finger a plain gold hoop, in the centre of which was an imperial eagle of the same metal. "This was given to me by Prince Louis Napoleon," she said, "on the occasion of my last journey to London.

He told me that it was a souvenir from his mother, and that he would not have parted with it to any one else but me."

I cannot remember the exact date of this conversation, but it must have been shortly after the Revolution, when the future emperor had just landed in France. About three or four weeks afterwards we were talking to Augustine Brohan, who had just returned from London, where she had fulfilled an engagement of one or two months. Rachel was not there that night, but some one asked her if she had seen Prince Louis in London. "Yes," she replied; "he was going away, and he gave me a present before he went." Thereupon she took from her finger a ring exactly like that of Rachel's. "He told me it was a souvenir from his mother, and that he would not have parted with it to any one but me."

We looked at one another and smiled. The prince had evidently a jeweller who manufactured "souvenirs from his mother" by the dozen, and which he, the prince, distributed at that time, "in remembrance of certain happy hours." The multiplicity of the rings on Rachel's wrist was no longer a puzzle to me. I was thinking of the story in the "Arabian Nights," where the lady with the ninety-eight rings bewitches the Sultans Shariar and Shahzenan, in spite of the jealousy and watchfulness of the monster to whom she belongs, and so makes the hundred complete.

Among the many stories Rachel told me there is one not generally known—that of her first appearance before Nicholas I. Though she was very enthusiastically received in London, and though she always spoke gratefully of the many acts of kindness shown her there, I am inclined to think that she felt hurt at the want of cordiality on the part of the English aristocracy when they invited her to recite at their entertainments. This may be a mere surmise of mine; I have no better grounds for it than an expression of hers one day when we were discussing London society. "Oui, les Anglais, ils sont très aimables, mais ils paraissent avoir peur des artistes, comme des bêtes sauvages, car ils vous parquent comme elles au Jardin des Plantes." I found out afterwards that it was a kind of grudge she bore the English for having invariably improvised a platform or enclosure by means of silken ropes. Certain is it that, beyond a few casual remarks at long intervals upon London, she seemed reluctant to discuss the subject with me. Not so with regard to Potsdam after her return whence in August, '51. In the beginning of July of that year she told me that she had a special engagement to appear before the court on the 13th of that month. I did not see her until a few weeks after she came back, and then she gave me a full account of the affair. I repeat, after the lapse of so many years, I cannot reproduce her own words, and I could not, even half an hour after her narrative, have reproduced the manner of her telling it; but I can vouch for the correctness of the facts.

"About six o'clock, Raphael [her brother], who was to give me my cues, and I arrived at Potsdam, where we were met by Schneider, who had made the engagement with me. You know, perhaps, that Schneider had been an actor himself, that afterwards he had been promoted to the directorship of the Royal Opera House, and that now he is the private reader to the king, with the title of privy or aulic councillor.

"Schneider is a very nice man, and I have never heard a German speak our language so perfectly. Perhaps it was as well, because I dread to contemplate what would have been the effect upon my nerves and ears of lamentations in Teutonized French."

"Why lamentations?" I asked.

"Ah, nous voilà!" she replied. "You remember I was in mourning. The moment I stepped out of the carriage, he exclaimed, 'But you are all in black, mademoiselle.' 'Of course I am,' I said, 'seeing that I am in mourning.' 'Great Heaven! what am I to do? Black is not admitted at court on such occasions.' I believe it was the birthday of the Czarina, but of course I was not bound to know that.

"There was no time to return to Berlin, and least of all to get a dress from there, so Raphael and he put their heads together; the result of which conference was my being bundled rather than handed into a carriage, which drove off at full speed to the Château de Glinicke. I could scarcely catch a glimpse of the country around Potsdam, which seemed to me very lovely.

"When we got to Glinicke, which belongs to Prince Charles, I was handed over to some of the ladies-in-waiting of the princess. Handed over is the only word, because I felt more like a prisoner than anything else, and they tried to make 'little Rachel' presentable according to their lights. One of them, after eyeing me critically, suggested my wearing a dress of hers. In length it would have done very well, only I happen to be one of the lean kine, and she decidedly was not, so that idea had to be abandoned. They may be very worthy women, these German ladies, but their inventiveness with regard to dress is absolutely *nil*. When the idea suggested by the first lady turned out to be impracticable, they were à bout de ressources. You may gather from this, mon ami, that the beginning and the end of their stratégie de la toilette are not far apart. There was one thing that consoled me for this sudden exhaustion of their limited ingenuity. Between the half-dozen—for they were half a dozen—they could not find a single word when the first and only device proved impossible of realization. Had there been the same number of French women assembled, it would have been a kind of little madhouse; in this instance there was a deep silence for at least ten minutes, eventually broken by the knocking at the door of one of the maids, with Herr Schneider's compliments, and wishing to know what had been decided upon. The doleful answer brought him to the room, and what six women could not accomplish, he, like the true artist, accomplished at once. 'Get Mdlle. Rachel a black lace mantilla, put a rose in her hair, and give her a pair of white gloves.' In less than ten minutes I was ready, and in another ten, Raphael, Schneider, and I embarked on a pretty little steam-yacht lying ready at the end of the magnificent garden for 'l'Île des Pâons' (Pfauen-Insul, Peacock Island), where we landed exactly at eight. But my troubles and surprises were not at an end. I made sure that there would be at least a tent, an awning, or a platform for me to stand under or upon. Ah, oui! not the smallest sign of either. 'Voilà votre estrade,' said Schneider, pointing to a small lawn, separated from the rest of the gardens by a gravelled walk three or four feet wide. I declined at once to act under such conditions, and insisted upon being taken back immediately to the station, and from thence to Berlin. Poor Schneider was simply in despair. In vain did he point out that to any one else the total absence of scenery and adjuncts might prove a drawback, but that to me it would only be an additional advantage, as it would bring into greater relief my own talent; I would not be persuaded. Finding that it was fruitless to play upon my vanity as an artist, he appealed to me as a femme du monde. 'The very absence of all preparations,' he said, 'proves that their majesties have not engaged Mdlle. Rachel of the Comédie-Française to give a recitation, but invited Mdlle. Rachel Félix to one of their soirées. That Mdlle. Rachel Félix should be kind enough, after having partaken of a cup of tea, to recite something, would only be another proof of her well-known readiness to oblige;' and so forth. Let me tell you, mon cher, that I have rarely met with a cleverer diplomatist, and Heaven knows I have seen a lot who imagined themselves clever. They could not hold a candle to this erstwhile actor; nevertheless I remained as firm as a rock, though I was sincerely distressed on Schneider's account."

"What made you give in at last?" I inquired. "Was it the idea of losing the magnificent fee?"

"For once you are mistaken," she laughed, "though Schneider himself brought that argument to bear as a big piece of artillery. 'Remember this, mademoiselle,' he said, when he could think of nothing else; 'remember this—that this soirée may be the means of putting three hundred thousand or four hundred thousand francs into your pocket. You yourself told me just now on board the yacht that you were very anxious for an engagement at St. Petersburg. I need scarcely tell you that, if you refuse to appear before their majesties to-night, I shall be compelled to state the reason, and Russia will be for ever closed to you. Apart from pecuniary considerations, it will be said by your enemies—and your very eminence in your profession causes you to have many—that you failed to please the Empress. After all, the fact that all the ordinary surroundings of the actress have been neglected proves that you are not looked upon as an actress by them, but as une femme du monde.'"

"That persuaded you?" I remarked.

"Not at all."

"Then it was the money."

"Of course you would think so, even if I swore the contrary a hundred times over; but if you were to guess from now till to-morrow, you would never hit upon the real reason that made me stay."

"Well, then, I had better not try, and you had better tell me at once."

"Strange as it may seem to you, it was neither the gratification of being treated en femme du monde nor the money that made me stay; it was the desire to see what I had been told was the handsomest man in Europe. I did see him, and for once in a way rumour had not exaggerated the reality. I had scarcely given my final consent to Schneider, when the yacht carrying the imperial and royal families came alongside the island, and the illustrious passengers landed, amidst an avalanche of flowers thrown from the other vessels. Schneider presented me to the King, who was also good-looking, and the latter presented me to the Czar.

"Immediately afterwards the recital began. At the risk of taxing your credulity still further, I may tell you that I, Rachel, who never knew what 'stage fright' meant, felt nervous. That man to me looked like a very god. Fortunately for my reputation, the shadows of night were gathering fast; in another twenty minutes it would be quite dark, and I felt almost rejoiced that my audience could scarcely distinguish my features. On the other hand, Raphael, who only knew the part of Hippolyte by heart, and who was obliged to read the others, declared that he could not see a line, and candles had to be brought in. It was a glorious evening, but there was a breeze nevertheless, and as fast as the candles were lighted, they were extinguished by the wind. To put ordinary lamps on the lawn at our feet was not to be thought of for a moment; luckily one of the functionaries remembered that there were some candelabra with globes inside, and by means of these a kind of 'float' was improvised. Still the scene was a curious one. Raphael close to me on the edge of the lawn, with one of these candelabra in his left hand. Behind, to the left and right of us, a serried crowd of generals, court dignitaries in magnificent uniforms. In front, and separated by the whole width of a gravel walk, the whole group of sovereigns and their relations, and behind them the walls of the mansion, against which the tea-table had been set, and around which stood the ladies-in-waiting of the Queen of Prussia and the Empress of Russia. A deep silence around, only broken by the soft soughing of the wind in the trees and the splashing of a couple of fountains near, playing a dirge-like accompaniment to Raphael's and my voice.

"The recital lasted for nearly an hour; if I had liked I could have kept them there the whole night, for never in my career have I had such an attentive, such a religiously attentive, audience. The King was the first to notice my fatigue, and he gave the signal for my leaving off by coming up and thanking me for my efforts. The Emperor followed his example, and stood chatting to me for a long while. In a few minutes I was the centre of a circle which I am not likely to forget as long as I live. Then came the question how Raphael and I were to get back to Berlin. The last train was gone. But Schneider simply suggested a special, and a mounted messenger was despatched then and there to order it. After everything had been arranged for my comfortable return, the sovereigns departed as they had come, only this time the yacht, as well as the others on the lake, were splendidly illuminated. This was my first appearance before Nicholas I."

There was no man to whom Rachel owed more than to Samson, or even as much; but for him, and in spite of her incontestable genius, the Comédie-Français might have remained closed to her for many years, if not for ever. Frédérick Lemaître and Marie Dorval were undoubtedly, in their own way, as great as she, yet the blue riband of their profession never fell to their lot. And yet, when she had reached the topmost rung of the ladder of fame, Rachel was very often not only ungrateful to him, but her ingratitude showed itself in mean, spiteful tricks. When Legouvé's "Adrienne Lecouvreur" was being cast, Samson, who had forgiven Rachel over and over again, was on such cool terms with her that the authors feared he would not accept the part of the Prince de Bouillon. Nevertheless, Samson, than whom there was not a more honourable and conscientious man on or off the stage, accepted; he would not let his resentment interfere with what he considered his duty to the institution of which he was so eminent a member. This alone ought to have been sufficient to heal the breach between the tutor and the pupil; any woman with the least spark of generosity, in the position of Rachel towards Samson, would have taken the first step towards a reconciliation. Rachel, as will be seen directly, was perfectly conscious of what she ought to do under the circumstances; she was too great an actress not to have studied the finer feelings of the human heart, and yet she did not do it. On the contrary, she aggravated matters. Every one knows the fable of "The Two Pigeons" which Adrienne recites at the soirée of the Princesse de Bouillon. Now, it so happened that the great barrister and orator, Berryer, was considered a most charming reciter of that kind of verse. Berryer, a most simple-minded man, took special delight in sharing the most innocent games of young children. He was especially fond of the game of "forfeits;" and so great was his fame as a diseur, that the penalty generally imposed upon him was the reciting of a fable. But great diseur as he was, he himself acknowledged that Samson could have given him a lesson.

At every new part she undertook, Rachel was in the habit of consulting with her former tutor; this time she went to consult Berryer instead, and, what was worse, took pains that every one should hear of it. "Then my heart smote me," she said afterwards, when by one of those irresistible tricks of hers she had obtained her tutor's pardon once more. It was as deliberate a falsehood as she ever uttered in her life, which in Rachel's case means a good deal. The fact was, the affair, as I have already said, had been bruited about, mainly by herself at first; the public showed a disposition to take Samson's part, and she felt afraid of a " warm reception " on the first night.

Under these circumstances she had recourse to one of her wiles, which, for being theatrical, was not less effective. At the first rehearsal, when Adrienne has to turn to Michonnet, saying, " This is my true friend, to whom I owe everything," she turned, not to Régnier, who played Michonnet, and to whom the words are addressed, but to Samson, at the same time holding out her hand to him. Samson, who, notwithstanding all their disagreements, felt very proud of his great pupil, who was, moreover, of a very affectionate disposition, notwithstanding his habitual reserve, fell into the trap. He took her proffered hand; then she flung herself into his arms, and the estrangement was at an end, for the time being. Rachel took great care to make the reconciliation as public as possible.

I was never very intimate with Samson, but the little I knew of him I liked. I repeat, he was essentially an honourable and honest man, and very tolerant with regard to the foibles of the fair sex. There was need for such tolerance in those days. Augustine Brohan, Sylvanie Plessy, Rachel, and half a dozen other women, all very talented, but all very wayward, made Buloz' life (he was the director of the Comédie-Française, as well as the editor of the *Revue* *des Deux Mondes*) a burden to him. He who could, and often did, dictate his will to men who already then were famous throughout Europe, frequently found himself powerless against women, who, however celebrated, were, with the exception of Rachel, nothing in comparison with the former. He was, it is true, overbearing to a degree, and disagreeable besides, but his temper proved of no avail with them; it only made matters worse. "Après tout," he said one day to Madame Allan, who was the most amenable of all, "je suis le maître ici." "Ça se peut, monsieur," was the answer, "mais nous sommes les contres maître." *

In nearly all such troubles Régnier and Samson had to act as buffers between the two contending parties; but, as Augustine Brohan explained once, the two were utterly different in their mode of casting oil upon the troubled waters. "Régnier," she said, "c'est le bon Dieu des Chrétiens, qui se fait très souvent mener par le nez par des mots. Du reste son nez s'y prête.† Samson c'est le Dieu juste, mais vengeur des Juifs, qui veut bien pardonner, mais seulement après soumission complète et entière. Samson ne vous promet pas le ciel, il vous offre des compensations solides ici bas."

It would be difficult to paint the contrast between two characters in fewer words. In 1845, when Mdlle. Sylvanie Plessy seceded from the Comédie-Française, Régnier wrote a kind epistle, recommending her to come and explain matters either personally or by letter. "Let your letter be kind and affectionate, and

---

* The play upon the word is scarcely translatable. "Contre-maître" in the singular means foreman; as it is used here it means against the master.—EDITOR.

† Régnier's nose was always a subject of jokes among his fellow-actors. "It is not because it is large," said Beauvallet, "but because it is his principal organ of speech."—EDITOR.

be sure that things will right themselves better than you expect."

Samson also wrote, but simply to say that if she did not come back *at once* all the terrors of the law would be invoked against her. Which was done. The Comédie-Française instituted proceedings, claiming two hundred thousand francs damages, and twenty thousand francs "à titre de provision." * The court cast Mdlle. Plessy in six thousand francs *provision*, deferring judgment on the principal claim. Two years later Mdlle. Plessy returned and re-entered the fold. Thanks to Samson, she did not pay a single farthing of damages, and the Comédie bore the costs of the whole of the lawsuit.†

Both Samson and Régnier were very proud of their profession, but their pride showed itself in different ways. Régnier would have willingly made every one an actor—that is, a good actor; he was always teaching a great many amateurs, staging and superintending their performances. Samson, on the other hand, had no sympathy whatsoever with that kind of thing, and could rarely be induced to give it aid, but he was very anxious that every public speaker should study elocution. "Eloquence and elocution are two different things," he said; "and the eloquent man who does not study elocution, is like an Apollo with a bad tailor, and who dresses without a looking-glass. I go further still, and say that every one ought to learn how to speak, not necessarily with the view of amusing his

* Damages claimed by one of the parties, pending the final verdict.—EDITOR.

† Curiously enough, it was Emile Augier's "Aventurière" that caused Mdlle. Plessy's secession, just as it did thirty-five years later, in the case of Mdlle. Sarah Bernhardt.—EDITOR.

friends and acquaintances, but with the view of not annoying them. I am a busy man, but should be glad to devote three hours a week to teach the rising generation, and especially the humbler ones, how to speak."

In connection with that wish of Samson, that every man whose duties compelled him, or who voluntarily undertook to speak in public, should be a trained elocutionist, I remember a curious story of which I was made the recipient quite by accident. It was in the year '60, one morning in the summer, that I happened to meet Samson in the Rue Vivienne. We exchanged a few words, shook hands, and each went his own way. In the afternoon I was sitting at Tortoni's, when a gentleman of about thirty-five came up to me. "Monsieur," he said, "will you allow me to ask you a question?" "Certainly, monsieur, if it be one I can answer," I replied. "I believe," he said, "that I saw you in the Rue Vivienne this morning talking to some one whose name I do not know, but to whom I am under great obligations. I was in a great hurry and in a cab, and before I could stop the cabman both of you had disappeared. Will you mind telling me his name?" "I recollect being in the Rue Vivienne and meeting with M. Samson of the Comédie-Française," I answered. "I thought so," remarked my interlocutor. "Allow me to thank you, monsieur." With this he lifted his hat and went out.

The incident had slipped my memory altogether, when I was reminded of it by Samson himself, about three weeks afterwards, in the green-room of the Comédie-Française. I had been there but a few moments when he came in. "You are the man who betrayed me," he said with a chuckle. "I have been cudgelling my brain for the last three weeks as to who it could have been, for I spoke to no less than half a dozen friends and acquaintances in the Rue Vivienne on the morning I met you, and they all wear imperials and moustaches. A nice thing you have done for me; you have burdened me with a grateful friend for the rest of my life!"

And then he told me the story, how two years before he had been at Granville during the end of the summer; how he had strolled into the Palais de Justice and heard the procureur-impérial make a speech for the prosecution, the delivery of which would have disgraced his most backward pupil at the Conservatoire. "I was very angry with the fellow, and felt inclined to write him a letter, telling him that there was no need to torture the innocent audience, as well as the prisoner in the dock. I should have signed it. I do not know why I did not, but judge of my surprise when, the same evening at dinner, I found myself seated opposite him. I must have scowled at him, and he repaid scowl for scowl. It appears that he was living at the hotel temporarily, while his wife and child were away. I need not tell you the high opinion our judges have of themselves, and I dare say he thought it the height of impertinence that I, a simple mortal, should stare at him. I soon came to the conclusion, however, that if I wanted to spare my fellow-creatures such an infliction as I had endured that day, I ought not to arouse the man's anger. So I looked more mild, then entered into conversation with him. You should have seen his face when I began to criticize his tone and gestures. But he evidently felt that I was somewhat of an authority on the subject, and at last I took him out on the beach and gave him a lesson in delivering a speech, and left him there without revealing my name. Next morning I went away, and never set eyes on him again until three weeks ago, when he left his card, asking for an interview. He is a very intelligent man, and has profited by the first lesson. During the three days he remained in Paris I gave him three more. He says that if ever I get into a scrape, he'll do better than defend me—prosecute me, and I'm sure to get off."

I have never seen Samson give a lesson at the Conservatoire, but I was present at several of Régnier's, thanks to Auber, whom I knew very well, and who was the director, and to Régnier himself, who did not mind a stranger being present, provided he felt certain that the stranger was not a scoffer. I believe that Samson would have objected without reference to the stranger's disposition; at any rate, Auber hinted as much, so I did not prefer my request in a direct form.

I doubt, moreover, whether a lesson of Samson to his pupils would have been as interesting to the outsider as one of Régnier's. Of all the gifts that go to the making of a great actor, Régnier had naturally only two—taste and intelligence; the others were replaced by what, for want of a better term, one might call the tricks of the actor; their acquisition demanded constant study. For instance, Régnier's appearance off the stage was absolutely insignificant; his voice was naturally husky and indistinct, and, moreover, what the French call nasillarde, that is, produced through the nose. His features were far from mobile; the eyes were not without expression, but these never twinkled with merriment nor shone with passion.

Consequently the smallest as well as largest effect necessary to the interpretation of a character had to be thought out carefully beforehand, and then to be tried over and over again materially. Each of his inflections had to be timed to a second; but when all this was accomplished, the picture presented by him was so perfect as to deceive the most experienced critic, let alone an audience, however intelligent. In fact, but for his own frank admission of all this, his contemporaries and posterity would have been never the wiser, for, to their honour be it said, his fellow-actors were so interested in watching him "manipulate himself," as they termed it, as to never breathe a word of it to the outside world. They all acknowledged that they had learned something from him during rehearsal. For instance, in one of his best-known characters, that of the old servant in Madame de Girardin's "La Joie fait peur," * there is a scene which, as played by Régnier and Delaunay, looked to the spectator absolutely spontaneous. The smallest detail had been minutely regulated. It is where the old retainer, while dusting the room, is talking to himself about his young master, Lieutenant Adrien Desaubiers, who is reported dead.

"I can see him now," says Noël, who cannot resign himself to the idea; "I can see him now, as he used to come in from his long walks, tired, starving, and shouting before he was fairly into the house. 'Here I am, my good Noël; I am dying with hunger. Quick!

---

* There are several English versions of the play, and I am under the impression that the late Tom Robertson was inspired by it when he adapted "Caste." I allude to that scene in the third act, where George d'Alroy returns unexpectedly, and where Polly Eccles breaks the news to her sister.—EDITOR.

an omelette.'" At that moment the young lieutenant enters the room, and having heard Noël's last sentence, repeats it word for word.

Short as was the sentence, it had been arranged that Delaunay should virtually cut it into four parts.

At the words, "*It is I*," Régnier shivered from head to foot; at "*Here I am, my good Noël,*" he lifted his eyes heavenwards, to make sure that the voice did not come from there, and that he was not labouring under a kind of hallucination; at the words, "*I am dying with hunger,*" he came to the conclusion that it was a real human voice after all; and at the final, "*Quick! an omelette,*" he turned round quickly, and fell like a log into the young fellow's arms.

I repeat, the whole of the scene had been timed to the fraction of a second; nevertheless, on the first night, Régnier, nervous as all great actors are on such occasions, forgot all about his own arrangements, and, at the first sound of Delaunay's voice, was so overcome with emotion that he literally tumbled against the latter, who of course was not prepared to bear him up, and had all his work to do to keep himself from falling also. Meanwhile Régnier lay stretched at full length on the stage, and the house broke into tumultuous applause.

"That was magnificent," said Delaunay after the performance. "Suppose we repeat the thing to-morrow?"

But Régnier would not hear of it; he stuck to his original conception in four tempi. He preferred trusting to his art rather than to the frank promptings of nature.

That is why a lesson of Régnier to his pupils was so

interesting to the outsider. The latter was, as it were, initiated into all the resources the great actor has at his command wherewith to produce his illusion upon the public. Among Régnier's pupils those were his favourites who never allowed themselves to be carried away by their feelings, and who trusted to these resources as indicated to them by their tutor. He was to a certain extent doubtful of the others. "Feelings vary; effects intelligently conceived, studied, and carried out ought never to vary," he said. Consequently it became one of his theories that those most plentifully endowed with natural gifts were not likely to become more perfect than those who had been treated niggardly in that respect, provided the vocation and the perseverance were there. The reverse of Samson, who was proudest of Rachel, Régnier was never half as proud of M. Coquelin as of others who had given him far more trouble. Augustine Brohan explained the feeling in her own inimitable way. Régnier est comme le grand seigneur qui s'énamourache d'une paysanne à qui il faut tout enseigner; si moi j'étais homme, j'aimerais mieux une demoiselle de bonne famille, qui n'aurait pas besoin de tant d'enseignement."

Mdlle. Brohan exaggerated a little bit. Régnier's pupils were not peasant children, to whom he had to teach everything; a great many, like Coquelin, required very little teaching, and all the others had the receptive qualities which make teaching a pleasure. The latter, boys and girls, had to a certain extent become like Régnier himself, "bundles of tricks," and, what is perhaps not so surprising to students of psychology and physiology, their features had contracted a certain likeness to his. At the first blush one might have mistaken them for his children. And they might have been, for the patience he had with them. It was rarely exhausted, but he now and then seemed to be waiting for a new supply. At such times there was a frantic clutch at the shock, grey-haired head, or else a violent blowing of the perky nose in a large crimson chequered handkerchief, its owner standing all the while on one leg; the attitude was irresistibly comic, but the pupils were used to it, and not a muscle of their faces moved.

Those who imagine that Régnier's courses were merely so many lessons of elocution and gesticulation would be altogether mistaken. Régnier, unlike many of his great fellow-actors of that period, had received a good education; he had been articled to an architect, he had even dabbled in painting, and there were few historical personages into whose characters he had not a thorough insight. He was a fair authority upon costume and manners of the Middle Ages, and his acquaintance with Roman and Greek antiquities would have done credit to many a professor. He was called "le comédien savant" and "le savant comédien." As such, whenever a pupil failed to grasp the social or political importance of one of the *dramatis personæ* of Racine's or Corneille's play, there was sure to be a disquisition, telling the youngster all about him, but in a way such as to secure the attention of the listener —a way that might have aroused the envy of a university lecturer. The dry bones of history were clothed by a man with an eye for the picturesque.

"Who do you think Augustus was?" he said one day when I was present to the pupil, who was declaiming some lines of "Cinna." "Do you think he was the concierge or le commissionnaire du coin?" And forthwith there was a sketch of Augustus. Absolutely quivering with life, he led his listener through the streets of Rome, entered the palace with him, and once there, became Augustus himself. After such a scene he would frequently descend the few steps of the platform and drop into his armchair, exhausted.

Every now and then, in connection with some character of Molière or Regnard, there would be an anecdote of the great interpreter of the character, but an anecdote enacted, after which the eyes would fill with tears, and the ample chequered handkerchief come into requisition once more.

Régnier was a great favourite with most of his fellow-actors and the employés of the Comédie-Française, but he was positively worshipped by Giovanni, the wigmaker of the establishment. They were in frequent consultation even in the green-room, the privilege of admission to which had been granted to the Italian Figaro. The consultations became most frequent when one of the members undertook a part new to him. It was often related of Balzac that he firmly believed in the existence of the characters his brain had created. The same might be said of Régnier with regard to the characters created by the great playwrights of his own time and those of the past. Of course, I am not speaking of those who had an historical foundation. But Alceste, Harpagon, Georges Dandin, Sganarelle, and Scapin were as real to him as Orestes and Œdipus, as Augustus and Mohammed. He would give not only their biographies, but describe their appearance, their manners, their gait, and even their complexion. The first time I heard him do so, I made sure that he was trying to mystify Giovanni; but Rachel, who was present, soon undeceived me. And the Italian would sit listening reverently, then start up and exclaim, "Ze sais ce qu'il vous faut, Monsu Régnier, ze vais faire oune parruque à étonner Molière lui-même." And he kept his word, because he considered that the wig contributed as much to, or detracted from, the success of an actor as his diction, and more than his clothes. When Delaunay became a sociétaire his first part was that of the lover in M. Viennet's "Migraine." "Voilà Monsu Delaunay, oune véritable parruque di sociétaire. Zouez à présent, vous êtes sour de votre affaire."

One day Beauvallet found him standing before the window of Brandus, the music-publisher in the Rue de Richelieu. He was contemplating the portrait of Rossini, and he looked sad.

"What are you standing there for, Giovanni?" asked Beauvallet.

"Ah, Monsu Bouvallet, I am looking at the portrait of Maëstro Giovanni Rossini, and when I think that his name is Giovanni like mine, when I see that abominable wig which looks like a grass-plot after a month of drought, I feel ashamed and sad. But I will go and see him, and make him a wig for love or money that will take twenty years off his age." He went, but Rossini would not hear of it, or rather Madame Rossini put a spoke in his wheel. Giovanni never mentioned his name again. It was Ligier who brought Giovanni to Paris, and for a quarter of a century he worked unremittingly for the glory of the Comédie-

Française, and when one of the great critics happened to speak favourably of the "make-up" of an actor, as Paul de St. Victor did when Régnier " created Noël," Giovanni used to leave his card at his house. It was Giovanni who made the wigs for M. Ancessy, the musical director at the Odéon, who, under the management of M. Edouard Thierry, occupied the same position at the Comédie-Française. M. Ancessy was not only a good chef d'orchestre, but a composer of talent; but he had one great weakness—he was as bald as a billiard-ball and wished to pass for an Absalom. Giovanni helped him to carry out the deception by making three artistic wigs. The first was of very short hair, and was worn from the 1st to the 10th of the month; from the 11th to the 20th M. Ancessy donned one with hair that was so visibly growing as to cover his ears. From the 20th to the last day of the month his locks were positively flowing, and he never failed to say on that last evening in the hearing of every one, "What a terrible nuisance my hair is to me! I must have it cut to-morrow."

CHAPTER VII.

Two composers, Auber and Félicien David—Auber, the legend of his youthful appearance—How it arose—His daily rides, his love of women's society—His mot on Mozart's "Don Juan"—The only drawback to Auber's enjoyment of women's society—His reluctance to take his hat off—How he managed to keep it on most of the time—His opinion upon Meyerbeer's and Halévy's genius—His opinion upon Gérard de Nerval, who hanged himself with his hat on—His love of solitude—His fondness of Paris—His grievance against his mother for not having given him birth there—He refuses to leave Paris at the commencement of the siege—His small appetite—He proposes to write a new opera when the Prussians are gone—Auber suffers no privations, but has difficulty in finding fodder for his horse—The Parisians claim it for food—Another legend about Auber's independence of sleep—How and where he generally slept—Why Auber snored in Véron's company, and why he did not in that of other people—His capacity for work—Auber a brilliant talker—Auber's gratitude to the artists who interpreted his work, but different from Meyerbeer's—The reason why, according to Auber—Jealousy or humility—Auber and the younger Coquelin—"The verdict on all things in this world may be summed up in the one phrase, 'It's an injustice'"—Félicien David—The man—The beginnings of his career—His terrible poverty—He joins the Saint-Simoniens, and goes with some of them to the East—Their reception at Constantinople—M. Scribe and the libretto of "L'Africaine"—David in Egypt at the court of Mehemet-Ali—David's description of him—Mehemet's way of testing the educational progress of his sons—Woe to the fat kine—Mehemet-Ali suggests a new mode of teaching music to the inmates of the harem—Félicien David's further wanderings in Egypt—Their effect upon his musical genius—His return to France—He tells the story of the first performance of "Le Désert"—An ambulant box-office—His success—Fame, but no money—He sells the score of "Le Désert"—He loses his savings—"La Perle du Brésil" and the Coup-d'Etat—"No luck"—Napoleon III. remains his debtor for eleven years—A mot of Auber, and one of Alexandre Dumas père—The story of "Aïda"—Why Félicien David did not compose the music—The real author of the libretto.

I KNEW Auber from the year '42 or '43 until the day of his death. He and I were in Paris during the siege and the Commune; we saw one another frequently, and I am positive that the terrible misfortunes of his country shortened his life by at least ten years. For though at the beginning of the campaign he was close upon ninety, he scarcely looked a twelvemonth older than when I first knew him, nearly three decades before; that is, a very healthy and active old man, but still an old man. So much nonsense has been written about his perpetual youth, that it is well to correct the error. But the ordinary French public, and many journalists besides, could not understand an octogenarian being on horseback almost every day of his life, any more than they understood later on M. de Lesseps doing the same. They did not and do not know M. Mackenzie-Grieves, and half a dozen English residents in Paris of a similar age, who scarcely ever miss their daily ride. If they had known them, they might perhaps have been less loud in their admiration of the fact.

What added, probably, to Auber's reputation of possessing the secret of perpetual youth was his great fondness for women's society, his very handsome appearance, though he was small comparatively, and his faultless way of dressing. He was most charming with the fairer sex, and many of the female pupils of the Conservatoire positively doted on him. Though polite to a degree with men—and I doubt whether Auber could have been other than polite with no matter whom—his smiles, I mean his benevolent ones, for he could smile very sceptically, were exclusively reserved for women. When he heard Mozart's "Don Juan" for the first time, he said, "This is the music of a lover of twenty, and if a man be not an imbecile, he may always have in a little corner of his heart the sentiment or fancy that he is only twenty."

There was but one drawback to Auber's enjoyment of the society of women—he was obliged to take off his hat in their presence, and he hated being without that article of dress. He might have worn a skull-cap at home, though there was no necessity for it, as far as his hair was concerned, for up to the last he was far from bald; but he wanted his hat. He composed with his hat on, he had his meals with his hat on, and though he would have frequently preferred to take his seat in the stalls or balcony of a theatre, he invariably had a box, and generally one on the stage, in order to keep his hat on. He would often stand for hours on the balcony of his house in the Rue Saint-Georges with his hat on. "I never feel as much at home anywhere, not even in my own apartment, as in the synagogue," he said one day. He frequently went there for no earthly reason than because he could sit among a lot of people with his hat on. In fact, those frequent visits, coupled with his dislike to be bareheaded, made people wonder now and then whether Auber was a Jew. The supposition always made Auber smile. "That would have meant the genius of a Meyerbeer, a Mendelssohn, or a Halévy," he said. "No, I have been lucky enough in my life, but such good fortune as that never fell to my lot." For there was no man so willing—nay, anxious—to acknowledge the merit of others as Auber. But Auber was not a Jew, and his mania for keeping on his hat had nothing to do with his religion. It was simply a mania, and nothing more. When, in January, '55, Gérard de Nerval was found suspended from a lamp-post in the

Rue de la Vieille-Lanterne, he had his hat on his head; his friends, and even the police, pretended to argue from this that he had not committed suicide, but had been murdered. "A man who is going to hang himself does not keep his hat on," they said. "Pourquoi pas, mon Dieu?" asked Auber, simply. "If I were going to kill myself, I should certainly keep my hat on." In short, it was the only thing about Auber which could not be explained.

Auber was exceedingly fond of society, and yet he was fond of solitude also. Many a time his friends reported that, returning home late from a party, they found Auber standing opposite his house in the Rue Saint-Georges, with apparently no other object than to contemplate it from below. After his return to Paris from London, whither he had been sent by his father, in order to become conversant with English business habits, he never left the capital again, though at the end of his life he regretted not having been to Italy. It was because Rossini, who was one of his idols, had said "that a musician should loiter away some of his time under that sky." But almost immediately he comforted himself with the thought that Paris, after all, was the only city worth living in. "I was very fond of my mother, but I have one grievance against her memory. What did she want to go to Caen for just at the moment when I was about to be born? But for that I should have been a real Parisian." I do not think it made much difference, for I never knew such an inveterate Parisian as Auber. When the investment of Paris had become an absolute certainty, some of his friends pressed him to leave; he would not hear of it. They predicted discomfort, famine, and what-not. "The latter contingency will not affect me much, seeing that I eat but once a day, and very little then. As for the sound of the firing disturbing me, I do not think it will. It has often been said that the first part of my overture to 'Fra Diavolo' was inspired by the retreating tramp of a regiment; there may be some truth in it. If it be vouchsafed to me to hear the retreating tramp of the Germans, I will write an overture and an opera, which will be something different, I promise you."

I do not suppose that, personally, Auber suffered any privations during the siege. A man in his position, who required but one meal a day, and that a very light one, was sure to find it somewhere; but he had great trouble to find sufficient fodder for his old faithful hack, that had carried him for years, and when, after several months of scheming and contriving to that effect, he was forced to give it up as food for others, his cup of bitterness was full. "Ils m'ont pris mon vieux cheval pour le manger," he repeated, when I saw him after the event; "je l'avais depuis vingt ans." It was really a great blow to him.

There is another legend about Auber which is not founded upon facts, namely, that he was pretty well independent of sleep. It was perfectly true that he went to bed very late and rose very early, but most people have overlooked the fact that during the evening he had had a comfortable doze, of at least an hour and a half or two hours, at the theatre. He rarely missed a performance at the Opéra or Opéra-Comique, except when his own work was performed. And during that time he slumbered peacefully, "en homme du monde," said Nestor Roqueplan, "without snoring."

"I never knew what it meant to snore," said Auber, apologetically, "until I took to sleeping in Véron's box; and as it is, I do not snore now except under provocation. But there would be no possibility of sleeping by the side of Véron without snoring. You have to drown his, or else it would awaken you."

Auber was a brilliant talker, but he scarcely ever liked to exert himself except on the subject of music. It was all in all to him, and the amount of work he did must have been something tremendous. There are few students of the history of operatic music, no matter how excellent their memories, who could give the complete list of Auber's works by heart. We tried it once in 1850, when that list was much shorter than it is now; there was not a single one who gave it correctly. The only one who came within a measureable distance was Roger, the tenor.

In spite of his world-wide reputation, even at that time, Auber was as modest about his work as Meyerbeer, but he had more confidence in himself than the latter. Auber was by no means ungrateful to the artists who contributed to his success; "but I don't 'coddle' them, and put them in cotton-wool, like Meyerbeer," he said. "It is perfectly logical that he should do so. The Nourrits, the Levasseurs, the Viardot-Garcias, and the Rogers, are not picked up at street-corners; but bring me the first urchin you meet, who has a decent voice, and a fair amount of intelligence, and in six months he'll sing the most difficult part I ever wrote, with the exception of that of Masaniello. My operas are a kind of warming-pan for great singers. There is something in being a good warming-pan."

At the first blush, this sounds something like

jealousy in the guise of humility, but I am certain that there was no jealousy in Auber's character. Few men have been so uniformly successful, but he also had his early struggles, "when perhaps I did better work than I have done since." The last sentence was invariably trolled out when a pupil of the Conservatoire complained to him of having been unjustly dealt with. I remember Coquelin the younger competing for the "prize of Comedy" in '65 or '66. He did not get it, and when we came out of Auber's box at the Conservatoire, the young fellow came up to him with tears in his eyes. I fancy they were tears of anger rather than of sorrow.

"Ah, Monsieur Auber," he exclaimed, "that's an injustice."

"Perhaps so, my dear lad," replied Auber; "but remember that the verdict on all things in this world may be summed up in the words you have just uttered, 'It's an injustice.' Let me give you a bit of advice. If you mean to become a good Figaro, you must be the first to laugh at an injustice instead of weeping over it." Wherewith he turned his back upon the now celebrated comedian. In the course of these notes I shall have occasion to speak of Auber again.

Auber need not have generalized to young Coquelin; he might have cited one instance of injustice in his own profession, to which, fortunately, there was no parallel for at least thirty years. In the forties the critics refused to recognize the genius of Félicien David, just as they had refused to recognize the genius of Hector Berlioz. In the seventies they were morally guilty of the death of Georges Bizet, the composer of "Carmen."

I knew little or nothing of Hector Berlioz, but I frequently met Félicien David at Auber's. It was a pity to behold the man even after his success—a success which, however, did not put money in his purse. His moral sufferings, his material privations, had left their traces but too plainly on the face as well as on the mind. David had positively starved in order to buy the few books and the paper necessary to his studies, and yet he had the courage to say, "If I had to begin over again, I would do the same." The respectability that drives a gig when incarnated in parents who refuse to believe in the power of soaring of their offspring because they, the parents, cannot see the wings, has assuredly much to answer for. Flotow's father stops the supplies after seven years, because his son has not come up to time like a race-horse. Berlioz' father does not give him so long a shrift; he allows him three months to conquer fame. Félicien David had no father to help or to thwart him in his ambition. He was an orphan at the age of five, and left to the care of a sister, who was too poor to help him; but he had an uncle who was well-to-do, and who allowed him the magnificent sum of fifty francs per month—for a whole quarter—and then withdrew it, notwithstanding the assurance of Cherubini that the young fellow had the making of a great composer in him. And the worst is that these young fellows suffer in silence, while there are hundreds of benevolent rich men who would willingly open their purses to them. When they do reveal their distressed condition, it is generally to some one as poor as themselves. These rich men buy the autographs of the deceased genius for small or large sums which would have provided the struggling ones with comforts for days and days. I have before me such a letter which I bought for ten francs. I would willingly have given ten times the amount not to have bought it. It is written to a friend of his youth. "As for money," it says, "seeing that I am bound to speak of it, things are going from bad to worse. And it is very certain that in a little while I shall have to give it up altogether. I have been ill for three weeks with pains in the back, and fever and ague everywhere. I dare say that my illness was brought on by my worries, and by the bad food of the Paris restaurants, also by the constant dampness. Why am I not a little better off? I fancy that the slight comforts an artist may reasonably expect would do me a great deal of good. I am not speaking of the body, though it is a part of ourselves which considerably affects our intellect, but my imagination would be the better for it, for how can my brain, constantly occupied as it is with the worry of material wants, act unhampered? Really, I do not hesitate to say that poverty and privation kill the imagination."

They did not kill the imagination in David's case, but they undermined his constitution. It was at that period that he fell in with the Saint-Simoniens, to the high priest of which, M. Enfantin, who eventually became the chairman of the Paris, Lyons, and Mediterranean Railway Company, he took me many years later. After their dispersion, the group to which he belonged went to the East, and it is to this apparently fortuitous circumstance that the world owes not only "Le Désert," "La Perle du Brésil," and "L'Eden," but probably also Meyerbeer's "Africaine." Meyerbeer virtually acknowledged that but for David's scores, so replete with the poetry of the Orient, he would have never thought of such a subject for one of his operas. M. Scribe, on the other hand, always maintained that the idea emanated from him, and that it dated from 1847, when the composer was given the choice between "Le Prophète" and "L'Africaine," and chose the former. One might almost paraphrase the accusation of the wolf against the lamb in La Fontaine's fable. "M. Scribe, if you did not owe your idea to Félicien David, you owed it to Montigny, the director of the Gymnase, who in the thirties produced a play with a curious name, and a more curious plot, at the Ambigu-Comique." * One thing is certain, that "L'Africaine" was discarded, if ever it was offered, and would never have been thought of again but for Meyerbeer's intense and frankly acknowledged admiration of Félicien David's genius.

To return for a moment to Félicien David, whose melancholy vanished as if by magic when he related his wanderings in the East. I do not mean the poetical side of them, which inspired him with his great compositions, but the ludicrous one. I do not remember the dress of the Saint-Simoniens, I was too young at

* I have taken some pains to unearth this play. It was called "Amazampo; or, The Discovery of Quinine." The scene was laid in Peru in 1636. Amazampo, the chief of a Peruvian tribe, is in love with Maïda, who on her part is in love with Ferdinand, the son of the viceroy. Amazampo is heart-broken, and is stricken down with fever. In his despair and partial delirium he tries to poison himself, and drinks the water of a pool in which several trunks of a tree called *kina*, reported poisonous, have been lying for years. He feels the effect almost immediately, but not the effect he expected. He recovers, and takes advantage of his recovered health to forget his love passion, and to be avenged upon the oppressors of his country, many of whom are dying with fever. Lima becomes a huge cemetery. Then the wife of the viceroy is stricken down. Maïda wishes to save her, but is forestalled by Amazampo, who compels Dona Theodora to drink the liquor, and so forth. But Amazampo and Maïda die.— EDITOR.

the time to have noticed it, but am told it consisted of a blue tunic and trousers to match, a scarlet jersey, which buttoned at the back, and could not be undone except with the aid of some one else. It was meant to symbolize mutual dependence upon one another. "As far as Marseilles everything went comparatively well," said David; "we lived by giving concerts, and though the receipts were by no means magnificent, they kept the wolf from the door. Our troubles began at Constantinople. Whether they did not like our music, or ourselves, or our dresses, I have never been able to make out, but we were soon denounced to the authorities, and marched off to prison, though our incarceration did not last more than a couple of hours, thanks to our ambassador, Admiral Roussin. Our liberation, however, was conditional; we had to leave at once. We made our way to Smyrna, where my music seemed to meet with a little more favour. I performed every night, but in the open air, and some one took the hat round, just as if we had been a company of ambulant musicians to the manner born. We were, however, not altogether unhappy, for we had enough to eat and to drink, which with me, at any rate, was a paramount consideration. Up till then sufficient food had not been a daily item in my programme of life. My companions, nevertheless, became restless; they said they had not come to eat and drink and play music, but to convert the most benighted part of Europe to their doctrines; so we moved to Jaffa and Jerusalem, then to Alexandria, and finally to Cairo. By the time we got there, only three of us were left; the rest had gone homeward. Koenig-Bey had just at that moment undertaken the tuition of Mehemet-Ali's children—there were between sixty and seventy at that time; it was he who presented me to their father, with a view of my becoming the professor of music to the inmates of the harem. 'It is of no use to try to get you the appointment of professor of music to the young princes, because Mehemet, though intelligent enough, would certainly not hear of it. He would not think it necessary that a man-child should devote himself to so effeminate an accomplishment. I am translating his own thoughts on the subject, not mine. When I tell you that my monthly eport about their intellectual progress is invariably waved off with the words, "Tell me how much they have gained or lost in weight," you will understand that I am not speaking at random. The viceroy thinks that hard study should produce a corresponding decrease in weight, which is not always the case, for those more or less inclined to obesity make flesh in virtue of their sitting too much. Consequently the fat kine have a very bad time of it, and among the latter is one of the most intelligent boys, Mohammed-Said.'"

"Those who would infer from this," said David one day, referring to the same subject, "that Mehemet-Ali was lacking in intelligence, would commit a grave error. I am convinced, from the little I saw of him, that he was a man of very great natural parts. His features, though not absolutely handsome, were very striking and expressive. He was over sixty then, but looked as if he could bear any amount of fatigue. His constitution must originally have been an iron one. Instead of the Oriental repose which I expected, there was a kind of semi-European, semi-military stiffness about him, which, however, soon wore off in conversation. I say advisedly conversation, albeit that he did not understand a word of French, which was the only language I spoke, and that I could not catch a word of his. But in spite of Koenig-Bey's acting the interpreter, it was a conversation between us both. He seemed to catch the meaning of my words the moment they left my lips, and every now and then smiled at my remarks. He as it were read the thoughts that provoked them, and I do not wonder at his having been amused, for I myself was never so amused in my life. Perhaps you will be, when I tell you that I was not to see the ladies I had to teach; my instruction was to be given to the eunuchs, who, in their turn, had to transmit them to the viceroy's wives and daughters. Of course, I tried to point out the impossibility of such a system, but Mehemet-Ali shook his head with a knowing smile. That was the only way he would have his womenkind initiated into the beauties of Mozart and Mendelssohn. I need not tell you that the arrangement came to nought."

Nearly all these conversations which I have noted down here, without much attempt at transition, took place at different times. One day, when he was relating some experiences of his wanderings through the less busy haunts of Egypt, I happened to say, "After all, Monsieur David, they did you good; they inspired you with the themes of your most beautiful works."

It was a very bitter smile that played on his lips, but only for a moment; the next his face resumed its usual melancholy expression. "Yes, they did me good. Do you know what occurred on the eve of the first performance of 'Le Désert,' on the morrow of which I may say without undue pride that I found myself famous? Well, I will tell you. But for Azevedo, I should have gone supperless that night.* I met him on the Boulevards, and I almost forced him to take some tickets, for I was hungry and desperate. I had been running about that morning to dispose of some tickets for love or money, for what I feared most was an empty house. I had sold half a dozen, perhaps, but no one had paid me. Azevedo said, 'Yes, send me some this afternoon.' 'I can give them to you now,' I replied, 'for I carry my box office upon me.' Then he understood, and gave me the money. May God bless him for it, for ever and ever!

"Now would you like to hear what happened after the performance?" he continued. "The place was full and the applause tremendous. Next morning the papers were full of my name; I was, according to most of them, 'a revelation in music.' But for all that I was living in an attic on a fifth floor, and had not sufficient money to pay my orchestra, let alone to arrange for another concert. As for the score of 'Le Désert,' it went the round of every publisher but one, and was declined by all these. At last the firm of Escudier offered me twelve hundred francs for it, which, of course, I was glad to take. They behaved handsomely after all, because they arranged for a series of performances of it, which I was to direct at a fee of a thousand francs per performance. Those good Saint-Simoniens, the Pereiras, Enfantin, Michel Chevalier, had not lifted

---

* Alexis Azevedo, one of the best musical critics of the time, as enthusiastic in his likes as unreasoning in his dislikes. He became a fervent admirer of Félicien David.—EDITOR.

a finger to help me in my need; nevertheless, I was not going to condemn good principles on account of the men who represented them not very worthily. Do you know what was the result of this determination not to be unjust if others were? I embarked my little savings in a concern presided over by one of them. I lost every penny of it; since then I have never been able to save a penny."

Félicien David was right—he never made money; first of all, "because," as Auber said, "he was too great an artist to be popular;" secondly, because the era of cantatas and oratorios had not set in in France; thirdly, because he composed very slowly; and fourthly, "because he had no luck." The performances of his principal theatrical work were interrupted by the Coup-d'Etat. I am alluding to "La Perle du Brésil," which, though represented at the Opéra-Comique in 1850, only ran for a few nights there, divergencies of opinion having arisen between the composer and M. Emile Perrin, who was afterwards director of the Grand Opéra, and finally of the Comédie-Française. When it was revived, on November 22, 1851, the great event which was to transform the second republic into the second empire was looming on the horizon. In 1862, Napoleon III. made Félicien David an officer of the Légion d'Honneur; Louis-Philippe had bestowed the knighthood upon him in '46 or '47, after a performance of his "Christophe Colomb" at the Tuileries. When Auber was told of the honour conferred, he said, "Napoleon is worse than the fish with the ring of Polycrates; it did not take him eleven years to bring it back." Alexandre Dumas opined that "it was a pearl hid in a dunghill for a decade or more." When, towards the end of the Empire, a street near the projected opera building was named after Auber, and when he could see his bust on the façade of the building, the scaffolding of which had been removed, Auber remarked that the Emperor had been good enough to give him credit. "Now we are quits," he added, "for he was David's debtor for eleven years. At any rate, I'll do my best to square the account, so you need not order any hatbands until '79." When '79 came, he had been in his tomb for nearly eight years.

I wrote just now that Félicien David composed very slowly. But for this defect, if it was one, Verdi would have never put his name to the score of "Aïda." The musical encyclopedias will tell you that Signor Ghislanzoni is the author of the libretto, and that the khedive applied to Signor Verdi for an opera on an Egyptian subject. The first part of that statement is utterly untrue, the other part is but partially true. Signor Ghislanzoni is at best but the adapter in verse and translator of the libretto. The original in prose is by M. Camille du Locle, founded on the scenario supplied by Mariette-Bey, whom Ismaïl-Pasha had given *carte blanche* with regard to the music and words. Mariette-Bey intended from the very first to apply to a French playwright, when one night, being belated at Memphis in the Serapeum, and unable to return on foot, he all at once remembered an old Egyptian legend. Next day he committed the scenario of it to paper, showed it to the khedive, and ten copies of it were printed in Alexandria. One of these was sent to M. du Locle, who developed the whole in prose.

M. du Locle had also been authorized to find a French composer, but it is very certain that Mariette-

Bey had in his mind's eye the composer of " Le Désert," though he may not have expressly said so. At any rate, M. du Locle applied to David, who refused, although the "retaining fee" was fifty thousand francs. It was because he could not comply with the first and foremost condition, to have the score ready in six months at the latest. Then Wagner was thought of. It is most probable that he would have refused. To Mariette-Bey belongs the credit furthermore of having entirely stage-managed the opera.

Thus Félicien David, who had revealed "the East in music" to the Europeans, no more reaped the fruits of his originality than Decamps, who had revealed it in painting. Was not Auber right when he said to young Coquelin that the verdict on all things in this world might be summed up in the one phrase, "It's an injustice"?

CHAPTER VIII.

Three painters, and a school for pifferari—Gabriel Decamps, Eugène Delacroix, and Horace Vernet—The prices of pictures in the forties—Delacroix' find no purchasers at all—Decamps' drawings fetch a thousand francs each—Decamps not a happy man—The cause of his unhappiness—The man and the painter—He finds no pleasure in being popular—Eugène Delacroix—His contempt for the bourgeoisie—A parallel between Delacroix and Shakespeare—Was Delacroix tall or short?—His love of flowers—His delicate health—His personal appearance—His indifference to the love-passion—George Sand and Delacroix—A miscarried love-scene—Delacroix' housekeeper, Jenny Leguillou—Delacroix does not want to pose as a model for one of George Sand's heroes—Delacroix as a writer—His approval of Carlyle's dictum, "Show me how a man sings," etc.—His humour tempered by his reverence—His failure as a caricaturist—His practical jokes on would-be art-critics—Delacroix at home—His dress while at work—Horace Vernet's, Paul Delaroche's, Ingrès'—Early at work—He does not waste time over lunch—How he spent his evenings—His dislike of being reproduced in marble or on canvas after his death—Horace Vernet—The contrast between the two men and the two artists—Vernet's appearance—His own account of how he became a painter—Moral and mental resemblance to Alexandre Dumas père—His political opinions—Vernet and Nicholas I.—A bold answer—His opinion on the mental state of the Romanoffs—The comic side of Vernet's character—He thinks himself a Vauban—His interviews with M. Thiers—His admiration of everything military—His worship of Alfred de Vigny—His ineffectual attempts to paint a scene in connection with the storming of Constantine—Laurent-Jan proposes to write an epic on it—He gives a synopsis of the cantos—Laurent-Jan lives "on the fat of the land" for six months—A son of Napoleon's companion in exile, General Bertrand—The chaplain of "la Belle-Poule"—The first French priest who wore the English dress—Horace Vernet and the veterans of "la grande armée"—His studio during their occupancy of it as models—His budget—His hatred of pifferari—A professor—The Quartier-Latin revisited.

A FEW weeks ago,* when rummaging among old papers, documents, memoranda, etc., I came upon

* Written in 1882.

some stray leaves of a catalogue of a picture sale at the Hôtel Bullion * in 1845. I had marked the prices realized by a score or so of paintings signed by men who, though living at that time, were already more or less famous, and many of whom have since then acquired a world-wide reputation. There was only one exception to this—that of Herrera the Elder, who had been dead nearly two centuries, and whose name was, and is still, a household word among connoisseurs by reason of his having been the master of Velasquez. The handiwork of the irascible old man was knocked down for three francs seventy-five centimes, though no question was raised as to the genuineness of it in my hearing. It was a saint—the catalogue said no more,—and I have been in vain trying to recollect why I did not buy it. There must have been some cogent reason for my not having done so, for "the frame was no doubt worth double the money," to use an auctioneer's phrase. Was it suspicion, or what? At any rate, two years later, I heard that it had been sold to an American for fourteen thousand francs, though, after all, that was no guarantee of its value.

In those days it was certainly better to be a live artist than a dead one, for, a little further on among these pages, I came upon a marginal note of the prices fetched by three works of Meissonier, "Le Corps de Garde," "Une partie de piquet," and "Un jeune homme regardant des dessins," all of which had been in the salon of that year,† and each of which fetched

* The Hôtel Bullion was formerly the town mansion of the financier of that name, and situated in the Rue Coquillière.—EDITOR.

† The annual salon was held in the Louvre then; in 1849 it was transferred to the Tuileries. In 1850, '51, and '52 it was removed to the galleries of the Palais-Royal; in 1853 and '54 the salon was held

3000 francs. I should not like to say what their purchasing price would be to-day, allowing for the difference in the value of money. Further on still, there is a note of a picture by Alfred de Dreux, which realized a similar amount. Allowing for that same difference in the value of money, that work would probably not find a buyer now among real connoisseurs at 200 francs.* At the same time, the original sketch of David's "Serment du Jeu de Paume" did not find a purchaser at 2500 francs, the reserve price. A landscape by Jules André, a far greater artist than Alfred de Dreux, went for 300 francs, and Baron's "Oies du Frère Philippe" only realized 200 francs more. There was not a single "bid" for Eugène Delacroix' "Marc-Aurèle," and when he did sell a picture it was for 500 or 600 francs; nowadays it would fetch 100,000 francs. On the other hand, the drawings of Decamps' admirable "Histoire de Samson" realized 1000 francs each.

Yet Gabriel Decamps was a far unhappier man than Eugène Delacroix. The pictures rejected by the public became the "apples" of Delacroix' eyes, with which he would not part, subsequently, at any price, as in the case of his "Marino Faliero." Decamps, one day, while he lived in the Faubourg Saint-Dénis, deliberately destroyed one hundred and forty drawings, the like of which were eagerly bought up for a

in the Hôtel des Menus-Plaisirs, in the Faubourg Poissonnière, which became afterwards the storehouse for the scenery of the Grand Opéra. In 1855 the exhibition took place in a special annex of the Palais de l'Industrie; after that, it was lodged in the Palais itself.—EDITOR.

* Alfred de Dreux was not an unknown figure in London society. He came in 1848. He was a kind of Comte d'Orsay, and painted chiefly equestrian figures. After the Coup-d'Etat he returned to Paris, and was patronized by society, and subsequently by Napoleon III. himself, whose portrait he painted. He was killed in a duel, the cause of which has never been revealed.—EDITOR.

thousand francs apiece, though at present they would be worth four times that amount. Delacroix was content with his God-given genius; "he saw everything he had made, and behold it was very good." Decamps fumed and fretted at the supposed systematic neglect of the Government, which did not give him a commission. "You paint with a big brush, but you are not a great painter," said Sir Joshua to a would-be Michael-Angelo. To Gabriel Decamps the idea of being allowed or invited by the State to cover a number of yards of canvas or wall or ceiling was so attractive that he positively lost his sleep and his appetite over it. It was, perhaps, the only bitter drop in his otherwise tolerably full cup of happiness, but that one drop very frequently embittered the whole. He had many good traits in his character, though he was not uniformly good-tempered. There was an absolute indifference as to the monetary results of his calling, and an inherent generosity to those who "had fallen by the way." But he was something of a bear and a recluse, not because he disliked society, but because he deliberately suppressed his sociable qualities, lest he should arouse the suspicion of making them the stepping-stone to his ambition. No man ever misread the lesson, "Do well and fear not," so utterly as did Decamps. He was never tired of well-doing; and he was never tired of speculating what the world would think of it. There is not a single picture from his brush that does not contain an original thought; he founded an absolutely new school—no small thing to do. The world at large acknowledged as much, and yet he would not enjoy the fruits of that recognition, because it lacked the "official stamp." When Decamps consented to forget his real or fancied grievances he became a capital companion, provided one had a taste for bitter and scathing satire. I fancy Jonathan Swift must have been something like Gabriel Decamps in his daily intercourse with his familiars. But he rarely said an ill-natured thing of his fellow-artists. His strictures were reserved for the political men of his time, and of the preceding reign. The Bourbons he despised from the bottom of his heart, and during the Restauration his contempt found vent in caricatures which, at the moment, must have seared like a red-hot iron. He had kept a good many of these ephemeral productions, and, I am bound to say, they struck one afterwards as unnecessarily severe. "If they" (meaning the Bourbons) "had continued to reign in France," he said one day, "I would have applied for letters of naturalization to the Sultan."

Decamps was killed, like Géricault, by a fall off his horse, but long before that he had ceased to work. "I cannot add much to my reputation, and do not care to add to my store," he said. In 1855, the world positively rang with his name, but I doubt whether this universal admiration gave him much satisfaction. He exhibited more than fifty works at the Exposition Universelle of that year, a good many of which had been rejected by the "hanging committees" of previous salons. True to his system, he rarely, perhaps never directly, called the past judgment in question, but he lived and died a dissatisfied man. Unlike Mirabeau, who had not the courage to be unpopular, Decamps derived no gratification from popularity.

I knew Eugène Delacroix better than any of the others in the marvellous constellation of painters of that period, and our friendship lasted till the day of his death, in December 1863. I was also on very good terms with Horace Vernet; but though the latter was perhaps a more lively companion, the stronger attraction was towards the former. I was one of the few friends whom he tolerated whilst at work. Our friendship lasted for nearly a quarter of a century, and during that time there was never a single unpleasantness between us, though I am bound to admit that Delacroix' temper was very uncertain. Among all those men who had a profound, ineradicable contempt for the bourgeois, I have only known one who despised him even to a greater extent than he; it was Gustave Flaubert. Though Delacroix' manners were perfect, he could scarcely be polite to the middle classes. With the exception of Dante and Shakespeare, Delacroix was probably the greatest poet that ever lived; a greater poet undoubtedly than Victor Hugo, in that he was absolutely indifferent to the material results of his genius. If Shakespeare and the author of the "Inferno" had painted, they would have painted like Delacroix; his "Sardanapale" is the Byronic poem, condensed and transferred to canvas.

Long as I knew Delacroix, I had never been able to make out whether he was tall or short, and most of his friends and acquaintances were equally puzzled. As we stood around his coffin many were surprised at its length. His was decidedly a curious face, at times stony in its immobility, at others quivering from the tip of chin to the juncture of the eyebrows, and with a peculiar movement of the nostrils that was almost pendulum-like in its regularity. It gave one the impression of their being assailed by some unpleasant smell, and, one day, when Delacroix was in a light mood, I remarked upon it. "You are perfectly right," he replied; "I always fancy there is corruption in the air, but it is not necessarily of a material kind."

Be this as it may, he liked to surround himself with flowers, and his studio was often like a hothouse, apart from the floral decorations. The temperature was invariably very high, and even then he would shiver now and again. I have always had an idea that Delacroix had Indian blood in his veins, which idea was justified to a certain extent by his appearance, albeit that there was no tradition to that effect in his family. But it was neither the black hair, the olive skin, nor the peculiar formation of the features which forced that conclusion upon me; it was the character of Delacroix, which for years and years I endeavoured to read thoroughly, without succeeding to any appreciable degree. There was one trait that stood out so distinctly that the merest child might have perceived it—his honesty; but the rest was apparently a mass of contradiction. It is difficult to imagine a poet, and especially a painter-poet, without an absorbing passion for some woman—not necessarily for the same woman; to my knowledge Delacroix had no such passion, for one can scarcely admit that Jenny Leguillou, his housekeeper, could have inspired such a feeling. True, when I first knew Delacroix he was over forty, but those who had known him at twenty and twenty-five never hinted at any romantic attachment or even at a sober, homely affection. And assuredly a man of forty is not invulnerable in that respect. And yet, the woman who positively bewitched, one after another, so many of Delacroix' eminent contemporaries, Jules Sandeau,

Alfred de Musset, Michel de Bourges, Chopin, Pierre Leroux, Cabet, Lammenais, etc., had no power over him.

Paul de Musset, perhaps as a kind of revenge for the wrongs suffered by his brother, once gave an amusing description of the miscarried attempt of George Sand "to net" Eugène Delacroix.

It would appear that the painter had shown signs of yielding to the charms which few men were able to withstand, or, at any rate, that George Sand fancied she could detect such signs. Whether it was from a wish on George Sand's part to precipitate matters or to nip the thing in the bud, it would be difficult to determine, but it is certain that she pursued her usual tactics—that is, she endeavoured to provoke an admission of her admirer's feeling. Though I subsequently ascertained that Paul de Musset's story was substantially true, I am not altogether prepared, knowing his animosity against her, to accept his hinted theory of the lady's desire "de brusquer les fiançailles."

One morning, then, while Delacroix was at work, George Sand entered his studio. She looked out of spirits, and almost immediately stated the purpose of her visit.

"My poor Eugène!" she began; "I am afraid I have got sad news for you."

"Oh, indeed," said Delacroix, without interrupting his work, and just giving her one of his cordial smiles in guise of welcome.

"Yes, my dear friend, I have carefully consulted my own heart, and the upshot is, I am grieved to tell you, that I feel I cannot and could never love you."

Delacroix kept on painting. "Is that a fact?" he said.

"Yes, and I ask you once more to pardon me, and to give me credit for my candour—my poor Delacroix."

Delacroix did not budge from his easel.

"You are angry with me, are you not? You will never forgive me?"

"Certainly I will. Only I want you to keep quiet for ten minutes; I have got a bit of sky there which has caused me a good deal of trouble, it is just coming right. Go and sit down or else take a little walk, and come back in ten minutes."

Of course, George Sand did not return; and equally, of course, did not tell the story to any one, but somehow it leaked out. Perhaps Jenny Leguillou had overheard the scene—she was quite capable of listening behind a screen or door—and reported it. Delacroix himself, when "chaffed" about it, never denied it. There was no need for him to do so, because theoretically it redounded to the lady's honour; had she not rejected his advances?

I have noted it here to prove that the poetry of Delacroix n'allait pas se faufiler dans les jupons, because, though we would not take it for granted that where George Sand failed others would have succeeded, it is nevertheless an authenticated fact that only one other man among the many on whom she tried her wiles remained proof against them. That man was Prosper Mérimée, the author of "Colomba" and "Carmen," the friend of Panizzi. "Quand je fais un roman, je choisis mon sujet; je ne veux pas que l'on me découpe pour en faire un. Madame Sand ne met pas ses amants dans son cœur, elle les mets dans ses livres; et elle le fait si diablement vite qu'on n'a pas le temps de la devancer." Mérimée was right, each of

George Sand's earlier books had been written with the heart's blood of one of the victims of her insatiable passions—for I should not like to prostitute the word "love" to her liaisons; and I am glad to think that Eugène Delacroix was spared that ordeal. It would have killed him; and the painter of "Sardanapale" was more precious to his own art than to hers, which, with all due deference to eminent critics, left an unpleasant sensation to those who were fortunate enough to be free from incipient hysteria.

A liaison with George Sand would have killed Eugène Delacroix, I am perfectly certain; for he would have staked gold, she would have only played with counters. It would have been the vitiated atmosphere in which the candle of his life and of his genius—which were one, in this instance—would have been extinguished.

As it was, that candle burned very low at times, because, during the years I knew Delacroix, he had nearly always one foot in the grave; the healthy breezes of art's unpolluted air made that candle burn brightly now and again; hence the difference in quality, as striking, of some of his pictures.

Perhaps on account of his delicate health, Delacroix was not very fond of society, in which, however, he was ever welcome, and particularly fitted to shine, though he rarely attempted to do so. I have said that Dante and Shakespeare, if they had painted, would have painted as Delacroix did; I am almost tempted to add that if Delacroix' vocation had impelled him that way, he would have sung as they sang—of course, I do not mean that he would have soared as high, but his name would have lived in literature as it does in painting, though perhaps not with so brilliant a halo around it. For, unlike many great painters of his time, Delacroix was essentially lettré. One has but to read some of his critical essays in the *Revue des Deux Mondes* of that period, to be convinced of that at once. Théophile Gautier said, one evening, that it was "the style of a poet in a hurry." The sentences give one the impression of newly-minted golden coins. Nearly every one contains a thought, which, if reduced to small change, would still make an admirable paragraph. He gives to his readers what he expects from his authors—a sensation, a shock in two or three lines. The sentences are modelled upon his favourite prose author, who, curious to relate, was none other than Napoleon I. I often tried to interest him in English literature. Unfortunately, he knew no English to speak of, and was obliged to have recourse to translations. Walter Scott he thought long-winded, and, after a few attempts at Shakespeare in French, he gave it up. "Ça ne peut pas être cela," he said. But he had several French versions of "Gulliver's Travels," all of which he read in turn. One day, I quoted to him a sentence from Carlyle's "Lectures on Heroes:" "Show me how a man sings, and I will tell you how he will fight." "C'est cela," he said; "if Shakespeare had been a general, he would have won his battles like Napoleon, by thunderclaps" (par des coups de foudre).

Delacroix had what a great many Frenchmen lack —a keen sense of humour, but it was considerably tempered by what, for the want of a better term, I may call the bump of reverence. He could not be humorous at the expense of those he admired or respected, consequently his attempts at caricature at the early period of his career in *Le Nain Jaune* were a failure; because Delacroix' admiration and respect were not necessarily reserved for those with whom he agreed in art or politics, but for every one who attempted something great or useful, though he failed. The man who, at the age of sixty, would enthusiastically dilate upon his meeting forty years before with Gros, whose hat he had knocked off by accident, was not the likely one to hold up to ridicule the celebrity of the hour or day *without* malice prepense. And this malice prepense never uprose within him, except in the presence of some bumptious, ignorant nobody. Then it positively boiled over, and he did not mind what trick he played his interlocutor. The latter might be a wealthy would-be patron, an influential Government official, or a well-known picture-dealer; it was all the same to Delacroix, who had an utter contempt for patronage, nepotism, and money. It was as good as a clever scene in a comedy to see him rise and draw himself up to his full height, in order to impress his victim with a sense of the importance of what he was going to say. To get an idea of him under such circumstances, one must go and see his portrait in the Louvre, painted by himself, with the semi-supercilious, semi-benevolent smile playing upon the parted lips, and showing the magnificent regular set of teeth, of which he was very proud, beneath the black bushy moustache, which reminds one curiously of that of Rembrandt. Of course, the victim was mesmerized, and stood listening with all attention, promising himself to remember every word of the spoken essay on art, with the view of reproducing it as his own at the first favourable opportunity. And he generally did, to his own discomfiture and the amusement of his hearers, who, if they happened to know Delacroix, which was the case frequently, invariably detected the source of the speaker's information. I once heard a spoken essay on Holbein reproduced in that way, which would have simply made the fortune of any comic writer. The human parrot had not even been parrot-like, for he had muddled the whole in transmission. I took some pains to reproduce his exact words, and I never saw Delacroix laugh as when I repeated it to him. For, as a rule, and even when he was mystifying that kind of numskull in the presence of half a dozen well-informed friends, Delacroix remained perfectly serious, though the others had to bite their lips lest they should explode. In fact, it would have been difficult at any time to guess or discover, beneath the well-bred man of the world, with his charming, courtly, though somewhat distant manner, the painter who gave us "La Barque de Dante," and "Les Massacres de Scio;" still, Delacroix was that man of the world, exceedingly careful of his appearance, particular to a degree about his nails, which he wore very long, dressed to perfection, and, in spite of the episode with George Sand, recorded above, most ingratiating with women.

Different altogether was he in his studio. Though he was "at home" from three till five, to visitors of both sexes, it was distinctly understood that he would not interrupt his work for them, or play the host as the popular painter of to-day is supposed to do. The atelier, encumbered with bric-à-brac and sumptuous hangings and afternoon tea, had not been invented: if the host wore a velvet coat, a Byronic collar, and gorgeous papooshes, it was because he liked these things himself, not because he intended to impress his visitors. As a rule, the host, though in his youth perhaps he had been fond of extravagant costumes, did not like them: Horace Vernet often worked in his shirt-sleeves, Paul Delaroche nearly always wore a blouse, and Ingrès, until he became "a society man," which was very late in life, donned a dressing-gown. Delacroix was, if anything, more slovenly than the rest when at work. An old jacket buttoned up to the chin, a large muffler round his neck, a cloth cap pulled over his ears, and a pair of thick felt slippers made up his usual garb. For he was nearly always shivering with cold, and had an affection of the throat, besides, which compelled him to be careful. "But for my wrapping up, I should have been dead at thirty," he said.

Nevertheless, at the stroke of eight, winter and summer, he was in his studio, which he did not leave until dark, during six months of the year, and a little before, during the other six. Contrary to the French habit, he never took luncheon, and generally dined at home a little after six—the fatigue of dining out being too much for him.

I may safely say that I was one of Delacroix' friends, with whom he talked without restraint. I often went to him of an evening when the weather prevented his going abroad, which, in his state of health, was very often. He always chafed at such confinement; for though not fond of society in a general way, he liked coming to the Boulevards, after his work was over, and mixing with his familiars. Delacroix smoked, but, unlike many addicted to tobacco, could not sit idle. His hands, as well as his brain, wanted to be busy; consequently, when imprisoned by rain or snow, he sat sketching figures or groups, talking all the while. By then his name had become familiar to every art student throughout the world, and he often received flattering letters from distant parts. One evening, shortly after the death of David d'Angers, to an episode in whose life I have devoted a considerable space in these notes, Delacroix received an American newspaper, the title of which I have forgotten, but which contained an exceedingly able article on the great sculptor, as an artist, and as a man. It wound up with the question, "And what kind of monument will be raised to him by the man who virtually shortened his life by sending him into exile, because David remained true to the republican principles which Napoleon only shammed—or, if not shammed, deliberately trod underfoot to ascend a tyrant's throne?"

I translated the whole of the article, and, when I came to the last lines, Delacroix shook his head sadly. "You remember," he said, "the answer of our friend Dumas, when they asked him for a subscription towards a monument to a man whom every one had reviled in the beginning of his career. 'They had better be content with the stones they threw at him during his existence. No monument they can raise will be so eloquent of their imbecility and his genius.' I may take it," he went on, "that such a question will be raised one day after my death, perhaps many years after I am gone. If you are alive you will, by my will, raise your voice against the project. I have painted my own portrait; while I am here, I will take care that it be not reproduced; I will forbid them to do so after I am at rest. There shall not be a bust on my tomb."

About a fortnight before his death he made a will to that effect, and up to the present hour (1883) its injunctions have been respected. Delacroix lies in a somewhat solitary spot in Père-Lachaise. Neither emblem, bust, nor statue adorns his tomb, which was executed according to his own instructions. "They libelled me so much during my life," he said one day, "that I do not want them to libel me after my death, on canvas or in marble. They flattered me so much afterwards, that I know their flattery to be fulsome, and, if anything, I am more afraid of it than of their libels."

It would be difficult to find a greater contrast than there existed between Eugène Delacroix, both as a man and an artist, and Horace Vernet. The one loved his art with the passionate devotion of an intensely poetical lover for his wayward mistress, whom to cease wooing for a moment might mean an irreparable breach or, at least, a long estrangement; the other loved his with the calm affection of the cherished husband for the faithful wife who had blessed him with a numerous offspring, whom he had known from his very infancy, a marriage with whom had been decided upon when he was a mere lad, whom he might even neglect for a little while without the bond being in any way relaxed. According to their respective certificates of birth, Vernet was the senior by ten years of Delacroix. When I first knew them, about 1840, Vernet looked ten years younger than Delacroix. If they had chosen to disguise themselves as musketeers of the Louis XIII.

period, Vernet would have reminded one of both Aramis and d'Artagnan; Delacroix, of Athos.

Montaigne spoke Latin before he could speak French; Vernet drew men and horses before he had mastered either French or Latin. His playthings were stumpy, worn-out brushes, discarded palettes, and sticks of charcoal; his alphabet, the pictures of the Louvre, where his father occupied a set of apartments, and where he was born, a month before the outbreak of the first Revolution. He once said to me, "Je suis peintre comme il y des hommes qui sont rois—parceque ils ne peuvent pas être autre chose. Il fallait un homme de génie pour sortir d'un pareil bourbier et malheureusement je n'ai que du talent." By the "bourbier" he meant his great-grandfather, his two grandfathers, and his father, all of whom were painters and draughtsmen.

Posterity will probably decide whether Horace Vernet was a genius or merely a painter of great talent, but it will scarcely convey an approximate idea of the charm of the man himself. There was only one other of his contemporaries who exercised the same spell on his companions — Alexandre Dumas *père*. Though Vernet was a comparative dwarf by the side of Dumas, the men had the same qualities, physical, moral, and mental. Neither of them knew what bodily fatigue meant; both could work for fourteen or fifteen hours a day for a fortnight or a month; both would often have "a long bout of idleness," as they called it, which, to others not endowed with their strength and mental activity, would have meant hard labour. Both were fond of earning money, fonder still of spending it; both created almost without an effort. Dumas roared with laughter while writing; Vernet sang at the top of his voice while painting, or bandied jokes with his visitors, who might come and go as they liked at all hours. Dumas, especially in the earlier days of his career, had to read a great deal before he could catch the local colour of his novels and plays—he himself has told us that he was altogether ignorant of the history of France. But when he had finished reading up the period in question, he wrote as if he had been born in it. Vernet was a walking cyclopædia on military costume; he knew, perhaps, not much more than that, but that he knew thoroughly, and never had to think twice about the uniforms of his models, and, as he himself said, "I never studied the thing, nor did I learn to paint or to draw. According to many people, I do not know how to paint or to draw now: it may be so; at any rate I have the comfort of having wasted nobody's time in trying to learn."

Like Dumas, he was very proud of his calling and of the name he had made for himself in it, which he would not have changed for the title of emperor—least of all for that of king; for, like his great contemporary, he was a republican at heart. It did not diminish either his or Dumas' admiration for Napoleon I. "I can understand an absolute monarchy, nay, a downright autocracy, and I can understand a republic," said Vernet, "but I fail to understand the use of a constitutional king, just because it implies and entails the principle of succession by inheritance. An autocracy means one ruler over so many millions of subjects; a constitutional monarchy means between five and six hundred direct rulers, so many millions of indirect ones, and one subject who is called king. Who would leave his child the inheritance of such slavery? A la bonne heure, give me a republic such as we understand it in France, all rulers, all natural-born kings, gods in mortals' disguise who dance to the piping of the devil. There have been two such since I was born; there may be another half-dozen like these within the next two centuries, because, before you can have an ideal republic, you must have ideal republicans, and Nature cannot afford to fritter away her most precious gifts on a lot of down-at-heels lawyers and hobnail-booted scum. She condescends now and then to make an ideal tyrant—she will never make a nation of ideal republicans. You may just as well ask her to make a nation of Raffaelles or Michael Angelos, or Shakespeares or Molières."

Both men, in spite of their republican opinions, were personally attached to some members of the Orleans family; both had an almost invincible objection to the Bourbons. Vernet had less occasion to be outspoken in his dislike than Dumas, but he refused to receive the Duc de Berri when the latter offered to come and see the battle-pieces Vernet was painting for the then Duke of Orleans (Louis-Philippe). Vernet had stipulated that his paintings should illustrate exclusively the campaigns of the first Republic and the Empire, though subsequently he depicted some episodes of the Algerian wars, in which the son of the King had distinguished himself. "Tricolour cockades or no pictures," he remarked, and Louis-Philippe good-humouredly acquiesced. Though courteous to a degree, he never minced matters to either king or beggar. While in Russia Nicholas took a great fancy to him. It appears that the painter, who must have looked even smaller by the side of the

Czar than he did by that of Dumas, had accompanied the former, if not on a perilous, at least on a very uncomfortable journey in the middle of the winter. He and the Emperor were the only two men who had borne the hardships and privations without grumbling, nay, with Mark Tapleyean cheerfulness. That kind of fortitude was at all times a passport to Nicholas' heart, doubly so in this instance, by reason of Vernet's by no means robust appearance. From that moment Nicholas became very attached to, and would often send for, him. They would often converse on subjects even more serious, and, one day, after the partition of Poland, Nicholas proposed that Vernet should paint a picture on the subject.

"I am afraid I cannot do it, sire," was the answer. "I have never painted a Christ on the cross."

"The moment I had said it," continued Vernet, when he told me the story, which is scarcely known, "I thought my last hour had struck. I am positively certain that a Russian would have paid these words with his life, or at least with lifelong exile to Siberia. I shall never forget the look he gave me; there was a murderous gleam in the eyes: but it was over in an instant. Nevertheless, I feel convinced that Nicholas was mad, and, what is more, I feel equally convinced that there is incipient madness throughout the whole of the Romanoff family. I saw a good many of its members during my stay in Russia. They all did and said things which would have landed ordinary men and women in a lunatic asylum. At the same time there was an unmistakable touch of genius about some of them. I often endeavoured to discuss the matter with the resident foreign physicians, but, as you may imagine, they were very reticent. But mark my words, one day there will be a terrible flare-up. Of course, the foreigner, who sees the superstitious reverence, the slavish respect with which they are surrounded, scarcely wonders that these men and women should, in the end, consider themselves above, and irresponsible to, the millions of grovelling mortals whom they rule; in spite of all this, the question can only be one of time, and when the Russian empire falls, the cataclysm will be unlike any other that has preceded it."

There was a comic side to Horace Vernet's character. By dint of painting battle-pieces he had come to consider himself an authority on strategy and tactics, and his criticisms on M. Thiers' system of fortifications used to set us roaring. I am under the impression—though I will not strictly vouch for it—that at the recommendation of one or two of the inveterate jokers of our set, Laurent-Jan * and Méry, he had a couple of interviews with M. Thiers, but we never ascertained the result of them. It is almost certain that the minister of Louis-Philippe, who at one period of his life considered himself a Napoleon and a Vauban rolled into one, did not entertain Vernet's suggestions with the degree of enthusiasm to which he thought them entitled; at any rate, from that time, the mention of M. Thiers' name generally provoked a contemptuous shrug of the shoulders on Vernet's part. "C'est tout à fait comme Napoleon et Jomini, mon cher Vernet,"

---

* Laurent-Jan was a witty, though incorrigibly idle journalist. He is entirely forgotten now save by such men as MM. Arsène Houssaye and Roger de Beauvoir, who were his contemporaries. He was the author of a clever parody on Kotzebue's "Menschenhasz und Reue," known on the English stage as "The Stranger."—EDITOR.

said Laurent-Jan; "mais, après tout, qu'est que cela vous fait? La postérité jugera entre vous deux, elle saura bien débrouiller la part que vous avez contribuée à ces travaux immortels."

Much as Horace Vernet admired his great contemporaries in art and literature, his greatest worship was reserved for Alfred de Vigny, the soldier-poet, though the latter was by no means a sympathetic companion. Next to his society, which was rarely to be had, he preferred that of Arthur Bertrand, the son of Napoleon's companion in exile. Arthur Bertrand had an elder brother, Napoleon Bertrand, who, at the storming of Constantine, put on a new pair of white kid gloves, brought from Paris for the purpose. Horace Vernet made at least fifty sketches of that particular incident, but he never painted the picture. "I could not do it justice," he said, when remonstrated with for his procrastination. "I should fail to realize the grandeur of the thing." Thereupon Laurent-Jan, who had no bump of reverence, proposed a poem, in so many cantos, to be illustrated by Vernet. I give the plan as developed by the would-be author.

1. The kid in its ancestral home among the mountains. A mysterious voice from heaven tells it that its skin will be required for a pair of gloves. The kid objects, and inquires why the skin of some other kid will not do as well. The voice reveals the glorious purpose of the gloves. The kid consents, and at the same moment a hunter appears in sight. The kid, instead of taking to its heels, assumes a favourable position to be shot. It makes a dying speech.

2. A glove-shop on the Boulevard. Enter Napoleon Bertrand, asking for a pair of gloves. The girl tells

him that she has only one pair left, and communicates the legend connected with it. The price is twenty francs. Napoleon Bertrand demurs at it, and tells her, in his turn, what the gloves are wanted for. The girl refuses to take the money, and her employer, overhearing the conversation, dismisses her there and then. He keeps the wages due to her as the price of the gloves. Napoleon Bertrand puts the latter in his pocket, offers the girl his arm, and invites her to breakfast in a *cabinet particulier*, "en tout bien, en tout, honneur." To prove his perfectly honourable intentions, he tells her the story of Jeanne d'Arc. The girl's imagination is fired by the recital, and after luncheon she goes in search of a book on the subject. An unscrupulous, dishonest second-hand bookseller palms off an edition of Voltaire's "La Pucelle." The girl writes to Napoleon Bertrand to tell him that he has made a fool of her, that Jeanne d'Arc was no better than she should be, and that she is going to join the harem of the Bey of Constantine.

3. Napoleon Bertrand stricken with remorse before Constantine. Orders given for the assault. Napoleon Bertrand looks for his gloves, and finds that they are too small. He can just get them on, but cannot grasp the handle of the sword. His servant announces a mysterious stranger, a veiled female stranger. She is admitted; she has made her escape from the harem; a mysterious voice from heaven—the same that spoke to the kid—having warned her the night before that the gloves would be too small, and that she was to let a piece in. Reconciliation. Tableau. The bugles are sounding "boot and saddle." Storming of Constantine.

I have reproduced the words of Laurent-Jan; I

will not attempt to reproduce his manner, which was simply inimitable. Horace Vernet and Arthur Bertrand shook with laughter, and the latter offered Laurent-Jan to keep him for a twelvemonth if he would write the poem. Jan consented, and lived upon the fat of the land during that time, but the poem never saw the light.

Arthur Bertrand was one of the most jovial fellows of his time. He, Eugène Sue, and Latour-Mézerai were the best customers of the florist on the Boulevards. It was he who accompanied the Prince de Joinville to St. Helena to bring back the remains of Napoleon. After their return, a new figure joined our set now and then. It was the Abbé Coquereau, the chaplain of "La Belle-Poule." The Abbé Coquereau was the first French Catholic priest who discarded the gown and the shovel hat, and adopted that of the English clergy. He was a charming man, and by no means straight-laced, but he drew the line at accompanying Arthur in his nightly perambulations. One evening he, Arthur Bertrand, and Alexandre Dumas were strolling along the Boulevards when the latter tried to make the abbé enter the Variétés. The abbé held firm, or rather took to his heels.

In those days there were still a great many veterans of the *grande armée* about, and a great deal of Horace Vernet's money went in entertaining them at the various cafés and restaurants—especially when he was preparing sketches for a new picture. The ordinary model, clever and eminently useful as he was at that period, was willingly discarded for the old and bronzed warrior of the Empire, some of whom were even then returning from Africa. "They may just as well earn the money I pay the others," he said; consequently it was not an unusual thing to see a general, a couple of colonels, half a dozen captains, and as many sergeants and privates, all of whom had served under Napoleon, in Vernet's studio at the same time. Of course the officers were only too pleased to give their services gratuitously, but Vernet had a curious way of making up his daily budget. Twenty models at four francs—for models earned no more then—eighty francs. Fifteen of them refuse their pay. The eighty francs to be divided between five. And the five veterans enjoyed a magnificent income for weeks and weeks at a time.

Truth compels me to state, however, that during those weeks "the careful mother could not have taken her daughter" to Vernet's studio. A couple of live horses, not unfrequently three, an equal number of stuffed ones, camp kettles, broken limbers, pieces of artillery, an overturned ammunition waggon, a collection of uniforms, that would have made the fortune of a costumier, scattered all over the place; drums, swords, guns and saddles: and, amidst this confusion, a score of veterans, some of whom had been comrades-in-arms and who seemed oblivious, for the time being, of their hard-earned promotion in the company of those who had been less lucky than they, every man smoking his hardest and telling his best garrison story: all these made up a scene worthy of Vernet himself, but somewhat appalling to the civilian who happened to come upon it unawares.

Vernet was never happier than when at work under such circumstances. Perched on a movable scaffolding or on a high ladder, he reminded one much more of an acrobat than of a painter. Like Dumas, he could work amidst a very Babel of conversation, but the sound of music, however good, disturbed him. In those days, itinerant Italian musicians and pifferari, who have disappeared from the streets of Paris altogether since the decree of expulsion of '81, were numerous, and grew more numerous year by year. I, for one, feel sorry for their disappearance, for I remember having spent half a dozen most delightful evenings listening to them.

The thing happened in this way. Though my regular visits to the Quartier-Latin had ceased long ago, I returned now and then to my old haunts during the years '63 and '64, in company of a young Englishman who was finishing his medical studies in Paris, who had taken up his quarters on the left bank of the Seine, and who has since become a physician in very good practice in the French capital. He had been specially recommended to me, and I was not too old to enjoy an evening once a week or a fortnight among my juniors. At a café, which has been demolished since to make room for a much more gorgeous establishment at the corners of the Boulevards Saint-Michel and Saint-Germain, we used to notice an elderly gentleman, scrupulously neat and exquisitely clean, though his clothes were very threadbare. He always sat at the same table to the right of the counter. His cup of coffee was eked out by frequent supplements of water, and meanwhile he was always busy copying music—at least, so it seemed to us at first. We soon came to a different conclusion, though, because every now and then he would put down his pen, lean back against the cushioned seat, look up at the ceiling and smile to himself—such a sweet smile; the smile of a poet or an artist, seeking inspiration from the spirits supposed to be hovering now and then about such.

That man was no copyist, but an obscure, unappreciated genius perhaps, biding his chance, hoping against hope, meanwhile living a life of jealously concealed dreams and hardship. For he looked sad enough at the best of times, with a kind of settled melancholy which apparently only one thing could dispel—the advent of a couple or trio of pifferari. Then his face would light up all of a sudden, he would gently push his music away, speak to them in Italian, asking them to play certain pieces, beating time with an air of contentment which was absolutely touching to behold. On the other hand, the young pifferari appeared to treat him with greater deference than they did the other customers; the little girl who accompanied them was particularly eager for his approval.

In a little while we became very friendly with the old gentleman, and, one evening, he said, "If you will be here next Wednesday, the pifferari will give us something new."

On the evening in question he looked quite smart; he had evidently "fait des frais de toilette," as our neighbours have it; he wore a different coat, and his big white neckcloth was somewhat more starched than usual. He seemed quite excited. The pifferari, on the other hand, seemed anxious and subdued. The café was very full, for all the habitués liked the old gentleman, and had made it a point of responding to his quasi-invitation. They were well rewarded, for I have rarely heard sweeter music. It was unlike anything we were accustomed to hear from such musicians; there was an old-world sound about it that went straight to the heart, and when we looked at the old gentleman amidst the genuine applause after the termination of the first piece, there were two big tears coursing down his wrinkled cheeks.

The pifferari came again and again, and though they never appealed to him directly, we instinctively guessed that there existed some connection between them. All our efforts to get at the truth of the matter were, however, in vain, for the old gentleman was very reticent.

Meanwhile my young friend had passed his examinations, and shifted his quarters to my side of the river. He did not abandon the Quartier-Latin altogether, but my inquiries about the old musician met with no satisfactory response. He had disappeared. Nearly two years went by, when, one afternoon, he called. "Come with me," he said; "I am going to show you a curious nook of Paris which you do not know, and take you to an old acquaintance whom you will be pleased to see again."

The "curious nook" of Paris still exists to a certain extent, only the pifferari have disappeared from it. It is situated behind the Panthéon, and is more original than its London counterpart—Saffron Hill. It is like a corner of old Rome, Florence, or Naples, without the glorious Italian sun shining above it to lend picturesqueness to the rags and tatters of its population; swarthy desperadoes with golden rings in their ears and on their grimy fingers, their greasy, soft felt hats cocked jauntily on their heads, or drawn over the flashing dark eyes, before which their womankind cower and shake; old men who but for the stubble on their chins would look like ancient cameos; girls with shapely limbs and handsome faces; middle-aged women who remind one of the witches in Macbeth; women younger still, who have neither shape nor make; urchins and little lassies who remind one of the pictures of Murillo: in short, a population of wood-carvers and modellers, vendors of plaster casts, artist-models, sugar-bakers and mosaic-workers, living in the streets the greater part of the day, retiring to their wretched attics at night, sober and peaceful generally, but desperate and unmanageable when in their cups.

The cab stopped before a six-storied house which had seen better days, in a dark, narrow street, into which the light of day scarcely penetrated. The moment we alighted we heard a charivari of string instruments and voices, and as we ascended the steep, slimy, rickety staircase the sound grew more distinct. When we reached the topmost landing, my friend knocked at one of the three or four doors, and, without waiting for an answer, we entered. It was a scantily furnished room with a bare brick floor, an old bedstead in one corner, a few rush-bottomed chairs, and a deal table; but everything was scrupulously clean. Behind the table, a cotton nightcap on his head, his tall thin frame wrapt in an old overcoat, stood our old friend, the composer; in front, half a dozen urchins, in costumes vaguely resembling those of the Calabrian peasantry, grimy like coalheavers, their black hair standing on end with attention, were rehearsing a new piece of music. Then I understood it all. He was the professor of pifferari, an artist for all that, an unappreciated genius, perhaps, who, rather than not be heard at all, introduced a composition of his own into their hackneyed programme, and tasted the sweets of popularity, without the accompanying rewards which, nowadays, popularity invariably brings. This one had known Paisiello and Rossini, had been in the thick of the excitement on the first night of the " Barbière," and had dreamt of similar triumphs. Perhaps his genius was as much entitled to them as that of the others, but he had loved not wisely, but too well, and when he awoke from the love-dream, he was too ruined in body and mind to be able to work for the realization of the artistic one. He would accept no aid. Three years later, we carried him to his grave. A simple stone marks the place in the cemetery of Montparnasse.

CHAPTER IX.

Louis-Philippe and his family—An unpublished theatrical skit on his mania for shaking hands with every one—His art of governing, according to the same skit—Louis-Philippe not the ardent admirer of the bourgeoisie he professed to be—The Faubourg Saint-Germain deserts the Tuileries—The English in too great a majority—Lord ——'s opinion of the dinners at the Tuileries—The attitude of the bourgeoisie towards Louis-Philippe, according to the King himself—Louis-Philippe's wit—His final words on the death of Talleyrand—His love of money—He could be generous at times—A story of the Palais-Royal—Louis-Philippe and the Marseillaise—Two curious stories connected with the Marseillaise — Who was the composer of it? — Louis-Philippe's opinion of the throne, the crown, and the sceptre of France as additions to one's comfort—His children, and especially his sons, take things more easily—Even the Bonapartists admired some of the latter—A mot of an Imperialist—How the boys were brought up—Their nocturnal rambles later on—The King himself does not seem to mind those escapades, but is frightened at M. Guizot hearing of them—Louis-Philippe did not understand Guizot—The recollection of his former misery frequently haunts the King—He worries Queen Victoria with his fear of becoming poor—Louis-Philippe an excellent husband and father—He wants to write the libretto of an opera on an English subject—His religion—The court receptions ridiculous—Even the proletariat sneer at them—The *entrée* of the Duchesse d'Orléans into Paris—The scene in the Tuileries gardens—A mot of Princesse Clémentine on her father's too paternal solicitude—A practical joke of the Prince de Joinville—His caricatures and drawings—The children inherited their talent for drawing and modelling from their mother—The Duc de Nemours as a miniature and water-colour painter—Suspected of being a Legitimist—All Louis-Philippe's children great patrons of art—How the bourgeoisie looked upon their intercourse with artists—The Duc de Nemours' marvellous memory—The studio of Eugène Lami—His neighbours, Paul Delaroche and Honoré de Balzac—The Duc de Nemours' bravery called in question—The Duc d'Aumale's exploits in Algeria considered mere skirmishes—A curious story of spiritism—The Duc d'Aumale a greater favourite with the world than any of the other sons of Louis-Philippe—His wit—The Duc d'Orléans also a great favourite—His visits to Decamps' studio

—An indifferent classical scholar—A curious kind of black-mail—His indifference to money—There is no money in a Republic—His death—A witty reply to the Legitimists.

As will appear by-and-by, I was an eye-witness of a good many incidents of the Revolution of '48, and a great many more have been related to me by friends, whose veracity was and still is beyond suspicion. Neither they nor I have ever been able to establish a sufficiently valid political cause for that upheaval. Perhaps it was because we were free from the prejudices engendered by what, for want of a better term, I must call "dynastic sentiment." We were not blind to the faults of Louis-Philippe, but we refused to look at them through the spectacles supplied in turns by the Legitimists, the Imperialists, and Republicans. How far these spectacles were calculated to improve people's vision, the following specimen will show.

I have lying before me a few sheets of quarto paper, sewn together in a primitive way. It is a manuscript skit, in the form of a theatrical duologue, professing to deal with the king's well-known habit of shaking hands with every one with whom he came in contact. The *dramatis personæ* are King Fip I., Roi des Epiciers-read, King of the Philistines or Shopkeepers, and his son and heir, Grand Poulot (Big Spooney). The monarch is giving the heir-apparent a lesson in the art of governing. "Do not be misled," he says, "by a parcel of theorists, who will tell you that the citizen-monarchy is based upon the sovereign will of the people, or upon the strict observance of the Charter; this is merely so much drivel from the political Rights or Lefts. In reality, it does not signify a jot whether France be free at home and feared and respected abroad, whether the throne be hedged round with republican institutions or supported by an hereditary peerage, whether the language of her statesmen be weighty and the deeds of her soldiers heroic. The citizen-monarchy and the art of governing consist of but one thing—the capacity of the principal ruler for shaking hands with any and every ragamuffin and out-of-elbows brute he meets." Thereupon King Fip shows his son how to shake hands in every conceivable position—on foot, on horseback, at a gallop, at a trot, leaning out of a carriage, and so forth. Grand Poulot is not only eager to learn, but ambitious to improve upon his sire's method. "How would it do, dad," he asks, "if, in addition to shaking hands with them, one inquired after their health, in the second person singular—'Comment vas tu, mon vieux cochon?' or, better still, 'Comment vas tu, mon vieux citoyen?'" "It would do admirably," says papa; "but it does not matter whether you say cochon or citoyen, the terms are synonymous."

I am inclined to think that beneath this rather clever banter there was a certain measure of truth. Louis-Philippe was by no means the ardent admirer of the bourgeoisie he professed to be. He did not foster any illusions with regard to their intellectual worth, and in his inmost heart he resented their so-called admiration of him, which he knew to be would-be patronage under another name. They had formed a hedge round him which prevented any attempt on his part at conciliating his own caste, the old noblesse. It is doubtful whether he would have been successful, especially in the earlier years of his reign; but their ostracism of him and his family rankled in his mind, and found vent now and again in an epigram that stung the author as much as the party against which it was directed. "There is more difficulty in getting people to my court entertainments from across the Seine than from across the Channel," he said.

The fact is, that the whole of the Faubourg St.-Germain was conspicuous by its absence from the Tuileries in those days, and that the English were in rather too great a majority. They were not always a distinguished company. I was little more than a lad at this time, but I remember Lord ———'s invariable answer when his friends asked him what the dinner had been like, and whether he had enjoyed himself: "The dinner was like that at a good table-d'hôte, and I enjoyed myself as I would enjoy myself at a good hotel in Switzerland or at Wiesbaden, where the proprietor knew me personally, and had given orders to the head waiter to look after my comforts. But," he added, "it is, after all, more pleasant dining there, when the English are present. At any rate, there is no want of respect. When the French sit round the table, it is not like a king dining with his subjects, but like half a hundred kings dining with one subject." Allowing for a certain amount of exaggeration, there was a good deal of truth in the remarks, as I found out afterwards. "The bourgeoisie in their attitude towards me," said Louis-Philippe, one day, to the English nobleman I have just quoted, "are always reminding me of Adalbéron of Rheims with Hugues Capet: 'Qui t'as fait roi?' asked the bishop. 'Qui t'as fait duc?' retorted the king. I have made them dukes to a greater extent, though, than they have made me king."

For Louis-Philippe was a witty king—wittier, perhaps, than any that had sat on the throne of France since Henri IV. Some of his mots have become historical, and even his most persistent detractors have been unable to convict him of plagiarism with regard to them. What he specially excelled in was the "mot de la fin" anglicé—the clenching of an argument, such as, for instance, his final remark on the death of Talleyrand. He had paid him a visit the day before. When the news of the prince's death was brought to him, he said, "Are you sure he is dead?"

"Very sure, sire," was the answer. "Why, did not your majesty himself notice yesterday that he was dying?"

"I did, but there is no judging from appearances with Talleyrand, and I have been asking myself for the last four and twenty hours what interest he could possibly have in departing at this particular moment."

To those who knew Louis-Philippe personally, it was very patent that he disliked those who had been instrumental in setting him on the throne, and who, under the cloak of "liberty, fraternity, and equality," were seeking their own interest only, namely, the bourgeoisie. He knew their quasi-goodwill to him to be so much sheer hypocrisy, and perhaps he and they were too much alike in some respects, in their love of money for the sake of hoarding it. It was, perhaps, the only serious failing that could be laid to the charge of the family, because none of its members, with the exception of the Duc d'Orléans, were entirely free from it. It must not be inferred, though, that

Louis-Philippe kept his purse closed to really deserving cases of distress. Far from it. I have the following story from my old tutor, to whom I am, moreover, indebted for a great many notes, dealing with events of which I could not possibly have had any knowledge but for him.

In 1829 the greater part of the Galerie d'Orléans in the Palais-Royal was completed. The unsightly wooden booths had been taken down, and the timber must have been decidedly worth a small fortune. Several contractors made very handsome offers for it, but Louis-Philippe (then Duc d'Orléans) refused to sell it. It was to be distributed among the poor of the neighbourhood for fuel for the ensuing winter, which threatened to be a severe one. One day, when the duke was inspecting the works in company of his steward, an individual, who was standing a couple of yards away, began to shout at the top of his voice, "Vive Louis-Philippe!" "Go and see what the fellow wants, for assuredly he wants something," said the duke, who was a Voltairean in his way, and had interpreted the man's enthusiasm aright. Papa Sournois was one of those nondescripts for whom even now there appear to be more resources in the French capital than elsewhere. At the period in question he mainly got his living by selling contre-marques (checks) at the doors of the theatre. He had heard of the duke's intention with regard to the wood, hence his enthusiastic cry of "Vive Louis-Philippe!" A cartload of wood was sent to his place; papa Sournois converted it into money, and got drunk with the proceeds for a fortnight. When the steward, horribly scandalized, told the duke of the results of his benevolence, the latter merely laughed, and sent for the wife, who made her appearance accompanied by a young brood of five. The duke gave her a five-franc piece, and told her to apply to the concierge of the Palais-Royal for a similar sum every day during the winter months. Of course, five francs a day was not as much as a drop of water out of the sea when we consider Louis-Philippe's stupendous income, and yet, when the Tuileries were sacked in 1848, documents upon documents were found, compiled with the sole view of saving a few francs per diem out of the young princes' "keep."

"I am so sick of the word 'fraternity,'" said Prince Metternich, after his return from France, "that, if I had a brother, I should call him cousin." Though it was to the strains of the Marseillaise that Louis-Philippe had been conducted to the Hôtel-de-Ville on the day when Lafayette pointed to him as "the best of all republics," a time came when Louis-Philippe got utterly sick of the Marseillaise.

But what was he to do, seeing that his attempt at introducing a new national hymn had utterly failed? The mob refused to sing "La Parisienne," composed by Casimir de la Vigne, after Alexandre Dumas had refused to write a national hymn; and they, moreover, insisted on the King joining in the chorus of the old hymn, as he had hitherto done on all public occasions.[*] They had grumblingly resigned themselves to his

[*] When there was no public occasion, his political antagonists or merely practical jokers who knew of his dislike invented one, like Edouard d'Ourliac, a well-known journalist and the author of several novels, who, whenever he had nothing better to do, recruited a band of street arabs to go and sing the Marseillaise under the king's windows. They kept on singing until Louis-Philippe, in sheer self-defence, was obliged to come out and join in the song.—EDITOR.

beating time no longer, but any further refusal of his co-operation might have been resented in a less peaceful fashion. On the other hand, there was the bourgeoisie who were of opinion that, now that the monarchy had entered upon a more conservative period, the intoning of the hymn, at any rate on the sovereign's part, was out of place, and savoured too much of a republican manifestation. "It was Guizot who told him so," said Lord ——, who had been standing on the balcony of the Tuileries on the occasion of the king's "saint's day," * and had heard the minister make the remark.

"And what did the king reply?" was the question.

"Do not worry yourself, monsieur le ministre; I am only moving my lips; I have ceased to pronounce the words for many a day."

These were the expedients to which Louis-Philippe was reduced before he had been on the throne half a dozen years. "I am like the fool between two stools," observed the king in English, afterwards, when speaking to Lord ——, "only I happen to be between the comfortably stuffed easy-chair of the bourgeois drawing-room and the piece of furniture seated on which Louis XIV. is said to have received the Dutch ambassadors."

While speaking of the Marseillaise, here are two stories in connection with it which are not known to the general reader. The first was told to me by the old tutor already mentioned; the second aroused a great deal of literary curiosity in the year 1860, and bears the stamp of truth on the face of it. It was,

* In France it is the Patron Saint's day, not the birthday, that is kept.

however, never fully investigated, or, at any rate, the results of the investigation were never published.*

"We were all more or less aware," said my informant, "that Rouget de l'Isle was not the author of the whole of the words of the Marseillaise. But none of us in Lyons, where I was born, knew who had written the last strophe, commonly called the 'strophe of the children,' and I doubt whether they were any wiser in Paris. Some of my fellow-students—for I was nearly eighteen at that time—credited André Chenier with the authorship of the last strophe, others ascribed it to Louis-François Dubois, the poet.† All this was, however, so much guess-work, when, one day during the Reign of Terror, the report spread that a ci-devant priest, or rather a priest who had refused to take the oath to the Republic, had been caught solemnizing a religious marriage, and that he was to be brought before the Revolutionary Tribunal that same afternoon. Though you may not think so, merely going by what you have read, the appearance of a priest before the Tribunal always aroused more than common interest, nor have you any idea what more than common interest meant in those days. A priest to the Revolutionaries and to the Terrorists, they might hector and bully as they liked, was not an ordinary being. They looked upon him either as something better than a man or worse than a devil. They had thrown the religious compass they had

* I have inserted them here in order not to fall into repetitions on the same subject.—EDITOR.

† Louis-François Dubois, the author of several heroic poems, "Ankarström," "Geneviève et Siegfried," etc., which are utterly forgotten. His main title to the recollection of posterity consists in his having saved, during the Revolution, a great many literary works of value, which he returned to the State afterwards.—EDITOR.

brought from home with them overboard, and they had not the philosophical one to take its place. You may work out the thing for yourself; at any rate, the place was crammed to suffocation when we arrived at the Hôtel de Ville. It was a large room, at the upper end of which stood an oblong table, covered with a black cloth. Seated around it were seven self-constituted judges. Besides their tricolour scarfs round their waists, they wore, suspended by a ribbon from their necks, a small silver axe.

"As a rule there was very little speechifying. 'La mort sans phrase,' which had become the fashion since Louis XVI.'s execution, was strictly adhered to. Half a dozen prisoners were brought in and taken away without arousing the slightest excitement, either in the way of commiseration or hatred. After having listened, the judges either extended their hands on the table or put them to their foreheads. The first movement meant acquittal and liberation, the second death; not always by the guillotine though, for the instrument was not perfect as yet, and did not work sufficiently quickly to please them. All at once the priest was brought in, and a dead silence prevailed. He was not a very old man, though his hair was snow-white.

"'Who art thou?' asked the president.

"The prisoner drew himself up to his full height. 'I am the Abbé Pessoneaux, a former tutor at the college at Vienne, and the author of the last strophe of the Marseillaise,' he said quietly.

"I cannot convey to you the impression produced by those simple words. The silence became positively oppressive; you could hear the people breathe. The president did not say another word; the priest's reply had apparently stunned him also: he merely turned round to his fellow-judges. Soldiers and gaolers stood as if turned into stone; every eye was directed towards the table, watching for the movement of the judges' hands. Slowly and deliberately they stretched them forth, and then a deafening cheer rang through the room. The Abbé Pessoneaux owed his life to his strophe, for, though his story was not questioned then, it was proved true in every particular. On their way to Paris to be present at the taking of the Tuileries on the 10th of August, the Marseillais had stopped at Vienne to celebrate the Fête of the Federation. On the eve of their arrival the Abbé Pessoneaux had composed the strophe, and but for his seizure the authorship would have always remained a matter of conjecture, for Rouget de l'Isle would have never had the honesty to acknowledge it."

My tutor was right, and I owe him this tardy apology; it appears that, after all, Rouget de l'Isle had not the honesty to acknowledge *openly* his indebtedness to those who made his name immortal, and that his share in the Marseillaise amounts to the first six strophes. He did not write a single note of the music. The latter was composed by Alexandre Boucher, the celebrated violinist, in 1790, in the drawing-room of Madame de Mortaigne, at the request of a colonel whom the musician had never met before, whom he never saw again. The soldier was starting next morning with his regiment for Marseilles, and pressed Boucher to write him a march there and then. Rouget de l'Isle, an officer of engineers, having been imprisoned in 1791, for having refused to take a second oath to the Constitution, heard the march from his cell, and, at the instance of his gaoler, adapted the words of a patriotic hymn he was then writing to it.

One may fancy the surprise of Alexandre Boucher, when he heard it sung everywhere and recognized it as his own composition, though it had been somewhat altered to suit the words. But the pith of the story is to come. I give it in the very words of Boucher himself, as he told it to a Paris journalist whom I knew well.

"A good many years afterwards, I was seated next to Rouget de l'Isle at a dinner-party in Paris. We had never met before, and, as you may easily imagine, I was rather interested in the gentleman, whom, with many others at the same board, I complimented on his production; only I confined myself to complimenting him on his *poem*.

"'You don't say a word about the music,' he replied; 'and yet, being a celebrated musician, that ought to interest you. Do not you like it?'

"'Very much indeed,' I said, in a somewhat significant tone.

"'Well, let me be frank with you. The music is not mine. It was that of a march which came, Heaven knows whence, and which they kept on playing at Marseilles during the Terror, when I was a prisoner at the fortress of St. Jean. I made a few alterations necessitated by the words, and there it is.'

"Thereupon, to his great surprise, I hummed the march as I had originally written it.

"'Wonderful!' he exclaimed; 'how did you come by it?' he asked.

"When I told him, he threw himself round my neck. But the next moment he said—

"'I am very sorry, my dear Boucher, but I am afraid that you will be despoiled for ever, do what you will; for your music and my words go so well together, that they seem to have sprung simultaneously from the same brain, and the world, even if I proclaimed my indebtedness to you, would never believe it.'

"'Keep the loan,' I said, moved, in spite of myself, by his candour. 'Without your genius, my march would be forgotten by now. You have given it a patent of nobility. It is yours for ever.'"

I return to Louis-Philippe, who, at the time of my tutor's story, and for some years afterwards, I only knew from the reports that were brought home to us. Of course, I saw him several times at a distance, at reviews and on popular holidays, and I was surprised that a king of whom every one spoke so well in private, who seemed to have so much cause for joy and happiness in his own family, should look so careworn and depressed in public. For, young as I was, I did not fail to see that, beneath the calm and smiling exterior, there was a great deal of hidden grief. But I was too young to understand the deep irony of his reply to one of my relatives, a few months before his accession to the throne: "The crown of France is too cold in winter, too warm in summer; the sceptre is too blunt as a weapon of defence or attack, it is too short as a stick to lean upon: a good felt hat and a strong umbrella are at all times more useful." Above all, I was too young to understand the temper of the French where their rulers were concerned, and though, at the time of my writing these notes, I have lived for fifty years amongst them, I doubt whether I could give a succinct psychological account of their mental attitude towards their succeeding régimes, except by borrowing the words of one of their cleverest countrywomen, Madame Emile de Girardin: "When Marshal Soult is in the Opposition, he is acknowledged to have won the battle of Toulouse; when he belongs to the Government, he is accused of having lost it." Since then the Americans have coined a word for that state of mind—"cussedness."

Louis-Philippe's children, and especially his sons, some of whom I knew personally before I had my first invitation to the Tuileries, seemed to take matters more cheerfully. Save the partisans of the elder branch, no one had a word to say against them. On the contrary, even the Bonapartists admired their manly and straightforward bearing. I remember being at Tortoni's one afternoon when the Duc d'Orléans and his brother, the Duc de Nemours, rode by. Two of my neighbours, unmistakable Imperialists, and old soldiers by their looks, stared very hard at them; then one said, "Si le petit au lieu de filer le parfait amour partout, avait mis tous ses œufs dans le même panier, il aurait eu des grands comme cela et nous ne serions pas dans l'impasse ou nous sommes."

"Mon cher," replied the other, "des grands comme cela ne se font qu'à loisir, pas entre deux campagnes." *

The admiration of these two veterans was perfectly

* It reminds one of the answer of the younger Dumas to a gentleman whose wife had been notorious for her conjugal faithlessness, and whose sons were all weaklings. "Ah, Monsieur Dumas, c'est un fils comme vous qu'il me fallait," he exclaimed. "Mon cher monsieur," came the reply, "quand on veut avoir un fils comme moi, il faut le faire soi-même."—EDITOR.

justified: they were very handsome young men, the sons of Louis-Philippe, and notably the two elder ones, though the Duc d'Orléans was somewhat more delicate-looking than his brother, De Nemours. The boys had all been brought up very sensibly, perhaps somewhat too strict for their position. They all went to a public school, to the College Henri IV., and I remember well, about the year '38, when I had occasion of a morning to cross the Pont-Neuf, where there were still stalls and all sorts of booths, seeing the blue-and-yellow carriage with the royal livery. It contained the Ducs d'Aumale and de Montpensier, who had not finished their studies at that time.

But though strictly brought up, they were by no means milksops, and what, for want of a better term, I may call "mother's babies:" quite the reverse. It was never known how they managed it, but at night, when they were supposed to be at home, if not in bed, they were to be met with at all kinds of public places, notably at the smaller theatres, such as the Vaudeville, the Variétés, and the Palais-Royal, one of which, at any rate, was a goodly distance from the Tuileries. It was always understood that the King knew nothing about these little escapades, but I am inclined to doubt this: I fancy he connived at them; because, when Lord —— told him casually one day that he had met his sons the night before, Louis-Philippe seemed not in the least surprised, he only anxiously asked, "Where?"

"At the Café de Paris, your majesty."

The king seemed relieved. "That's all right," he said, laughing. "As long as they do not go into places where they are likely to meet with Guizot, I don't mind; for if he saw them out in the evening, it might cost me my throne. Guizot is so terribly respectable. I am afraid there is a mistake either about his nationality or about his respectability; they are badly matched."

The fact is, that though Louis-Philippe admired and respected Guizot, he failed to understand him. To the most respectable of modern kings—not even Charles I. and William III. excepted—if by respectability we mean an unblemished private life—Guizot's respectability was an enigma. The man who, in spite of his advice to others, " Enrichissez vous, enrichissez vous," was as poor at the end of his ministerial career as at the beginning, must have necessarily been a puzzle to a sovereign who, with a civil list of £750,000, was haunted by the fear of poverty, and haunted to such a degree as to harass his friends and counsellors with his apprehensions. " My dear minister," he said one day to Guizot, after he had recited a long list of his domestic charges—" My dear minister, I am telling you that my children will be wanting for bread." The recollection of his former misery uprose too frequently before him like a horrible nightmare, and made him the first bourgeois instead of the first gentilhomme of the kingdom, as his predecessors had been. When a tradesman drops a shilling and does not stoop to pick it up, his neglect becomes almost culpable improvidence; when a prince drops a sovereign and looks for it, the deed may be justly qualified as mean. The *leitmotif* of Louis-Philippe's conversation, witty and charming as it was, partook of the avaricious spirit of a Thomas Guy and a John Overs rather than of that of the great adventurer John Law. The chinking of the money-bags is audible through both, but in the one case the orchestration is strident, disagreeable, depressing; in the other, it is generous, overflowing with noble impulses, and cheering. I recollect that during my stay at Tréport and Eu, in 1843, when Queen Victoria paid her visit to Louis-Philippe, the following story was told to me. Lord —— and I were quartered in a little hostelry on the Place du Château. One morning Lord —— came home laughing till he could laugh no longer. "What do you think the King has done now?" he asked. I professed my inability to guess. "About an hour ago, he and Queen Victoria were walking in the garden, when, with true French politeness, he offered her a peach. The Queen seemed rather embarrassed how to skin it, when Louis-Philippe took a large clasp-knife from his pocket. 'When a man has been a poor devil like myself, obliged to live upon forty sous a day, he always carries a knife. I might have dispensed with it for the last few years; still, I do not wish to lose the habit—one does not know what may happen,' he said. Of course, the tears stood in the Queen's eyes. He really ought to know better than to obtrude his money worries upon every one."

I must confess that I was not as much surprised as my interlocutor, who, however, had known Louis-Philippe much longer than I. Not his worst enemies could have accused the son of Philippe Egalité of being a coward: the bulletins of Valmy, Jemmappes, and Neerwinden would have proved the contrary. But the contempt of physical danger on the battle-field does not necessarily constitute heroism in the most elevated sense of the term, although the world in general frequently accepts it as such. A man can die but once, and the semi-positivism, semi-Voltaireanism of Louis-Philippe had undoubtedly steeled him against the fear of death. His religion, throughout life, was not even skin-deep; and when he accepted the last rites of the Church on his death-bed, he only did so in deference to his wife. "Ma femme, es-tu contente de moi?" were his words the moment the priests were gone.

Nevertheless, he was too good a husband to grieve his wife, who was deeply religious, by any needless display of unbelief. He always endeavoured, as far as possible, to find an excuse for staying away from church. He, as well as the female members of his family, were very fond of music; and Adam, the composer, was frequently invited to come and play for them in the private apartments. In fact, after his abdication, he seriously intended to write, in conjunction with Scribe, the libretto of an opera on an English historical subject, the music of which should be composed by Halévy. The composer of "La Juive" and the author of "Les Hugenots" came over once to consult with the King, whose death, a few months later, put an end to the scheme.

On the occasion of Adam's visits the princesses worked at their embroidery, while the King often stood by the side of the performer. Just about that period the chamber organ was introduced, and, on the recommendation of Adam, one was ordered for the Tuileries. The first time Louis-Philippe heard it played he was delighted: "This will be a distinct gain to our rural congregations," he said. "There must be a great many people who, like myself, stay away from church on account of their objection to that horrible instrument, the serpent. Is it not so, my wife?"

The ideal purpose of life, if ever he possessed it, had been crushed out of him—first, by his governess, Madame de Genlis; secondly, by the dire poverty he suffered during his exile: and, notwithstanding all that has been said to the contrary, France wanted at that moment an ideal ruler, not the rational father of a large family who looked upon his monarchy as a suitable means of providing for them. He was an usurper without the daring, the grandeur, the lawlessness of the usurper. The lesson of Napoleon I.'s method had been thrown away upon him, as the lesson of Napoleon III.'s has been thrown away upon his grandson. When I said France, I made a mistake,—I should have said Paris; for since 1789 there was no longer a King of France, there was only a King of Paris. Such a thing as a Manchester movement, as a Manchester school of politics, would have been and is still an impossibility in France.

And, unfortunately, Paris, which had applauded the glorious *mise-en-scène* of the First Empire, which had even looked on approvingly at some of the pomp and state of Louis XVIII. and Charles X., jeered at Louis-Philippe and his court with its ridiculous gatherings of tailors, drapers, and bootmakers, " ces gardes nationaux d'un pays où il n'y a plus rien de national à garder," and their pretentious spouses " qui," according to the Duchesse de la Trémoïlle, " ont plus de chemises que nos aïeules avaient des robes."* She and the

* She had unconsciously borrowed the words from the Duchesse de Coislin, who, under similar circumstances a few years before, said to Madame de Chateaubriand, " Cela sent la parvenue; nous autres, femmes de la cour, nous n'avions que deux chemises; on les renou-

Princesse Bagration were the only female representatives of the Faubourg St. Germain who attended these gatherings; for the Countess Le Hon, of whom I may have occasion to speak again, and who was the only other woman at these receptions that could lay claim to any distinction, was by no means an aristocrat. And be it remembered that in those days ridicule had still the power to kill.

Nor was the weapon wielded exclusively by the aristocracy; the lower classes could be just as satirical against the new court element. I was in the Tuileries gardens on that first Sunday in June, 1837, when the Duchesse d'Orléans made her entrée into Paris. The weather was magnificent, and the set scene—as distinguished from some of the properties, to use a theatrical expression—in keeping with the weather. The crowd itself was a pleasure to look at, as it stood in serried masses behind the National Guards and the regular infantry lining the route of the procession from the Arc de Triomphe to the entrance of the Château. All at once an outrider passes, covered with dust, and the crowd presses forward to get a better view. A woman of the people, in her nice white cap, comes into somewhat violent contact with an elegantly dressed elderly lady, accompanied by her daughter. The woman, instead of apologizing, says aloud that she wishes to see the princess: "You will have the opportunity of seeing her at court, mesdames," she adds. The elegant lady vouchsafes no reply, but turns to her daughter: "The good woman," says the latter, shrug-

velait quand elles étaient usées; nous étions vetues de robes de soie et nous n'avions pas l'air de grisettes comme ces demoiselles de maintenant."—EDITOR.

ging her shoulders, "is evidently not aware that she has got a much greater chance of going to that court than we have. She has only got to marry some grocer or other tradesman, and she will be considered a grande dame at once." Then the procession passes—first the National Guards on horseback, then the king and M. de Montalivet, followed by Princesse Hélène, with her young husband riding by the side of the carriage. So far so good: the first three or four carriages were more or less handsome, but Heaven save us from the rest, as well as from their occupants! They positively looked like some of those wardrobe-dealers so admirably described by Balzac.

When all is over, the woman of the people turns to the elegant lady: "I ask your pardon, madame; it was really not worth while hurting you. If these are *grandes dames*, I prefer *les petites* whom I see in my neighbourhood, the Rue Notre-Dame de Lorette. Comme elles étaient attifées!"—*Anglice*, "What a lot of frumps they looked!"

In fact, Louis-Philippe and his queen sinned most grievously by overlooking the craving of the Parisians for pomp and display. No one was better aware of this than his children, notably the Duc d'Orléans, Princess Clementine,[*] and the Duc de Nemours. They

[*] The mother of Prince Ferdinand of Saxe-Coburg, the present ruler of Bulgaria. She was a particular favourite of Queen Victoria, and Louis-Philippe himself not only considered her the cleverest of his three daughters, but the most likely successor to his sister Adelaide, as his private adviser. That the estimate of her abilities was by no means exaggerated, subsequent events have proved. The last time I saw the princess was at the garden party at Sheen-House, on the occasion of the silver wedding of the Count and Countess de Paris. I did not remember her for the moment, for a score of years had made a difference. I asked an Austrian attaché who she was. The answer came pat, "Alexander III.'s nightmare, Francis-Joseph's bogy, and Bismarck's sleeping draught; one of the three clever women in Europe; Bulgaria's mother."—EDITOR.

called him familiarly "le père." "Il est trop père," said the princess in private; "il fait concurrence au Père Eternel." She was a very clever girl—perhaps a great deal cleverer than any of her brothers, the Solon of the family, the Duc de Nemours, included—but very fond of mischief and practical joking. She found her match, though, in her brother, the Prince de Joinville, the son of Louis-Philippe of whom France heard most and saw least, for he was a sailor. One day, his sister asked him to bring her a complete dress of a Red-Skin chieftain's wife. His absence was shorter than usual, and, a few days before his return, he told her in a letter that he had the costume she wanted. "Here, Clementine, this is for you," he said, at his arrival, putting a string of glass beads on the table.

"Very pretty," said Clementine, "but you promised me a complete dress."

"This is the complete dress. I never saw them wear any other."

I did not see the Prince de Joinville very often, perhaps two or three times in all; once on the occasion of his marriage with Princess Françoise de Bourbon, the daughter of Dom Pedro I. of Brazil, and sister of the present emperor, when the prince brought his young bride to Paris. He was a clever draughtsman and capital caricaturist; but if the first of these talents proved an unfailing source of delight to his parents, the second frequently inspired them with terror, especially his father, who never knew which of his ministers might become the next butt for his third son's pencil. I have seen innumerable sketches, ostensibly done to delight his young wife and brothers, which, had they been published, would have been much more telling against his father's pictorial satirists than anything they produced against the sovereign. For in those days, whatever wisdom or caution they may have learnt afterwards, the sons of Louis-Philippe were by no means disposed to sit down tamely under the insults levelled at the head of their house. In fact, nearly the whole of Louis-Philippe's children had graphic talents of no mean order. The trait came to them from their mother, who was a very successful pupil of Angelica Kauffman. Princesse Marie, who died so young, executed a statue of Jeanne d'Arc, which was considered by competent judges, not at all likely to be influenced by the fact of the artist's birth, a very creditable piece of work indeed. I never saw it, so I cannot say, but I have seen some miniatures by the Duc de Nemours, which might fairly rank with performances by the best masters of that art, short of genius.

It is a curious, but nevertheless admitted fact that the world has never done justice to the second son of Louis-Philippe. He was not half as great a favourite with the Parisians as his elder brother, although, in virtue of his remarkable likeness to Henri IV., whom the Parisians still worship—probably because he is dead,—he ought to have commanded their sympathies. This lukewarmness towards the Duc de Nemours has generally been ascribed by the partisans of the Orléanist dynasty to his somewhat reticent disposition, which by many people was mistaken for *hauteur*. I rather fancy it was because he was suspected of being his father's adviser, and, what was worse, his father's adviser in a reactionary sense. He was accused of being an anti-parliamentarian, and he never took the trouble to refute the charge, probably because he was too honest to tell a lie.* I met the Duc de Nemours for the first time in the studio of a painter, Eugène Lami, just as I met his elder brother in that of Decamps. In fact, all these young princes were sincere admirers and patrons of art, and, if they had had their will, the soirées at the Tuileries would have been graced by the presence of artists more frequently than they were; but, preposterous and scarcely credible as it may seem, the bourgeoisie looked upon this familiar intercourse of the king's sons with artists, literary men, and the like, as so much condescension, if not worse, of which they, the bourgeoisie, would not be guilty if they could help it. It behoves me, however, to be careful in this instance, for the English aristocracy at home was not much more liberal in those days.

The first thing that struck one in the Duc de Nemours was the vast extent of his general information and the marvellous power of memory. Eugène Lami had just returned from London, and, in the exercise of his profession, had come in contact with some members of the oldest families. The mere mention of the name sufficed as the introduction to the general and anecdotal history of such a family, and I doubt whether the best official at Herald's College could have dissected a pedigree as did the Duc de Nemours. Eugène

* There was a similar divergence of dynastic opinion during the Second Empire between the sovereign and those placed very near him on the throne. When Alphonse Daudet came to Paris to make a name in literature, the Duc de Morny offered him a position as secretary. "Before I accept it, monsieur le duc, I had better tell you that I am a Legitimist," replied the future novelist. "Don't let that trouble you," laughed De Morny; "so am I to a certain extent, and the Empress is even more of a Legitimist than I am."—EDITOR.

Lami was at that time engaged upon designing some new uniforms for the army, many of which disappeared only after the war of 1870. He lived in the Rue des Marais, the greater part of which was subsequently demolished to make room for the Boulevard de Magenta, and in the same house with two men whose names have become immortal, Honoré de Balzac and Paul Delaroche. I have already spoken of both, but I did not mention the incident that led to the painter's acquaintance with the novelist, an incident so utterly fanciful that the boldest farce-writer would think twice before utilizing it in a play. It was told to me by Lami himself. One morning, as he and Paul Delaroche were working, there was a knock at the door, and a stout individual, dressed in a kind of monastic garb, appeared on the threshold. Delaroche remembered that he had met him on the staircase, but neither knew who he was, albeit that Balzac's fame was not altogether unknown to them. "Gentlemen," said the visitor, "I am Honoré Balzac, a neighbour and a confrère to boot. My chattels are about to be seized, and I would ask you to save a remnant of my library."

Of course, the request was granted. The books were stowed away behind the pictures; and, after that, Balzac often dropped in to have a chat with them, but neither Delaroche nor Lami, the latter least of all, ever conceived a sincere liking for the great novelist. Their characters were altogether dissimilar. I have seen a good many men whose names have become household words among the refined, the educated, and the art-loving all the world over; I have seen them at the commencement, in the middle, and at the zenith of their career: I have seen none more indifferent to the material benefits of their art than Eugène Lami and Paul Delaroche, not even Eugène Delacroix and Decamps. Balzac was the very reverse. To make a fortune was the sole ambition of his life.

To return for a moment to Louis-Philippe's sons. I have said that the Duc de Nemours was essentially the grand seigneur of the family; truth compels me to add, however, that there was a certain want of pliability about him which his social inferiors could not have relished. It was Henri IV. minus the bonhomie, also perhaps minus that indiscriminate galanterie which endeared Ravaillac's victim to all classes, even when he was no longer young. In the days of which I am treating just now, the Duc de Nemours was very young. As for his courage, it was simply above suspicion; albeit that it was called in question after the revolution of '48, to his father's intense sorrow. No after-dinner encomium was ever as absolutely true as that of Sir Robert Peel on the sons and daughters of the last King of France, when he described them as respectively brave and chaste. Nevertheless, had the Duc de Nemours and his brothers been a thousand times as brave as they were, party spirit, than which there is nothing more contemptible in France, would have found the opportunity of denying that bravery.

If these notes are ever published, Englishmen will smile at what I am about to write now, unless their disgust takes another form of expression. The exploits of the Duc d'Aumale in Algeria are quoted by independent military authorities as so many separate deeds of signal heroism. They belong to history, and not a single historian has endeavoured to impair their value. Will it be believed that the Opposition journals of those days spoke of them with ill-disguised contempt as mere skirmishes with a lot of semi-savages? And, during the Second Republic, many of these papers returned to the charge because the Duc d'Aumale, being the constitutionally-minded son of a constitutionally-minded king, resigned the command of his army instead of bringing it to France to coerce a nation into retaining a ruler whom, ostensibly at least, she had voluntarily accepted, and whom, therefore, she was as free to reject.

In connection with these Algerian campaigns of the Duc d'Aumale, I had a story told to me by his brother, De Montpensier, which becomes particularly interesting nowadays, when spiritualism or spiritism is so much discussed. He had it from two unimpeachable sources, namely, from his brother D'Aumale and from General Cousin-Montauban, afterwards Comte de Palikao, the same who was so terribly afraid, after the expedition in China, that the emperor would create him Comte de Pékin, and who sent an aide-de-camp in advance to beg the sovereign not to do so.*

It was to General Montauban that Abdel-Kader surrendered after the battles of Isly and Djemma-Gazhouat. It was in the latter engagement that a Captain de Géreaux fell, and when the news of his death reached his family they seemed almost prepared for it. It transpired that, on the very day of the engagement, and at the very hour in which Captain de Géreaux was struck down, his sister, a young

* In order to understand this dread on Montauban's part, the English reader should be told that the term *pékin* is the contemptuous nickname for the civilian, with the French soldier.—EDITOR.

and handsome but very impressionable girl, started all of a sudden from her chair, exclaiming that she had seen her brother, surrounded by Arabs, who were felling him to the ground. Then she dropped to the floor in a dead swoon.

A few years elapsed, when General Montauban, who had become the military Governor of the province of Oran, received a letter from the De Géreaux family, requesting him to make some further inquiries respecting the particulars of the captain's death. The letter was written at the urgent prayer of Mdlle. de Géreaux, who had never ceased to think and speak of her brother, and who, on one occasion, a month or so before the despatch of the petition, had risen again from her chair, though in a more composed manner than before, insisting that she had once more seen her brother. This time he was dressed in the native garb, he seemed very poor, and was delving the soil. These visions recurred at frequent intervals, to the intense distress of the family, who could not but ascribe them to the overstrung imagination of Mdlle. de Géreaux. A little while after, she maintained having seen her brother in a white robe and turban, and intoning hymns that sounded to her like Arabic. She implored her parents to institute inquiries, and General Montauban was communicated with to that effect. He did all he could; the country was at peace, and, after a few months, tidings came that there was a Frenchman held prisoner in one of the villages on the Morocco frontier, who for the last two or three years had entirely lost his reason, but that, previous to that calamity, he had been converted to Islamism. His mental derangement being altogether harmless, he was an attendant at the Mosque. As a matter of course, the information had been greatly embellished in having passed through so many channels, nor was it of so definite a character as I have noted it down, but that was the gist of it.

Meanwhile, Montauban had been transferred to another command, and for a twelvemonth after his successor's arrival the inquiry was allowed to fall in abeyance. When it was finally resumed, the French prisoner had died, but, from a document written in his native language found upon him and brought to Oran, there remained little doubt that he was Captain de Géreaux.

To return for a moment to the Duc d'Aumale, who, curiously enough, exercised a greater influence on the outside world in general than any of his other brethren—an influence due probably to his enormous wealth rather than to his personal qualities, though the latter may, to some people, have seemed remarkable. I met him but seldom during his father's lifetime. He was the beau-ideal of the preux chevalier, according to the French notion of the modern Bayard—that is, handsome, brave to a fault, irresistibly fascinating with women, good-natured in his way, and, above all, very witty. It was he who, after the confiscation of the d'Orléans' property by Napoleon III., replied to the French Ambassador at Turin, who inquired after his health, "I am all right; health is one of the things that cannot be confiscated." Nevertheless, upon closer acquaintance, I failed to see the justifying cause for the preference manifested by public opinion, and, upon more minute inquiry, I found that a great many people shared my views. I am at this moment convinced that, but for his having been the heir of that ill-fated Prince de Condé, and consequently the real defender in the various suits resulting from the assassination of that prince by Madame de Feuchères, he would have been in no way distinguished socially from the rest of the D'Orléans.

The popularity of his eldest brother, the Duc d'Orléans, was, on the contrary, due directly to the man himself. As far as one can judge of him, he was the reverse of Charles II., in that he never said a wise thing and never did a foolish one. He was probably not half so clever as his father, nor, brave as he may have been, would he have ever made so dashing a soldier as his brother D'Aumale, or so rollicking a sailor as his brother De Joinville. He did not pretend to the wisdom of his brother De Nemours, nor to the mystic tendencies of his youngest sister, nor to the sprightly wit of Princesse Clementine, and yet withal he understood the French nation better than any of them. Even his prenuptial escapades, secrets to no one, were those of the grand seigneur, though by no means affichées; they endeared him to the majority of the people. "Chacun colon-ise à sa façon," was the lenient verdict on his admiration for Jenny Colon, at a moment when colonization in Algeria was the topic of the day. On the whole he liked artists better, perhaps, than art itself, yet it did not prevent him from buying masterpieces as far as his means would allow him. Though still young, in the latter end of the thirties, I was already a frequent visitor to the studios of the great French painters, and it was in that of Decamps' that I became alive to his character for the first time. I was talking to the great painter when the duke came in. We had met before, and shook hands, as he had been taught to do by his father when he met with an Englishman. But I could not make out why he was carrying a pair of trousers over his arm. After we had been chatting for about ten minutes, I wondering all the while what he was going to do with the nether garment, he caught one of my side glances, and burst out laughing. "I forgot," he said; "here, Decamps, here are your breeches." Then he turned to me to explain. "I always bring them up with me when I come in the morning. The concierge is very old, and it saves her trudging up four flights of stairs." The fact was, that the concierge, before she knew who he was, had once asked him to take up the painter's clothes and boots. From that day forth he never failed to ask for them when passing her lodge.

I can but repeat, the Duc d'Orléans was one of the most charming men I have known. I always couple him in my mind with Benjamin Disraeli, and Alexandre Dumas the elder. I knew the English statesman almost as well during part of my life as the French novelist. Though intellectually wide apart from them, the duke had one, if not two traits in common with both; his utter contempt for money affairs and the personal charm he wielded. I doubt whether this personal charm in the other two men was due to their intellectual attainments; with the Duc d'Orléans it was certainly not the case. He rarely, if ever, said anything worth remembering; in fact, he frankly acknowledged his very modest scholarship, and his inability either to remember the epigrams of others or to condense his thoughts into one of his own. "I should not like to admit as much to my father, who, it appears, is a very fine Greek and Latin scholar," he said—"that is, if I am to believe my brothers, De Nemours and D'Aumale, who ought to know; for, notwithstanding the prizes they took at college, I believe they are very clever. Ah, you may well look surprised at my saying, 'notwithstanding the prizes they took,' because I took ever so many, although, for the life of me, I could not construe a Greek sentence, and scarcely a Latin one. I have paid very handsomely, however, for my ignorance." And then he told us an amusing story of his having had to invent a secretaryship to the duchess for an old schoolfellow. "You see, he came upon me unawares with a slip of paper I had written him while at college, asking him to explain to me a Greek passage. There was no denying it, I had signed it. What is worse still, he is supposed to translate and to reply to the duchess's German correspondence, and, when I gave him the appointment, he did not know a single word of Schiller's language, so I had to pay a German tutor and him too."

I have said that the Duc d'Orléans was absolutely indifferent with regard to money, but he would not be fleeced with impunity. What he disliked more than anything else, was the greed of the shop-keeping bourgeois. One day, while travelling in Lorraine, he stopped at the posting-house to have his breakfast, consisting of a couple of eggs, a few slices of bread and butter, and a cup of coffee. Just before proceeding on his journey, his valet came to tell him that mine host wanted to charge him two hundred francs for the repast. The duke merely sent for the mayor, handed him a thousand-franc note, gave him the particulars of his bill of fare, told him to pay the landlord according to the tariff, and to distribute the remainder of the money among the poor. It is more than probable that mine host was among the first, in '48, to hail the republic: princes and kings, according to him, were made to be fleeced; if they objected, what was the good of having a monarchy?

The popular idol in France must distribute largesse, and distribute it individually, or be profitable in some other way. Greed, personal interest, underlies most of the political strife in France. During one of the riots, so common in the reign of Louis-Philippe, Mimi-Lepreuil, a well-known clever pickpocket, was shouting with all his might, "Vive Louis-Philippe! à bas la République!" As a rule, gentlemen of his profession are found on the plebeian side, and one of the superintendents of police on duty, who had closely watched him, inquired into the reason of his apostasy. "I am sick of your Republicans," was the answer. "I come here morning after morning"—it happened on the Place de la Bourse,—" and dip my hands into a score of pockets without finding a red cent. During the Revolution of July, at the funeral of General Lamarque, I did not make my expenses. Give me a royal procession to make money." These were his politics.

It would be difficult to say what the Duc d'Orléans would have done, had he lived to ascend the throne. One thing is certain, however, that, on the day of his death, genuine tears stood in the eyes of all classes, except the Legitimists. As I have already said, they ascribed the fatal accident to God's vengeance for the usurpation of his father. "If this be the case," said an irreverent but witty journalist, "it argues but very little providence on the part of *your Providence,* for now He will have to keep the peace between the Duc de Berri, the Duc de Reichstadt, and the Duc d'Orléans."

CHAPTER X.

The Revolution of '48—The beginning of it—The National Guards in all their glory—The Café Grégoire on the Place du Caire—The price of a good breakfast in '48—The palmy days of the Cuisine Bourgeoise—The excitement on the Boulevards on Sunday, February 20th, '48—The theatres—A ball at Poirson's, the erstwhile director of the Gymnase—A lull in the storm—Tuesday, February 22nd—Another visit to the Café Grégoire—On my way thither—The Comédie-Française closes its doors—What it means, according to my old tutor—We are waited upon by a sergeant and corporal—We are no longer "messieurs," but "citoyens"—An eye to the main chance—The patriots do a bit of business in tricolour cockades—The company marches away—Casualties—"Le patriotisme" means the difference between the louis d'or and the écu of three francs—The company bivouacs on the Boulevard Saint-Martin—A tyrant's victim "*malgre lui*"—Wednesday, February 23rd—The Café Grégoire once more—The National Guards *en negligé*—A novel mode of settling accounts—The National Guards fortify the inner man—A bivouac on the Boulevard du Temple—A camp scene from an opera—I leave—My companion's account—The National Guards protect the regulars—The author of these notes goes to the theatre—The Gymnase and the Variétés on the eve of the Revolution—Bouffé and Déjazet—Thursday, February 24th, '48—The Boulevards at 9.30 a.m.—No milk—The Revolutionaries do without it—The Place du Carrousel—The sovereign people fire from the roofs on the troops—The troops do not dislodge them—The King reviews the troops—The apparent inactivity of Louis-Philippe's sons—A theory about the difference in bloodshed—One of the three ugliest men in France comes to see the King—Seditious cries—The King abdicates—Chaos—The sacking of the Tuileries—Receptions and feasting in the Galerie de Diane—"Du café pour nous, des cigarettes pour les dames"—The dresses of the princesses—The bourgeois feast the gamins who guard the barricades—The Republic proclaimed—The riff-raff insist upon illuminations—An actor promoted to the Governorship of the Hôtel de Ville—Some members of the "provisional Government" at work—Méry on Lamartine—Why the latter proclaimed the Republic.

I WAS returning home earlier than usual on Saturday night, the 19th of February, '48, when, at the corner of the Rue Lafitte, I happened to run against a young Englishman who had been established for some years in Paris as the representative of his father, a wealthy cotton-spinner in the north. We had frequently met before, and a cordial feeling had sprung up between us, based at first—I am bound to say—on our common contempt for the vanity of the French.

"Come and breakfast with me to-morrow morning," he said; "I fancy you will enjoy yourself. We will breakfast in my quarter, and you will see the National Guards in all their glory. They will muster very strong to-morrow, if it be fine."

"But why to-morrow?" I replied. "I was under the impression that the idea of the Reformist banquet in the Champs-Elysées had been abandoned, so there will be no occasion for them to parade? Besides, that would be on Tuesday only."

"It has been abandoned, but if you think that it will prevent them from turning out, you are very much mistaken; at any rate, come and listen to the preliminaries."

I promised him to come, but I had not the slightest idea that I was going to witness a kind of mild prologue to a revolution.

Next morning turned out very fine—balmy spring weather—and as I sauntered along the Boulevards Montmartre and Poissonière to the place of appointment the streets were already crowded with people in their Sunday clothes. The place where I was to meet my English friend was situated in the midst of a busy quarter, scarcely anything but warehouses where they sold laces, and flowers, and silks; something like the neighbourhood at the back of Cheapside. The wealthy tradesmen of those days did not live in the outskirts of Paris, as they did later on; and when my friend and I reached the principal café and restaurant on the Place du Caire—I think it was called the Café Grégoire—there was scarcely a table vacant. The habitués were, almost to a man, National Guards, prosperous business men, considerably more anxious, as I found out in a short time, to play a political part than to maintain public tranquillity. If I remember rightly, one of them, a chemist and druggist, who was pointed out to me then, became a deputy after the fall of the Second Empire; and I may notice en passant that this same spot was the political hothouse which produced, afterwards, Monsieur Tirard, who started life as a small manufacturer of imitation jewellery, and who rose to be Minister of Finances under the Third Republic.

The breakfast was simply excellent, the wine genuine throughout, the coffee and cognac all that could be wished; and, when I asked my friend to let me look at the bill, out of simple curiosity, or, rather, for the sake of comparing prices with those of the Cafés de Paris and Riche, I found that he had spent something less than eleven francs. At the Café Riche it would have been twenty-five francs, and, at the present time, one would be charged double that sum. These were the palmy days of the Cuisine Française, or, to call it by another name, the Cuisine Bourgeoise, for which, a few years later, a stranger in Paris would have almost sought in vain. Luckily, however, for my enjoyment and digestive organs, I was no stranger to Paris and to the French; if I had been, both the former would have been spoilt, the excitement of those around me being such as to lead the alien to believe that there would be an instantaneous departure for the Tuileries, and a revival of the bloody scenes of the first revolution. It has been my lot, in after-years, to hear a great deal of political drivel in French and English, but it was sound philosophy compared to what I heard that morning. I have spoken before of the Hôtel des Haricots, where men like Hugo, Balzac, Béranger, and Alfred de Musset chose to be imprisoned rather than perform their *duties* as National Guards. After that, I could fully appreciate their reluctance to be confounded with such a set of pompous windbags.

It came to nothing that day, but I had become interested, and made an appointment with my friend for the Tuesday, unless something should happen in the interval. Still, I did not think that the monarchy of July was doomed, though, on returning to the Boulevards, I could not help noticing that the excitement had considerably increased during the time I had been at breakfast. By twelve o'clock that night I was convinced that I had been mistaken, and that the dynasty of the D'Orléans had not a week to live. All the theatres were still open, but I had an invitation to a ball, given by Poirson, the then late director of the Gymnase Théâtre, at his house in the Faubourg Poissonnière. "Nous ne danserons plus jamais sous Louis-Philippe!" was the general cry, which did not prevent the guests from thoroughly enjoying themselves.

Next morning, Monday, there seemed to be a lull in the storm, but on the Tuesday the signs of the coming hurricane were plainly visible on the horizon.

The Ministry of Marine was guarded by a company of linesmen. I had some business in the Rue de Rivoli, which at that time ended almost abruptly at the Louvre; and, on my way to the Café Grégoire, I met patrol upon patrol of National Guards beating the "assembly." I had occasion to pass before the Comédie-Française. The ominous black-lettered slip of yellow paper, with the word *Relache*, was pasted across the evening's bill. That was enough for me. I remembered the words of my old tutor: "When the Comédie-Française shuts its doors in perilous times, it is like the battening down of the hatches in dirty weather. There is mischief brewing." When I got to the Place du Caire, I was virtually in the thick of it. With the exception of my friend and I, there was not a man in mufti. Even the proprietor had donned his uniform. Our fillet of beef was brought to us by a corporal, and our coffee poured out by a sergeant. Whether these warrior-waiters meant to strike one blow for freedom and to leave the place to take care of itself, we were unable to make out; but their patrons were no longer "messieurs," but had already become " citoyens." I was tempted to say, in the words of Dupin—the one who was President of the Chamber on the day of the Coup d'Etat, and who was Louis-Philippe's personal friend, " Soyons citoyens, mais restons messieurs," but I thought it better not. My friend had given up all idea of attending to business. " It will not be of the least use," he said. " If I had ribbons to sell instead of cottons, I might make a lot of money, though; for I am open to wager that some of our patriotic neighbours, while they are going to bell the cat outside, have given orders to their workpeople to manufacture tricolour cockades and rosettes with the magic R. F. (République Française) in the centre.

"You do not mean that they would think of such a thing at such a critical moment, even if the republic were a greater probability than it appears to be?" I remonstrated.

"I do mean to say so," he replied, beckoning at the same time to a sleek, corpulent lieutenant, standing a few paces away. "Can you do with a nice lot of narrow silk ribbon?" he asked, as the individual walked up to our table.

"What colour?" inquired the lieutenant.

My friend gave me a significant look, and named all the hues of the rainbow except white, red, and blue.

"Won't do," said the lieutenant, shaking his head. "If it had been red, white, and blue I would have bought as much as you like, because I am manufacturing rosettes for the good cause." After this he walked away.

On the Thursday afternoon the Boulevards and principal thoroughfares swarmed with peripatetic vendors of the republican insignia, and some of my friends expressed their surprise as to where they had come from in so short a time. Seeing that they were Frenchmen, I held my tongue, even when one professed to explain, "They have come from England; they are always speculating upon our misfortunes, though they do it cleverly enough. They got scent of what was coming, and sent them over as quickly as they could. Truly they are a great nation—of shopkeepers!" I was reminded of Béranger's scapegrace, when he was accused of being drunk.

> "Qu'est que cela me fait, a moi ?
> Que l'on m'appelle ivrogne ?"

he sings.

As the afternoon wore on, the excitement increased; the news from the Boulevards became alarming, and at about three o'clock the company marched away. As a matter of course we followed, and equally, as a matter of course, did not leave them until 2.30 next morning. Casualties to report. A large scratch in one of the drummer's cheeks, made by an oyster-shell, flung at the company as it turned round the corner of the Rue de Cléry. No battles, no skirmishes, a great deal of fraternizing with "le peuple souverain," whom, in their own employ, the well-to-do tradesmen would have ordered about like so many mangy curs.

From that day forth I have never dipped into any history of modern France, professing to deal with the political causes and effects of the various upheavals during the nineteenth century in France. They may be worth reading; I do not say that they are not. I have preferred to look at the men who instigated those disorders, and have come to the conclusion that, had each of them been born with five or ten thousand a year, their names would have been absolutely wanting in connection with them. This does not mean that the disorders would not have taken place, but they would have always been led by men in want of five or ten thousand a year. On the other hand, if the D'Orléans family had been less wealthy than they are there would have been no firmly settled third republic; if Louis-Napoleon had been less poor, there would, in all probability, have been no second empire; if the latter had lasted another year, we should have found Gambetta among the ministers of Napoleon III., just like Emile Ollivier, of the "light heart." "Les convictions politiques en France sont basées sur le fait que le louis d'or vaut sept fois plus que l'écu de trois francs." This is the dictum of a man who never wished to be anything, who steadfastly refused all offers to enter the arena of public life.

My friend and I had been baulked of the drama we expected—for we frankly confessed to one another that the utter annihilation of that company of National Guards would have left us perfectly unmoved,—and got instead, a kind of first act of a military spectacular play, such as we were in the habit of seeing at Franconi's. The civic warriors were ostensibly bivouacking on the Boulevard St. Martin; they stacked their muskets and fraternized with the crowd; it would not have surprised us in the least to see a troupe of ballet dancers advance into our midst and give us the entertainment de rigueur—the intermède. It was the only thing wanting to complete the picture, from which even the low comedy incident was not wanting. An old woebegone creature, evidently the worse for liquor, had fallen down while a patrol of regulars was passing. He was not a bit hurt; but there and then the rabble proposed to carry him to the Hôtel de Ville, and to give him an apotheosis as a martyr to the cause. They had already fetched a stretcher, and were, notwithstanding his violent struggles, hoisting him on it, when prevented by the captain of the National Guards.

Still, we returned next day to the Café Grégoire. In the middle of the place there lay an old man—that one, stark dead, who had been fired upon without rhyme or reason by a picket of the National Guards. It was only about eleven o'clock, and those valiant defenders of public order were still resting from their fatigue—at any rate, there were few of them about. There was a discussion going on whether they should go out or not—a discussion confined to the captain, two lieutenants, and as many sub-lieutenants. They appeared not to have the least idea of the necessity to refer for orders to the colonel or the head-quarters of the regiment or the legion, as it was called. They meant to settle the matter among themselves. The great argument in favour of calling out the men was that one of them, while standing at his window that very morning, was fired at by a passing ragamuffin, who, instead of hitting him, shattered his window-panes.

"Well," said one of the lieutenants, who had been opposed to the calling out of the men, "then we are quits after all; for look at the old fellow lying out there."

"No, we are not," retorts the captain; "for he was shot by a mistake, so he doesn't count."

"L'esprit ne perd jamais ses droits en France;" so, in another moment or two, the bugle sounded lustily throughout the quarter. We followed the buglers for a little while, it being still too early for our breakfast, and consequently enjoyed the felicity of seeing a good many of the warriors "in their habit as they lived" indoors—namely, in dressing-gown and slippers and smoking-caps. For most of them opened their windows on the first, second, and third floors, to inquire whether the call was urgent. The buglers entered into explanations. No, the call was not urgent, but the captain had decided on a military promenade, just to reassure the neighbourhood, and to stimulate the martial spirit of the lagging members of the company. The explanation invariably provoked the same answer, and in a voice not that of the citizen-warrior: " Que le capitaine attende jusqu'après le déjeuner."

Davoust has said that the first condition of the fitness of an army is its commissariat. In that respect every one of these National Guards was fit to be a Davoust, for their fortifying of the inner man was not accomplished until close upon two o'clock. By that time they marched out, saluted by the cries of " Vive la Réforme ! " of all the ragtag and bobtail from the Faubourgs du Temple and St. Antoine, who had invaded the principal thoroughfares. The " Marseillaise," the " Chant des Girondins," " La République nous appelle " resounded through the air; and I was wondering whether they were packing their trunks at the Tuileries, also what these National Guards had come out for. They only seemed to impede the efficient patrolling of the streets by the regulars, and, instead of dispersing the rabble, they attracted them. They were evidently under the impression that they made a very goodly show, and at every word of command I expected to see the captain burst asunder. When we got to the Boulevard St. Martin, the latter was told that the sixth legion was stationed on the Boulevard du Temple. A move was made in that direction.

Now " Richard is himself again ; " he is among the crowd he likes best—the crowd of the Boulevard du Crime, with its theatres, large and small, its raree and puppet shows, its open-air entertainments, its cafés and mountebanks; and, what is more, he is there in his uniform, distinguished from the rest, and consequently the cynosure of all the little actresses and pretty *figurantes* who have just left the rehearsal—for by this time it is after three—and who are but too willing to be entertained. Appointments are made to dine or to sup together, without the slightest reference as to what may happen in the interval. All at once there is an outcry and a rush towards the Porte Saint-Martin; our warriors are obliged to leave their inamoratas, and when they come to look for their muskets, which they have placed in a corner for convenience' sake, they find that a good many have disappeared. The customers belonging to the sovereign people have slunk off with them. Nevertheless they join the ranks, for the bugle has sounded. At the corner of the Faubourg Saint-Martin, whence the noise proceeded, they are met by three or four score of the sovereign people, ragged, unkempt, who are pushing in front of them two of the students of the Ecole Polytechnique. The two young fellows are very pale, and can scarcely speak. Still they manage to explain that the Municipal Guard at the Saint-Martin barracks have fired upon the people: then they go their way. Whither? Heaven only knows. But our captain, in the most stentorian of voices, gives the word of command, "To the right, wheel!" and we are striding up the faubourg, which is absolutely deserted as far as the Rue des Marais. A collision seems pretty inevitable now, the more that the Municipal Guards are already taking aim, when all at once our captain and one of the lieutenants rush forward, and fling themselves into the arms of the officers of the Municipal Guards. Tableau; and I am baulked once more of a good fight. I leave my friend to see the rest of this ridiculous comedy, and take my departure there and then.

The following is my companion's account of what happened after I left. I am as certain that every word of it is true as if I had been there myself, though it seems almost incredible that French officers, whose worst enemies have never accused them of being deficient in courage, should have acted so inconsiderately.

"The officers of the National Guards appear to have assumed at once the office of protectors of the regulars against the violence of the crowd. Why the regulars should have submitted to this, seeing that they were far better armed than their would-be guardians, I am unable to say. Be this as it may, the regulars consented, the flag floating above the principal door of the barracks was taken down, and I really believed that the Municipal Guards stacked their arms and virtually handed them over to the others. But I will not vouch for it. At any rate, a few hours afterwards, while the company had gone to dinner, the barracks were assailed, the men and officers knocked down by the people, and the building set on fire. When the fifth legion returned about eleven o'clock to the Faubourg Saint-Martin, the flames were leaping up to the sky, so they turned their heels contentedly in the direction of the Boulevard du Temple, where they bivouacked between the Théâtre de la Gaîté and the Ambigu-Comique, while those who had made appointments with the little actresses went round by the stage doors to keep them. That, as far as I could judge, was the part of the fifth legion in the day's proceedings.

I left them in all their glory, thinking themselves, no doubt, very fine fellows.

"On the Thursday morning"—my companion told me all this on Saturday evening, the 26th of February—"I was up betimes, simply because the drumming and bugling prevented my sleeping. At eight, the Café Grégoire was already very full, the heroes of the previous night had returned to perform their ablutions, and also, I suppose, to reassure their anxious spouses; but they had no longer that conquering air I noticed when I left them the night before. Whether they had come to the conclusion that both in love and war they had reaped but barren victories, I cannot say, but their republican ardour, it seemed to me, had considerably cooled down. I am convinced that, notwithstanding the events of Wednesday night in the Faubourg Saint-Martin, they were under the impression that neither the people nor the military would resort to further extremities. I cannot help thinking that, after I left, not a single man could have remained at his post, because not one amongst them seemed to have an idea of the horrible slaughter on the Boulevard des Capucines.* They were not left very long in

* The author, as will be seen directly, saw nothing of that massacre, though he must have passed within a few hundred yards of the spot immediately before it began. It would have been the same if he had; he could not have explained the cause, seeing that the most painstaking historians who have consulted the most trustworthy eye-witnesses have failed to do so. It will always remain a mystery whence the first shot came, whether from the military who were drawn up across the Boulevard des Capucines, on the spot where now stands the Grand Café, or from the crowd that wanted to pass, in order to proceed to Odilon-Barrot's to serenade him, because, notwithstanding the opposition of the king, he was to be included in the new ministry, which Molé had been instructed to form. It may safely be said, however, that, but for that shot and the slaughter consequent upon it, the revolution might have been averted then—after all, perhaps, only temporarily.—EDITOR.

ignorance of the real state of affairs, and then they saw at once that they had roused a spectre they would be unable to lay. From that moment, it is my opinion, they would have willingly drawn back, but it was too late. While they were still debating, an individual rushed in, telling them that one or two regiments, commanded by a general (who turned out to be General Bedeau), had drawn up in front of the barricade which had been thrown up during the night in the Boulevard Bonne-Nouvelle, and was being defended by a detachment of the fifth legion. They all ran out, and I ran with them. When we got to the boulevard, matters had already been arranged, and they were just in time to join the escort General Bedeau had accepted, after having consented not to execute the orders with which he had been entrusted. By that time I began to perceive which way the wind was blowing: the canaille had unceremoniously linked their arms in those of the National Guards, and insisted, courteously but firmly, on carrying their firearms. When we got to the Rue Montmartre, they took the horses out of the gun-carriages, and the soldiers looked tamely on, notwithstanding the commands of their officers. When the latter endeavoured to enforce their orders by hitting them with the flat of their swords, they simply left the ranks and joined the rabble. I had had enough of it, and made my way home by the back streets. I had had enough of it, and kept indoors until this afternoon."

Thus far my informant. As for myself, I saw little on the Wednesday night of what was going on. It was my own fault: I was too optimistic. I had scarcely gone a few steps, after my dinner, when, just in front of the Gymnase, they began shouting, "*La Patrie*,

Journal du soir; achetez *La Patrie.* Voyez le nouveau ministère de Monsieur Molé." I remember giving the fellow half a franc, at which he grumbled, though it was three times the ordinary price. On opening the paper, I rashly concluded from what I read that the revolution was virtually at an end, and I was the more confirmed in my opinion by the almost instantaneous lighting up of the Boulevards. It was like a fairy scene: people were illuminating—a little bit too soon, as it turned out. Being tired of wandering, and feeling no inclination for bed, I turned into the Gymnase. There were Bressant and Rose Chéri and Arnal; I would surely be able to spend a few pleasant hours. But alack and alas! the house presented a very doleful appearance—dead-heads, to a man; and very few of these, people who, if they could not fiddle themselves, like Nero while Rome was burning, would go to hear fiddling under no matter what circumstances, provided they were not asked to pay. I did not stay long, but when I came out into the streets the noise was too deafening for me. The "Marseillaise" has always had a particularly jarring effect upon my nerves. There are days when I could be cruel enough to prefer "the yells of those ferocious soldiers, as they murder in cold blood the sons and the companions" of one section of defenceless patriots, to the stirring strains of the other section as they figuratively rush to the rescue; and on that particular evening I felt in that mood. So, when I got to the Boulevard Montmartre, I turned into the Théâtre des Variétés. I remember the programme up to this day. They were playing "Le Suisse de Marly," "Le Marquis de Lauzun," "Les Extrèmes se touchent," and "Les Vieux Péchés." I had seen the second and the last piece at least a dozen times, but I was always ready to see them again for the sake of Virginie Déjazet in the one, of Bouffé in the other. The lessee at that time was an Englishman. Bouffé and I had always kept up our friendship; so I made up my mind to go and have a chat with him, hoping that Déjazet, whose conversation affected one like a bottle of champagne, would join us. The house, like the Gymnase, was almost empty, but I made my way behind the scenes, and in about half an hour forgot all about the events outside. Bouffé was telling me anecdotes about his London performances, and Déjazet was imitating the French of some of the bigwigs of King Leopold's court; so the time passed pleasantly enough. At the end of the performance we proposed taking supper, and turned down the Rue Montmartre. It was late when I returned home, consequently I saw nothing of the slaughter on the Boulevard des Capucines.

Though I had gone to bed late, I was up betimes on the Thursday morning. A glance at the Boulevards, as I turned the corner of my street about half-past nine, convinced me that the illuminations of the previous night had been premature, and that before the day was out there would be an end of the monarchy of July. A slight mist was still hanging over the city as I strolled in the direction of the Madeleine, and the weather was damp and raw, but in about half an hour the sun broke through. A shot was heard now and then, but I myself saw no collision then between the troops and the people. On the contrary, it looked to me as if the former would have been glad to be left alone. As I had been obliged to leave home without my usual cup of tea for want of milk—the servant had told me there was none—I went back a little way to Tortoni's, where I was greeted with the same answer. I could have tea or coffee or chocolate made with water, but milk there was none on that side of Paris, and, unless things took a turn, there would be no butter. The sovereign people had thrown up barricades during the night round all the northern and north-western issues, and would not let the milk-carts pass. They, no doubt, had some more potent fluids to fall back upon, for a good many, even at that early hour, were by no means steady in their gait. The Boulevards were swarming with them. Since then, I have seen these sovereign people getting the upper hand twice, viz. on the 4th of September, '70, and on the 18th of March, '71. I have seen them during the siege of Paris, and I have no hesitation in saying that, for cold-blooded, apish, monkeyish, tigerish cruelty, there is nothing on the face of God's earth to match them, and that no concessions wrung from society on their behalf will ever make them anything else but the fiends in human shape they are.

After my fruitless attempt to get my accustomed breakfast, I resumed my perambulations, this time taking the Rue Vivienne as far as the Palais-Royal. It must have been between half-past ten and eleven when I reached the Place du Carrousel, which, at a rough guess, was occupied by about five thousand regular infantry and horse and National Guards. The Place du Carrousel was not then, what it became later on, a large open space. Part of it was encumbered with narrow streets of very tall houses, and from their windows and roofs the sovereign people—according to an officer who had been on duty from early morn—had been amusing themselves by firing on the troops,—not in downright volleys, but with isolated shots, picking out a man here and there. "But," I remonstrated, "half a dozen pompiers and a score of linesmen could dislodge them in less than ten minutes, instead of returning their shots one by one." "So they could," was the reply, "but orders came from the Château not to do so, and here we are. Besides," added my informant, "I doubt very much, if I gave my men the word of command to storm the place, whether they would do so; they are thoroughly demoralized. On our way hither I had the greatest difficulty in keeping them together. Without a roll-call I could not exactly tell you how many are missing, but as we came along I noticed several falling out and going into the wine-shops with the rabble. They did not come back again. I had to shut my eyes to it. If I had attempted to prevent it, there would have been a more horrible slaughter than there was last night on the Boulevards, and, what is worse, the men who remained staunch would have been in a minority, and not able to stand their ground. The mob have got hold of the muskets of the National Guards. I dare say, as you came along, you noticed on many doors, written up in chalk, 'Arms given up,' and on some the words 'with pleasure' added to the statement." It was perfectly true; I had noticed it.

I was still talking to the captain when the drums began to beat and the buglers sounded the salute. At the same moment I saw the King, in the uniform of a general of the National Guards, cross the courtyard on horseback. I noticed a great many ladies at the ground-floor windows of the palace, but could not distinguish their faces. I was told afterwards that they were the Queen and the princesses, endeavouring to encourage the septuagenarian monarch. Louis-Philippe was seventy-five then.

I have often heard and seen it stated by historians of the revolution of '48, that the Duke d'Aumale and the Prince de Joinville, had they been in Paris, would have saved their father's crown. This is an assumption which it is difficult to disprove, seeing how popular these young princes were then. But if the assumption is meant to convey that the mob at the sight of these brave young fellows would have laid down their arms without fighting, I can unhesitatingly contradict it. What the National Guard might have done it is impossible to say. The regulars, no doubt, would have followed the princes into battle, as they would have followed their brother, De Nemours, notwithstanding the latter's unpopularity. There would have been a great deal of bloodshed, but the last word would have remained with the Government. Louis-Philippe's greatest title to glory is that of having prevented such bloodshed. But to show how little such abnegation of self is understood by even the most educated Frenchmen, I must relate a story which was told to me many years afterwards by a French officer who, at that time, had just returned from the Pontifical States, where he had helped to defeat the small army of Garibaldi. He was describing the battle-field of Mentana to Napoleon III., and mentioned a prisoner he had made who turned out to be an old acquaintance from the Boulevards. "He was furious against

Garibaldi, sire," said the officer, "because the latter had placed him in the necessity, as it were, of firing upon his own countrymen in a strange land. Said the prisoner, 'I am not an emigré; I would not have gone to Coblenz; I am a Frenchman from the crown of my head to the sole of my foot. If it came to fighting my countrymen in the streets of Paris, that would be a different thing. I should not have the slightest scruple of firing upon the Imperial Guards or upon the rabble, as the case might be, for that would be civil war.' That's what he said, sire."

Napoleon nodded his head, and with his wonderful, sphinx-like smile, replied, "Your prisoner was right; it makes all the difference." The Orléans princes, save perhaps one, never knew these distinctions; if they had known them, the Comte de Paris might be King of France to-day.

To return for a moment to Louis-Philippe as I saw him at the last moments of his reign. He felt evidently disappointed at the lukewarm reception he received, for though there was a faint cry among the regulars of " Vive le Roi ! " it was immediately drowned by the stentorian one of the rabble of " Vive la Réforme ! " in which a good many of the National Guards joined. He was evidently in a hurry to get back to the Tuileries, and, when he disappeared in the doorway, I had looked upon him for the last time in my life. An hour and a half later, he had left Paris for ever.

* * * * *

Personally I saw nothing of the flight of the King, nor of the inside of the Tuileries, until the royal family were gone. The story of that flight was told to me several years later by the Duc de Montpensier. What is worse, in those days it never entered my mind that a time would come when I should feel desirous of committing my reminiscences to paper, consequently I kept no count of the hours that went by, and cannot, therefore, give the exact sequence of events. I do not know how long I stood among the soldiers and the crowd, scarcely divided from one another even by an imaginary line. It was not a pleasant crowd, though to my great surprise there were a great many more decently dressed persons in it than I could have expected, so I stayed on. About half an hour after the King re-entered the Tuileries, I noticed two gentlemen elbow their way through the serried masses. I had no difficulty in recognizing the one in civilian's clothes. Though he was by no means so famous as he became afterwards, there was hardly a Parisian who would not have recognized him on the spot. His portrait had been drawn over and over again, at least as many times as that of the King, and it is a positive fact that nurses frightened their babies with it. He was the ugliest man of the century. It was M. Adolphe Cremieux.* His companion was in uniform. I learnt afterwards that it was General Gourgaud, but I did not know him then except by name, and in connection with his polemics with the Duke of Wellington, in which the latter did not altogether behave with the generosity one expects from an English gentleman towards a fallen foe. As they passed, the old soldier must have been recog-

* The author is slightly mistaken. The two ugliest men in France in the nineteenth century were Andrieux, who wrote "Les Etourdis," and Littré; but Cremieux ran them very hard.—EDITOR.

nized, because not one, but at least a hundred cries resounded, "Vive la grande armée! Vive l'Empereur!" In after years I thought that these cries sounded almost prophetic, though I am pretty sure that those who uttered them had not the slightest hope of, and perhaps not even a desire for, a Napoleonic restoration; at any rate, not the majority. There is one thing, however, which could not have failed to strike the impartial observer during the next twenty years. I have seen a good many riots, small and large, during the Second Republic and the Second Empire. "Seditious cries," as a matter of course, were freely shouted. I have never heard a single one of "Vivent les D'Orléans!" or "Vivent les Bourbons!" I have already spoken more than once about the powerful influence of the Napoleonic legend in those days; I shall have occasion to refer to it again and again when speaking about the nephew of the first Napoleon.

Cremieux and Gourgaud could not have been inside the Tuileries more than a quarter of an hour when they rushed out again. They evidently made a communication to the troops, because I beheld the latter waving their arms, but, of course, I did not catch a word of what they said; I was too far away. It was, I learnt afterwards, the announcement of the advent of a new ministry, and the appointment of a new commander of the National Guards. When I saw hats and caps flung into the air, and heard the people shouting, I made certain that the revolution was at an end. I was mistaken. It was not Cremieux's communication at all that had provoked the enthusiasm; it was a second communication, made by some one from the doorway of the Tuileries immediately after the eminent barrister had disappeared among the crowd, to the effect that the King had abdicated in favour of the Comte de Paris, with the Duchesse d'Orléans as regent. Between the first and second announcements there could not have elapsed more than five or six minutes, ten at the utmost, because, before I had time to recover from my surprise, I saw Cremieux and Gourgaud battle through the tightly wedged masses once more, and re-enter the Tuileries to verify the news. I am writing this note especially by the light of subsequent information, for, I repeat, it was impossible to understand events succinctly by the quickly succeeding effects they produced at the time. Another ten minutes elapsed — ten minutes which I shall never forget, because every one of the thousands present on the Place du Carrousel was in momentary danger of having the life crushed out of him. It was no one's fault; there was, if I recollect rightly, but one narrow issue on the river-side, and there was a dense seething mass standing on the banks, notwithstanding the danger of that position, for the insurgents were firing freely and recklessly across the stream. Egress on the opposite side of the Place du Carrousel, that of the Place du Palais-Royal, had become absolutely impossible, for at that moment a fierce battle was raging there between the people and the National Guards for the possession of the military post of the Château d'Eau;* and those of the non-combatants who did not think it necessary to pay for the fall or the maintenance of the monarchy of

* So called after a large ornamental fountain; the same, I believe, which subsequently was transferred to what is now called the Place de la République, and which finally found its way to the Avenue Daumesnil, where it stands at present.—EDITOR.

July with life or limb, tried to get out of the bullets' reach. There was but one way of doing so, by a stampede in a southerly direction; the Rue de Rivoli, at any rate that part which existed, was entirely blocked to the west, the congeries of streets that have been pulled down since to make room for its prolongation to the east were bristling with barricades: hence the terrible, suffocating crush, in which several persons lost their lives. The most curious incident connected with these awful ten minutes was that of a woman and her baby. When Cremieux issued for the second time from the Tuileries, it was to confirm the news of the King's abdication. Almost immediately afterwards, the masses on the quay were making for the Place de la Concorde and the Palais-Bourbon, whither, it was rumoured, the Duchesse D'Orléans and her two sons were going; and gradually the wedged in mass on the Place du Carrousel found breathing space. Then the woman was seen to fall down like a ninepin that has been toppled over; she was dead, but her baby, which she had held above the crowd, and which they had, as it were, to wrench from her grasp, was alive and well.

I stood for a little while longer on the Place du Carrousel, trying to make up my mind whether to proceed to the Place de la Concorde or to the Place de l'Hôtel de Ville. I knew that the newly-elected powers, whosoever they might be, would make their appearance at the latter spot, but how long it would be before they came, I had not the least idea. I was determined, however, to see at any rate one act of the drama or the farce; for even then there was no knowing in what guise events would present themselves. I could hear the reports of firearms on both sides of me, though why there should be firing when the King had thrown up the sponge, I could not make out for the life of me. I did not know France so well then as I know her now. I did not know then that there is no man or, for that matter, no woman on the civilized earth so heedlessly and obdurately bloodthirsty when he or she works himself into a fury as the professedly débonnaire Parisian proletarian. Nevertheless, I decided to go to the Hôtel de Ville, and had carefully worked my way as far as the site of the present Place du Châtelet, when I was compelled to retrace my steps. The élite of the Paris scum was going to dictate its will to the new Government; it was marching to the Chamber of Deputies with banners flying. One of the latter was a red-and-white striped flannel petticoat, fastened to a tremendously long pole. I had no choice, and if at that moment my friends had seen me they might have easily imagined that I had become one of the leaders of the revolutionary mob. We took by the Quai de la Mégisserie, and just before the Pont des Arts there was a momentary halt. The vanguard, which I was apparently leading, had decided to turn to the right; in other words, to visit the abode of the hated tyrant. Had I belonged to the main division, I should have witnessed a really more important scene, from the historical point of view; as it was, I witnessed—

The Sacking of the Tuileries.

The idea that "there is a divinity that hedgeth round a king" seemed, I admit, preposterous enough at that moment; but I could not help being struck with its partial truth on seeing the rabble invade the palace. When I say the rabble, I mean the rabble, though there were a great many persons whom it would be an insult to class as such, and who from sheer curiosity, or because they could not help themselves, had gone in with them. The doors proved too narrow, and those who could not enter by that way, entered by the windows. The whole contingent of the riff-raff, male and female, weltering in the adjacent streets—and such streets!—was there. Well, for the first ten minutes they stood positively motionless, not daring to touch anything. It was not the fear of being caught pilfering and punished summarily that prevented them. The minority which might have protested was so utterly insignificant in numbers, as to make action on their part impossible. No, it was neither fear nor shame that stayed the rabble's hands; it was a sentiment for which I can find no name. It was the consciousness that these objects had belonged to a king, to a royal family, which made them gaze upon them in a kind of superstitious wonder. It did not last long. We were on the ground floor, which mainly consisted of the private apartments of the household of Louis-Philippe. We were wandering, or rather squeezing, through the study and bedroom of the King himself, through the sitting-rooms of the princes and princesses. I do not think that a single thing was taken from there at that particular time. But as if the atmosphere their rulers had breathed but so very recently became too oppressive, the crowd swayed towards the vestibule, and ascended the grand staircase. Then the spell was broken. The second batch that entered through the windows, when we had made room for them, were apparently not affected by wonder and respect, for, half an hour later, when I came down again, every cupboard, every wardrobe, had been forced, though it is but fair to say that very little seems to have been taken; the contents, books, clothing, linen, etc., were scattered on the floors; but the cellars, containing over four thousand bottles of wine, were positively empty. Two hours later, however, the clothing, especially that of the princesses, had totally disappeared. It had disappeared on the backs of the inmates of St. Lazare, the doors of which had been thrown open, and who had rushed to the Tuileries to deck themselves with these fine feathers which, in this instance, did not make fine birds. I saw some of them that same evening on the Boulevards, and a more heart-rending spectacle I have rarely beheld.

The three hours I spent at the Tuileries were so crowded with events as to make a succinct account of them altogether impossible. I can only give fragments, because, though at first the wearers of broadcloth were not molested, this tolerance did not last long on the part of the new possessors of the Tuileries; and consequently the former gradually dropped off, and those of them who remained had to be very circumspect, and, above all, not to linger long in the same spot. This growing hostility might have been nipped in the bud by our following the example of the National Guards, and taking off our coats and fraternizing with the rabble; but I frankly confess that I had neither the courage nor the stomach to do so. I have read descriptions of mutinous sailors stowing in casks of rum and gorging themselves with victuals; revolting as such scenes must be to those who take no active part in them, I doubt whether they could be as revolting as the one I witnessed in the Gallerie de Diane.

The Gallerie de Diane was one of the large reception rooms on the first floor, but it generally served as the dining and breakfast room of the royal family. The table had been laid for about three dozen persons, because, as a rule, Louis-Philippe invited the principal members of his military and civil households to take their repasts with him. The breakfast had been interrupted, and not been cleared away. When I entered the apartment some sixty or seventy ruffians of both sexes were seated at the board, while a score or so were engaged in waiting upon them. They were endeavouring to accomplish what the Highest Authority has declared impossible of accomplishment, namely, the making of silken purses out of sows' ears. They were "putting on" what they considered "company manners," and, under any other circumstances but these, the attempt would have proved irresistibly comic to the educated spectator; as it was, it brought tears to one's eyes. I have already hinted elsewhere that the cuisine at the Tuileries during Louis-Philippe's reign was execrable, though the wine was generally good. Bad as was the fare on that abandoned breakfast-table, it must, nevertheless, have been superior to that usually partaken of by the convives who had taken the place of the fugitive king and princes. They, the convives, however, did not think so; they criticized the food, and ordered the improvised attendants "to give them something different;" then they turned to their female companions, filling their glasses and paying them compliments. But for the fact of another batch eagerly claiming their turn, the repast would have been indefinitely prolonged; as it was, the provisions in the palace were running short, and the deficiency had to be made up by supplies from outside. The inner man being refreshed, the ladies were invited to take a stroll through the apartments, pending the serving of the café and liqueurs. The preparation of the mocha was somewhat difficult, seeing the utensils necessary for the supply of so large a company were probably not at hand, and the ingredients themselves in the store-rooms of the palace. Nothing daunted, one of the self-invited guests rose and said, in a loud voice, "Permettez moi d'offrir le café à la compagnie," which offer was received with tumultuous applause. Suiting the action to the word, he pulled out a small canvas bag, and took from it two five-franc pieces. "Qu'on aille chercher du café et du meilleur," he said to one of the guests who had stepped forward to execute his orders, for they sounded almost like it; and I was wondering why those professed champions of equality did not tell him to fetch the coffee himself. Then he added, "Et pendant que tu y es, citoyen, apporte des cigarres pour nous et des cigarettes pour les dames." The "citoyen" was already starting on his errand, when the other "citoyen" called him back. "Écoute," he said; "tu n'acheteras rien à moins d'y être forcé. Je crois que tu n'auras qu'à demander à la première épicerie venue ce que t'il faut, et ainsi au premier bureau de tabac. Ils ont si peur, ces sales bourgeois qu'ils n'oseront pas te refuser. En tout cas prends un fusil; on ne sait pas ce qui peut arriver; mais ne t'en sers pas qu'en cas de necessité:"—which meant plainly enough, "If they refuse to give you the coffee and the tobacco, shoot them down."

Of course, I am unable to say how these two commodities were eventually procured; but I have every reason to believe that this messenger had only "to ask and have," without as much as showing his musket. There is no greater cur at troublous times than the Paris shopkeeper. The merest urchin will terrify him. Even on the previous day I had seen bands of gamins who had constituted themselves the guardians of the barricades—and there was one in nearly every street—levy toll without the slightest resistance, when a few well-administered cuffs would have sent them flying, so I have not the slightest doubt that our friend had all the credit of his generosity without disbursing a penny—unless his delegate fleeced him also, on the theory that a man who could "fork out" ten francs at a moment's notice was nothing more or less than a bourgeois. However, when I returned after about forty minutes' absence, it was very evident that both the coffee and the tobacco had arrived, because the Galerie de Diane, large as it was, was full of smoke, and three saucepans, filled with water, were standing on the fire, while two or three smaller ones were arranged on the almost priceless marble mantelpiece. Another batch of ravenous republicans had taken their seats at the board, their predecessors whiling the time away in sweet converse with the "ladies." Some of the latter were more usefully engaged; they were rifling the cabinets of the most rare and valuable Sèvres, and arranging the cups, saucers, platters on their tops to be ready for the beverage that was being brewed. I was wondering how they had got at these art-treasures, having noticed an hour before that their receptacles were locked and the keys taken away. The doors had simply been battered in with the hammer of the great clock of the Tuileries.

It was of a piece with the wanton destruction I had witnessed elsewhere, during my absence from the Galerie de Diane. Before I returned thither, I had seen the portrait of General Bugeaud in the Salle des Maréchaux, literally stabbed with bayonets; the throne treated to a similar fate, and carried off to the Place de la Bastille to be burned publicly; the papers of the royal family mercilessly flung to the winds; the dresses of the princesses torn to ribbons or else put on the backs of the vilest of the vile.

There was only one comic incident to relieve the horror of the whole. In one of the private apartments the rabble had come upon an aged parrot screeching at the top of its voice, "A bas Guizot!" The bird became a hero there and then, and was absolutely crammed with sweets and sugar. That one comic note was not enough to dispel my disgust, and after the scene in the Galerie de Diane which I have just described, I made my way into the street.

I had scarcely proceeded a few steps, when I heard the not very startling news that the republic had been formally proclaimed in the Chamber by M. de Lamartine, who had afterwards repaired to the Hôtel de Ville. At the same time, people were shouting that the King had died suddenly. I endeavoured to get as far, but, though the distance was certainly not more than half a mile, it took me more than an hour. At every few yards my progress was interrupted by barricades, the self-elected custodians of which were particularly anxious to show their authority to a man like myself, dressed in a coat. At last I managed to get to the corner of the Rues des Lombards and Saint-Martin, and just in time to enjoy a sight than which I have witnessed nothing more comic during the succeeding popular uprisings in subsequent years. I was just crossing, when a procession hove in sight, composed mainly of ragged urchins, dishevelled women, and riff-raff of both sexes. In their midst was an individual on horseback, dressed in the uniform of a general of the First Republic, whom they were cheering loudly. The stationary crowd made way for them, and mingled with the escort. The moment I had thrown in my lot with the latter, retreat was no longer possible, and in a very short time I found myself in the courtyard of the Hôtel de Ville, and, in another minute or so, in the principal gallery on the first floor, where, it appears, *some members* of the Provisional Government were already at work. I had not the remotest notion who they were, nor did I care to inquire, having merely come to look on. The work of the members of the Provisional Government seemed mainly to consist in consuming enormous quantities of charcuterie and washing them down with copious libations of cheap wine. The place was positively reeking with the smell of both, not to mention the fumes of tobacco. Every one was smoking his hardest. The entrance of the individual in uniform caused somewhat of a sensation; a *member*—whom I had never seen before and whom I have never beheld since—

stepped forward to ask his business. The new-comer did not appear to know himself; at any rate, he stammered and stuttered, but his escort left him no time to betray his confusion more plainly. "C'est le citoyen gouverneur de l'Hôtel de Ville," they shouted as with one voice; and there and then the new governor was installed, though I am perfectly sure that not a soul of all those present knew as much as his name.

Subsequent inquiries elicited the fact that the man was a fourth or fifth-rate singer, named Chateaurenaud, and engaged at the Opéra National (formerly the Cirque Olympique) on the Boulevard du Temple. On that day they were having a dress rehearsal of a new piece in which Chateaurenaud was playing a military part. He had just donned his costume when, hearing a noise on the Boulevards, he put his head out of the window. The mob caught sight of him. "A general, a general!" cried several urchins; and in less time than it takes to tell, the theatre was invaded, and notwithstanding his struggles, Chateaurenaud was carried off, placed on horseback, and conducted to the Hôtel de Ville, where, for the next fortnight, he throned as governor. For, curious to relate, M. de Lamartine ratified his appointment (?) on the morning of the 25th of February. Chateaurenaud became an official of the secret police during the Second Empire. I often saw him on horseback in the Bois de Boulogne, when the Emperor drove in that direction.

I did not stay long in the Hôtel de Ville, but made my way back to the Boulevards as best I could; for by that time darkness had set in, and the mob was shouting for illuminations, and obstructing the thoroughfares everywhere. Every now and then one came upon a body which had been lying there since the morning, but they took no notice of it. Their principal concern seemed the suitable acknowledgment of the advent of the Second Republic by the bourgeoisie by means of coloured devices, or, in default of such, by coloured lamps or even candles. Woe to the houses, the inhabitants of which remained deaf to their summons to that effect. In a very few minutes every window was smashed to atoms, until at last a timid hand was seen to arrange a few bottles with candles stuck into them on the sill, and light them. Then they departed, to impose their will elsewhere.

That night, after dinner, the first person of my acquaintance I met was Méry. He had been in the Chamber of Deputies from the very beginning of the proceedings; it was he who solemnly assured me that the first cry of " Vive la République! " had been uttered by M. de Lamartine. I was surprised at this, because I had been told that early in the morning the poet had paid a visit to the Duchesse d'Orléans to assure her of his devotion to her cause. "That may be so," said Méry, to whom I repeated what I had heard; "but you must remember that Lamartine is always hard up, and closely pursued by duns. A revolution with the prospect of becoming president of the republic was the only means of staving off his creditors. He clutched at it as a last resource."

Alexander Dumas was there also, but I have an idea that he would have willingly passed the sponge over that incident of his life, for I never could get him to talk frankly on the subject. This does not mean that he would have recanted his republican principles, but that he was ashamed at having lent his countenance to such a republic as that. I fancy there were a great many like him.

END OF VOL. I.

www.ingramcontent.com/pod-product-compliance
Lightning Source LLC
Chambersburg PA
CBHW060455170426
43199CB00011B/1206